POSTCARD HISTORY SERIES

Marion

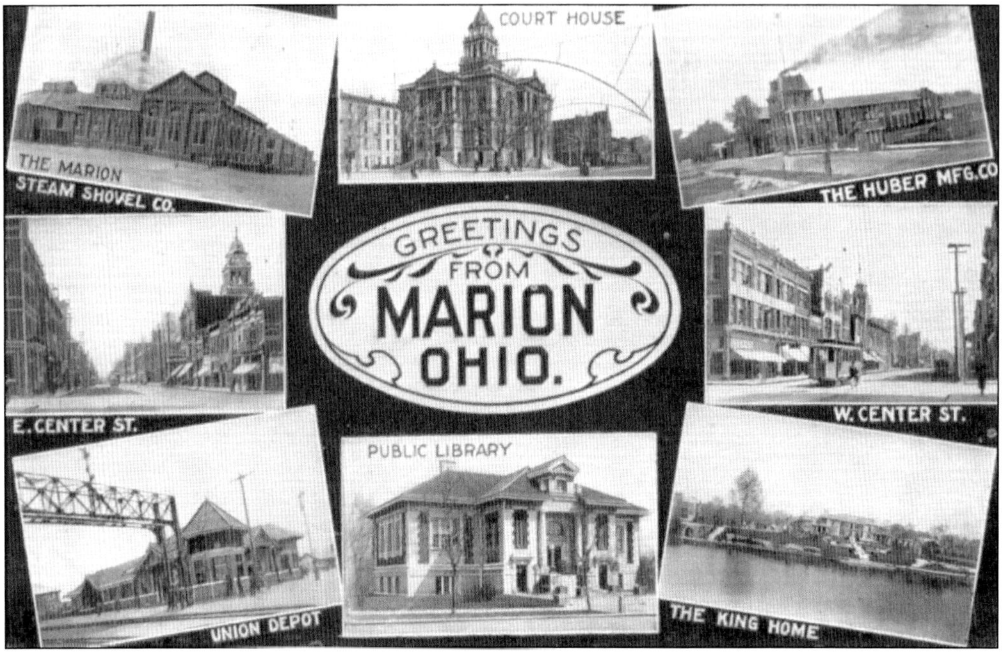

Postcards featuring a collage of significant structures and scenes were a popular way of providing a quick overview of what a town had to offer. This c. 1910 card included samples of Marion's industry, housing, street views, and public services. (Author's collection.)

ON THE COVER: The Huber Manufacturing Company was one of Marion's leading industries around 1900. Products included steam engines, threshers, hay rakes, road graders, and other farm and industrial equipment. This real-photo postcard shows a Huber steam engine powering a straw baler while several workers take a break to pose for the photographer. (Courtesy of Mike and Linda Perry.)

POSTCARD HISTORY SERIES

Marion

Randy Winland

ARCADIA PUBLISHING

ISBN 978-1-4671-1060-0

Published by Arcadia Publishing
Charleston, South Carolina

Printed in the United States of America

Library of Congress Control Number: 2013941802

For all general information contact Arcadia Publishing at:
Telephone 843-853-2070
Fax 843-853-0044
E-mail sales@arcadiapublishing.com
For customer service and orders:
Toll-Free 1-888-313-2665

Visit us on the Internet at www.arcadiapublishing.com

Dedicated to the collectors of memories of Marion—
be they past, present, or future.

CONTENTS

Acknowledgments		6
Introduction		7
1.	For the Price of a One-Cent Stamp	9
2.	Uptown, Downtown, All Around the Town	17
3.	The Business of Business	35
4.	Made in Marion	53
5.	Now Leaving the Station	69
6.	Houses of Worship and Places of Rest	77
7.	Bells, Books, and Blackboards	91
8.	For a Good Time	105

ACKNOWLEDGMENTS

The best results often come from the efforts of many combined into one finished product. Such was the case with this publication. The postcard collectors and historians of Marion generously contributed their collections, knowledge, and advice to help make this compilation of images and information a resource to be used and enjoyed.

Stuart Koblentz Haley's insight and suggestions, combined with his knowledge of Marion's history, served as a resource that is greatly valued. Richard Carey, Mike Perry, and Bob Turner all graciously shared their expansive postcard collections, including many very unique and perhaps one-of-a-kind images.

Others who shared their collections are Maureen Cole, Michael Crane, Ellis and Marjorie Hudson, Stuart Koblentz Haley, T.J. Kohler, Shelby Needham, Carol Robinson, and the Marion County Historical Society. My thanks are extended to all for their generosity and willingness to share.

Research and background assistance were provided by Devon Hardwick, Keith Kohler, Carroll Neidhardt, Phil Reid, Rich Tubbs, and Willis Thomas. I thank them for their assistance.

Marion is fortunate to have the Marion County Historical Society with its dedicated and insightful volunteers and employees. Mary Gross, Alex Profitt, Mark Revere, and director Gale Martin assisted with the research efforts.

Appreciation is extended to Jill Nunn, Mary Margaret Schley, and Liz Gurley, my acquisitions editors at Arcadia Publishing. They helped guide me through the writing and publishing process.

Finally, and most importantly, I truly thank Sandy Winland, my wife of 37 years and my best friend. Her acceptance of the many days I spent scanning, researching, compiling, and writing—as well as the numerous requests of, would you mind just taking a quick look at this?—were done without complaint, or at least not that I heard. In addition, her suggestions for possible improvements in the grammar and content of my captions certainly made for a better end product.

Introduction

The city of Marion is no different in many ways than hundreds of other small towns across the United States. It has enjoyed times of prosperity and of distress. Employers have come, while others have gone. Social causes have risen to the forefront only to retreat. Many other small towns share similar legacies.

Yet Marion is unique in several regards. One of the most notable is that Marion is the home of both a president of the United States and a Miss America. Warren G. Harding was elected the 29th president in 1920, while Marilyn Meseke was chosen as Miss America in 1938.

Marion became the adopted home of an inventor who held nearly 100 patents. Edward Huber moved to Marion in 1865 because of the availability of the resources needed to build his invention of a revolving hay rake. Huber's success with this endeavor, as well as many more, led to his becoming known as the "Father of Marion Industry." He was also the primary backer of various cultural and social causes such as a free public library and the Grand Opera House.

Once nicknamed Lime City due to the large number of limestone quarries, Marion later became recognized for the number of steam shovel manufacturers located in the town. Companies such as Marion Steam Shovel, Osgood, Fairbanks, and General Excavator all contributed to help Marion earn the title of Shovel City. By the early 1900s, over 90 percent of all steam shovels in the world were made by Marion companies.

With a centralized location for much of the Midwest, Marion grew into a rail transportation hub with numerous routes passing through the city. This availability of a substantial rail system continues to be a draw, as intermodal facilities and industrial development utilize the rail network.

This publication shows many aspects of Marion's past via the use of postcards. In an effort to provide a resource that is as historically accurate as possible, extensive research was undertaken. As is true in most historical research, discrepancies in the recording of Marion's past were discovered. This was especially so in areas such as specific dates, locations, and sometimes even people. Some of these discrepancies are perhaps due to the lack of attention to detail by those who recorded the events. Other differences exist because of changes made by city leaders as their town grew and expanded. For example, the original plat map made in 1822 was redrawn in 1872. This created changes such as lots that were originally on South Main Street being on North Main Street after the revision.

Some street names were changed in 1874 when East Street became State Street, West Street became Prospect Street, North Street became Mill Street (although sometimes also identified as Railroad Street) before changing again to Huber Street in 1988, South Street became Church Street, Centre Street became Center Street, and Canal Street became Columbia Street. Other name changes throughout the years included Garden City Pike to Fairgrounds Street and the Claridon Pike becoming Mount Vernon Avenue. For clarity, the revised names are used in this book.

Perhaps the most confusing of all these changes came about as the result of a 1917 city ordinance that renumbered the city lots. Essentially overnight, 145 North State Street became 160 North State, 118 North Main Street became 130 North Main Street, and so forth. Changes such as these made the task of locating the exact locations of former businesses and residences using city directories and other resources more of a challenge.

Marion is fortunate to have had numerous histories written, including two previous volumes published by Arcadia. This publication continues with the task of preserving Marion's legacy, but in a somewhat unique fashion. First, the primary focus is on the city of Marion, with the county and villages reserved for a subsequent publication. In addition, all views were taken from postcards, which somewhat limited the scope of possibilities as opposed to the use of photographs. Marion's postcard collectors generously shared their collections, which contain thousands of unique views including many real-photo, one-of-a-kind cards. Finally, and perhaps most challenging, was the necessity of telling only snippets of the history of interesting and unusual subjects in 70 words or less when pages could easily have been written.

A large number of the cards originally came from the Wiant's Bookseller, Stationer & Souvenirs Store in Marion. It was opened in 1886 by Charles G. Wiant, who operated it until his death in 1929. Originally located at 144 West Center Street, the store moved to various locations throughout downtown Marion until closing in the late 1980s. Known as the House of Postcards, the store featured a selection of postcards numbering in the thousands, including many printed exclusively for Wiant's. Different series of cards issued throughout the years by Wiant's can be identified by the various font types used on the reverse. To the passionate Marion postcard collector, finding that one missing Red Letter Serif Vivid or Brown Letter Sans Serif Wiant card can be an enticing and elusive process. Additional information is included in a historical summary and overview of postcard development in chapter one.

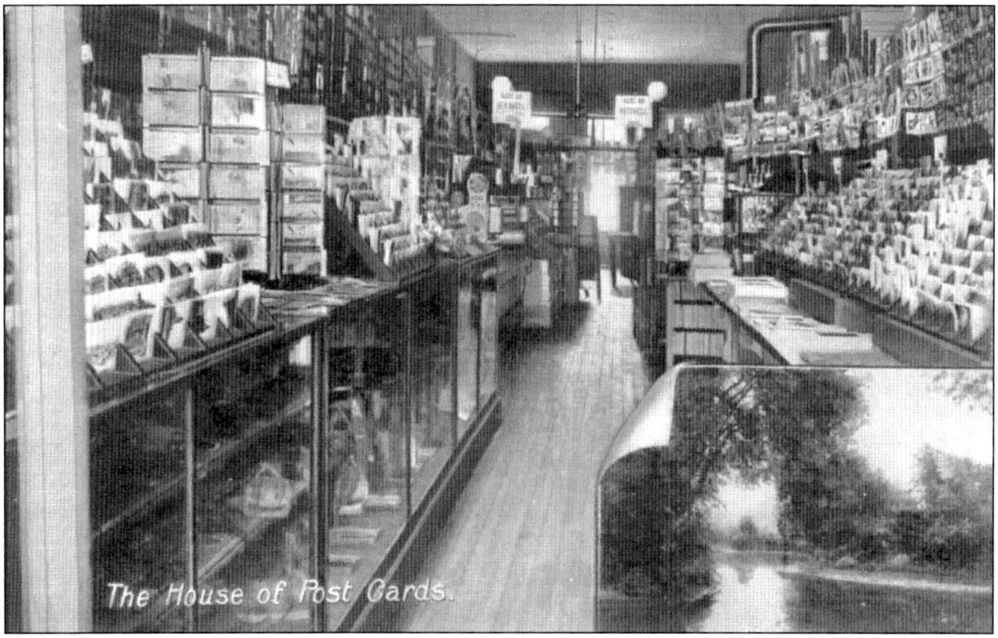

WIANT'S HOUSE OF POSTCARDS. This is an interior view of the store. (Author's collection.)

One

For the Price of a One-Cent Stamp

In the days before telephones, e-mail, and texting, communicating was often accomplished with a piece of paper and a one-cent stamp. The use of postcards for sending messages was a simple, quick, and inexpensive method especially if the sender did not mind an occasional inquisitive postman.

An early version of postcards began in Europe in the middle of the 19th century when printers put pictures on the outsides of mailing envelopes. Common themes were holidays, music, and comics. In Great Britain, early cards without images were issued by the postal service, had a stamp printed as part of the design, and were known as postal cards.

Many of the first cards with images were printed in France. By 1889, cards with images of the newly built Eiffel Tower started the trend of using postcards as souvenirs. Some of the first souvenir cards printed in the United States were created in 1893 to help advertise the World's Columbian Exposition in Chicago. These cards were pre-stamped "penny postcard" and were printed by the United States Post Office Department, which held monopoly rights on the printing of such cards in the country.

In 1898, legislation was passed that allowed private publishers to produce postcards, but they could not be identified as such. They were required to be labeled as "private mailing cards." This changed in 1901 when the law was modified to permit private companies to use the term postcard or "post card" to describe their products.

Rural Free Delivery (RFD) mail service was adopted on a national basis by the United States Post Office Department in 1902 after a six year experimental trial. More than 10,000 petitions had been received seeking the establishment of rural delivery. This service brought the convenience of home-delivered mail to the majority of Americans who lived outside of cities. As a result, the market for postcards increased significantly as people used them to communicate with friends and relatives across the nation. Businesses also found them to be an effective means of advertising.

In the early 1900s, the sale of postcards in the United States became a craze as the cards also became very popular with collectors. Many postcard clubs were created with their members seeking out examples from the numerous different forms and printing techniques utilized by the postcard publishers.

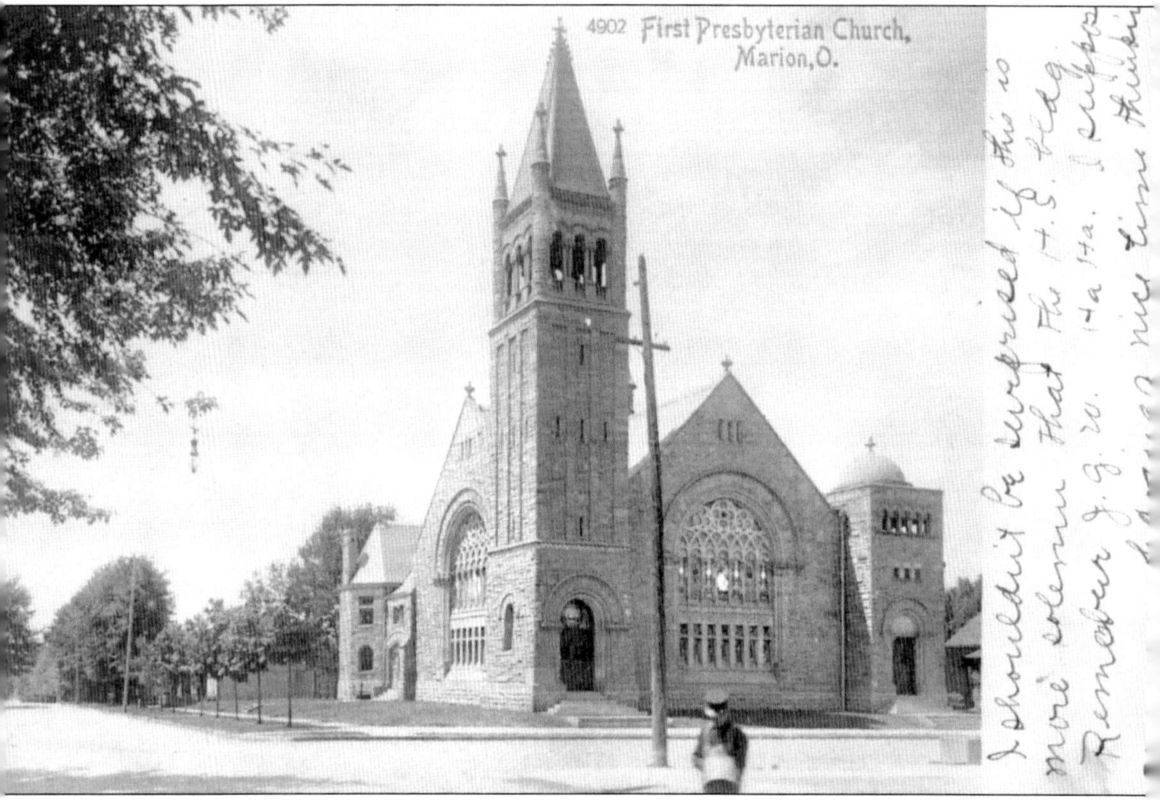

UNDIVIDED BACK POSTCARD. First Presbyterian Church, known as "The Great Stone Church," stands on the northwest corner of Church and Prospect Streets. Built in 1893 at a cost of $56,900, it is located on the former site of the Wigwam entertainment house. (Author's collection.)

Postal regulations prohibited writing anything other than the recipient's name and address on the backs of the cards. This resulted in messages being written on the front, or picture side, of the card, either in space left beside the image or around the border. Lasting from 1901 to 1907, this was the so-called undivided back era of postcards.

The use of postcards with a divided back was permitted beginning in 1907. The address was written on the right side of the card back, while the left side was reserved for messages. It was no longer necessary for messages to be written over the card image or jammed into the blank area left beside it. The popularity of postcards skyrocketed as the difficulty of trying to write a message in a small space was eliminated.

Official figures from the Post Office Department in 1908 showed over 677 million postcards mailed. The population of the United States was approximately 89 million. This meant that more than seven postcards were mailed for every man, woman, and child in the country. With twice-a-day mail delivery in many areas, a card could be mailed in the morning and possibly arrive at the recipient's address in the evening mail. Due to the tremendous volume of postcards being mailed and collected, the years from 1905 to 1909 became known as the golden age of postcards.

In 1909, Congress authorized a tariff on imported postcards as a result of a campaign led by American publishers. Most of the cards sold in the United States were printed in Germany or other European countries utilizing a process that American publishers had not mastered. The resulting lower quality cards were not well-accepted and the postcard craze slowed significantly.

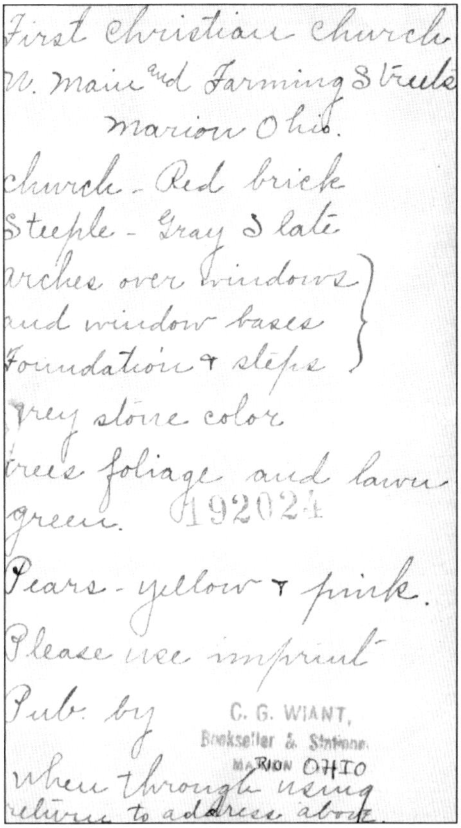

First Christian church
N. Main and Farming Streets
Marion Ohio.
church - Red brick
Steeple - Gray Slate
arches over windows
and window bases
Foundation & steps
grey stone color
trees foliage and lawn
green. 192024
Pears - yellow & pink.
Please use imprint
Pub. by C. G. WIANT,
Bookseller & Stationer
MARION OHIO
when through using
return to address above

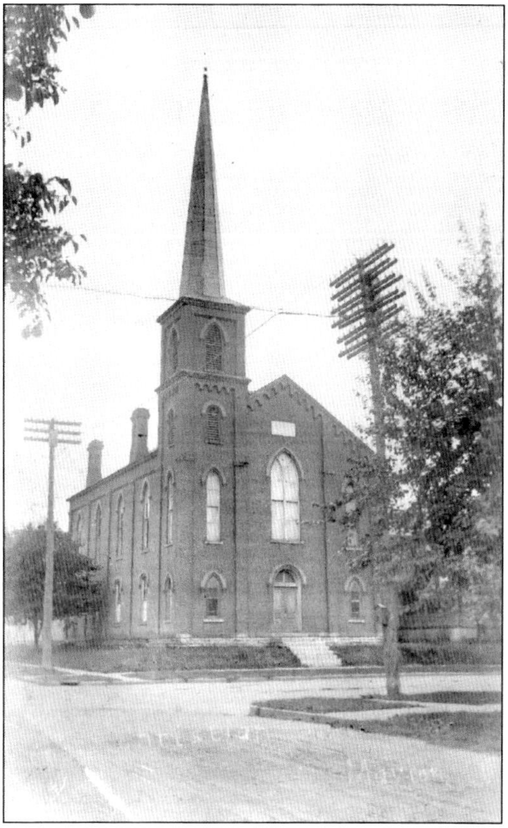

ORIGINAL PHOTOGRAPH AND INSTRUCTIONS FOR CONVERTING TO COLOR. The First Christian Church of Marion held services beginning in 1880 in this building on North Main Street. Several members split from the congregation in 1902 and established the Central Christian Church. In 1965, the First Christian congregation moved to a new location on Richland Road and became the Richland Road Church of Christ. The building on North Main is still standing but abandoned. (Courtesy of Mike and Linda Perry.)

As color photography was not readily available, the process of getting colored images for postcards required several steps. The first was to take a black-and-white photograph of the subject. Specific instructions were devised for coloring each aspect of the photograph. The photograph and instructions were then sent to the postcard publishers in Germany or Belgium where cards were printed using a lithographic process. This process involved using separate stones or plates to apply each of the bright colors, resulting in a completely colored card. Once the printing was done, the cards were shipped back and made ready for distribution.

While the process worked well for the most part, it was not without issues. Discrepancies in interpreting what a color description actually meant occasionally made for some interesting final results. For example, the instruction to color a building as "red brick" left a wide range of final choices as to what "red" should be used. While accuracy in color selection was important, the main concern was having a bright, vibrant color to attract the eye of a potential customer.

European publishers accounted for the large majority of the postcards sold in the United States. Many of them opened offices in large cities to help with the importation and sales which were handled through a nationwide distribution network.

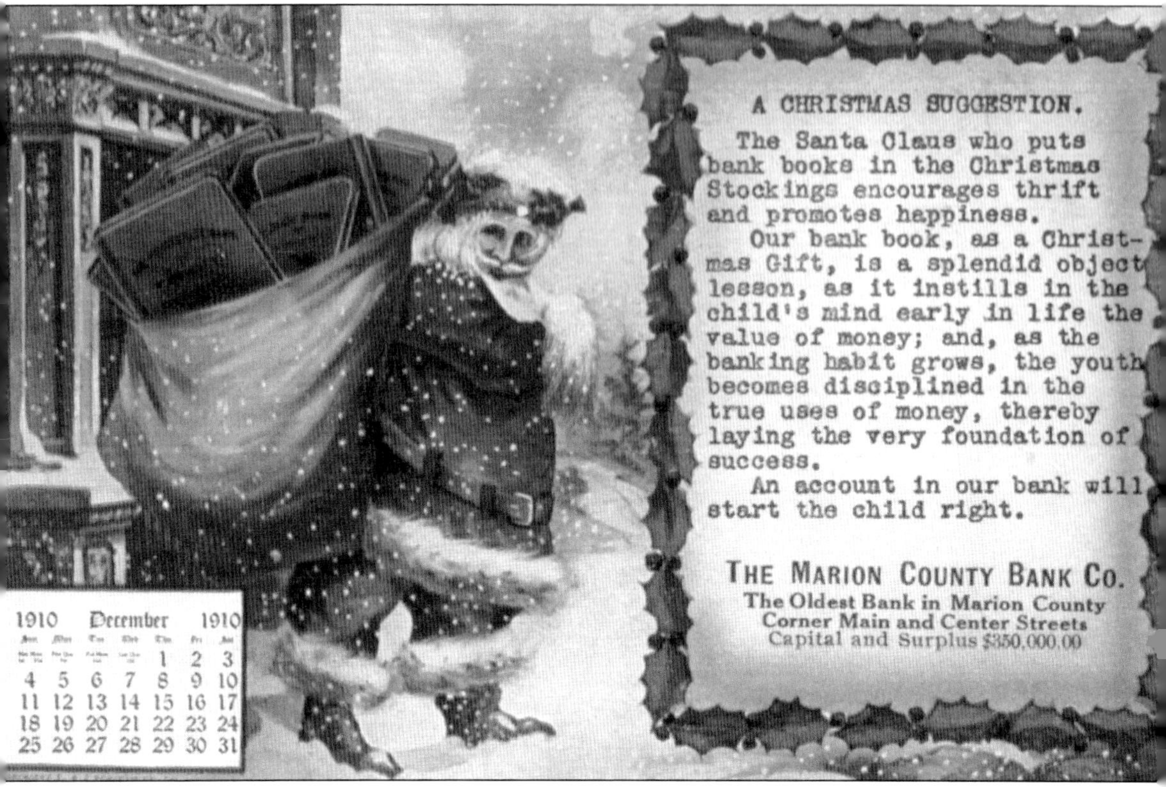

LITHOGRAPHIC POSTCARD. An early example of a lithographic postcard, this card was one in a monthly series sent by the Marion County Bank as part of an advertising promotion. The bank was established in 1857 as a successor to the J.S. Reed and Company, which had started business in 1839. (Author's collection.)

Lithographic postcards greatly increased the popularity of postcards as images could now be seen in a more lifelike and colorful view. Some postcards were actually colored by hand using an assembly-line process. Known as hand tinted cards, they were colored by hand to lend a realistic or stylized look. Many of the first hand tinted cards were of young ladies from exotic countries as well as actresses and other celebrities. Patriotic themes were also popular. In some instances, only specific parts of the image were tinted in order to show a stylized view.

Coloring of the postcards was done by a group of trained women artists who each added a color to the card with the result being a small work of art. To help with the fine detail needed, the women would often use their lips to wet the tip of their brush. Eventually, many became ill and developed problems with their mouth and gums, later determined to be the result of ingesting lead used in the paints. This led to the discontinuation of hand-tinted cards and also to their relative scarcity for collectors.

People began to collect unmailed postcards and save them in albums to display in their homes. Postcards became one of the first items collected by Americans for something other than monetary value. This led to the creation of the hobby of deltiology or postcard collecting. Deltiologists divide postcard collecting into several general types. Among these are view, greeting, historical, art, photographic, and novelty cards. Postcards also vary in size with continental (4 by 6 inches), regular or standard (3.5 by 5.5 inches), modern (6.5 by 4.75 inches) and oversized (anything larger than continental) being the most common.

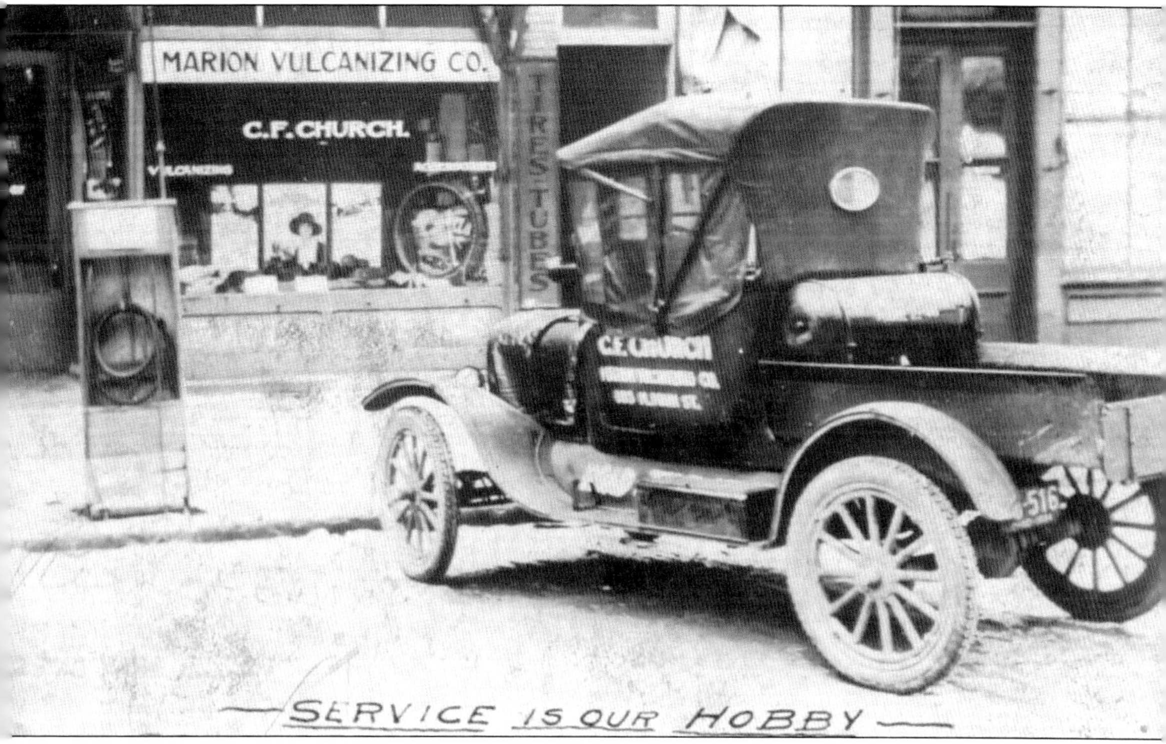

REAL-PHOTO POSTCARD. The Marion Vulcanizing Company advertised its services and modern equipment, which included a service truck complete with a compressed-air tank and toolbox mounted on the running board. Located on North Main Street, the company sold Firestone tires in solid, pneumatic, and balloon versions as well as offering vulcanizing repairs for flat tires. (Courtesy of Richard Carey.)

The Eastman-Kodak company took notice of this growing business opportunity. Around 1913, the company offered a unique option for photographers. Known as the Folding Pocket Kodak camera, it used the newly developed Autographic film. The system, which could also be retrofitted to existing Kodak cameras, consisted of a special camera back with a small, sliding door opening to reveal a red, tissue-like carbon paper sandwiched between the film and the paper backing. Text could be written on the film using a special metal stylus with the results appearing on the margin of the finished print. The film was specially designed to produce a negative that was postcard size. This resulted in very clear images, which could be printed directly onto postcard stock, with the product being a real-photo postcard. The cameras were relatively inexpensive for the time with a cost of $6 for a Vest Pocket Autographic Kodak although a No. 1 Autographic Special with Zeiss Anastigmatic Lens would cost $45. Instructions for using the Autographic film suggested writing the date and title on the film each time an exposure was made.

The cost of printing real-photo postcards was reasonable. An advertisement in the 1915 *Photographic Times Magazine* quotes prices ranging from 100 postcards made from one negative for $2 to 500 made from five different negatives for $8. Photographers were encouraged to take pictures of local landmarks and set up postcards sales displays in stores in the area. Businesses also saw the advantage of being able to increase sales opportunities by sending potential customers photo postcards.

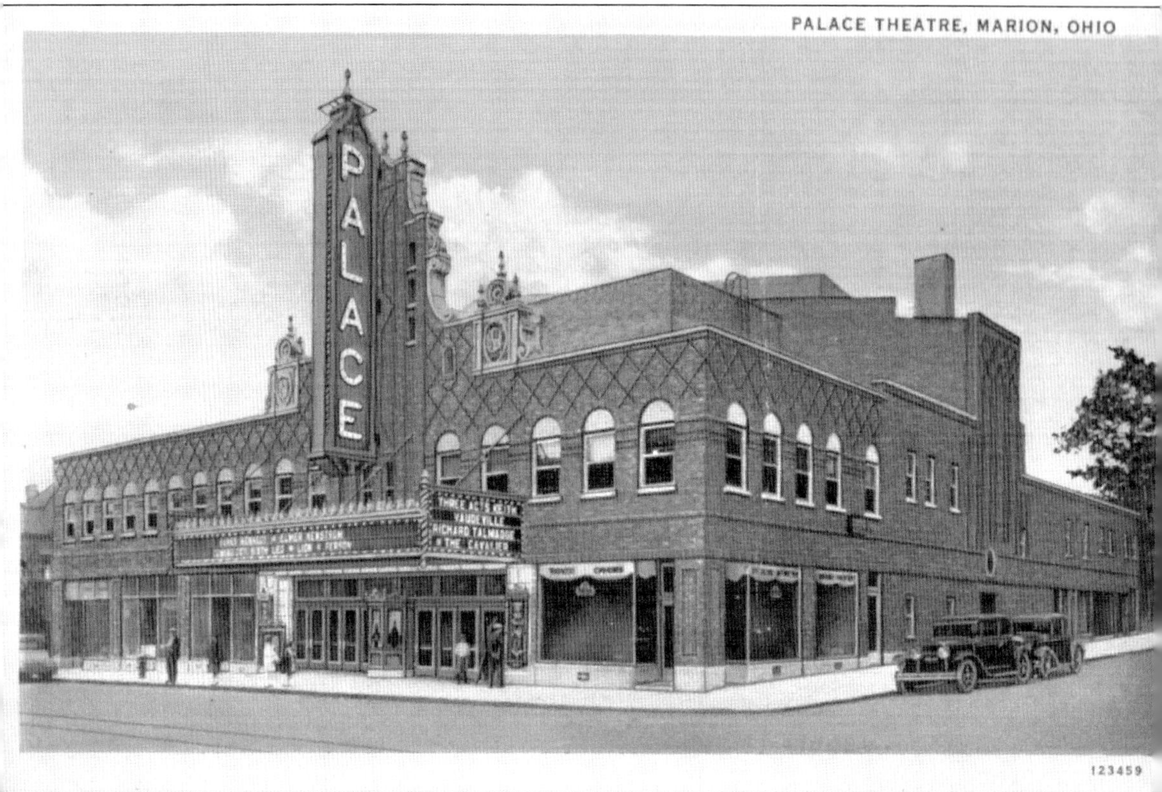

White-Border Postcard. Guests entering Marion's Palace Theatre upon its opening in 1928 found themselves in a Moorish-style courtyard complete with twinkling stars and moving clouds on the ceiling. Designed by renowned architect John Eberson, the Palace's walls were covered with classic sculptures, including one of George Washington in Masonic regalia. Fictional family crests were displayed on the proscenium arch. Each of the 1,445 seats had an unobstructed view of the stage, while outstanding acoustics allowed the massive Page Theatre Organ to be enjoyed to its fullest. The Palace underwent a major refurbishing in 1976, along with the later addition of a large pavilion used for smaller shows and events. (Author's collection.)

At the height of the postcard craze, World War I caused a sharp decline in the use of postcards as they were no longer available from the German printers. After the war, the German publishing industry was left in a shambles. Replacements by American and British publishers were of much lower quality due to the unavailability of the specialized dyes used by the Germans as well as a lack of understanding of the intricacies of the printing processes. The reduced quality of the available cards, combined with the increased availability of the telephone as a faster and more convenient means of communicating, led to a drastic reduction in the volume of postcard usage.

From 1915 to 1930, American postcards were known as white-border cards because of the white space left around the image to save on ink usage. While the overall demand for postcards was shrinking, a new development in rotary drum negative imprinters allowing an image to be easily printed on thousands of real-photo postcards helped reverse the trend. Views of local scenes were among the favorites, with sales racks set up in stores and roadside stands across the nation with a resulting resurgence in sales.

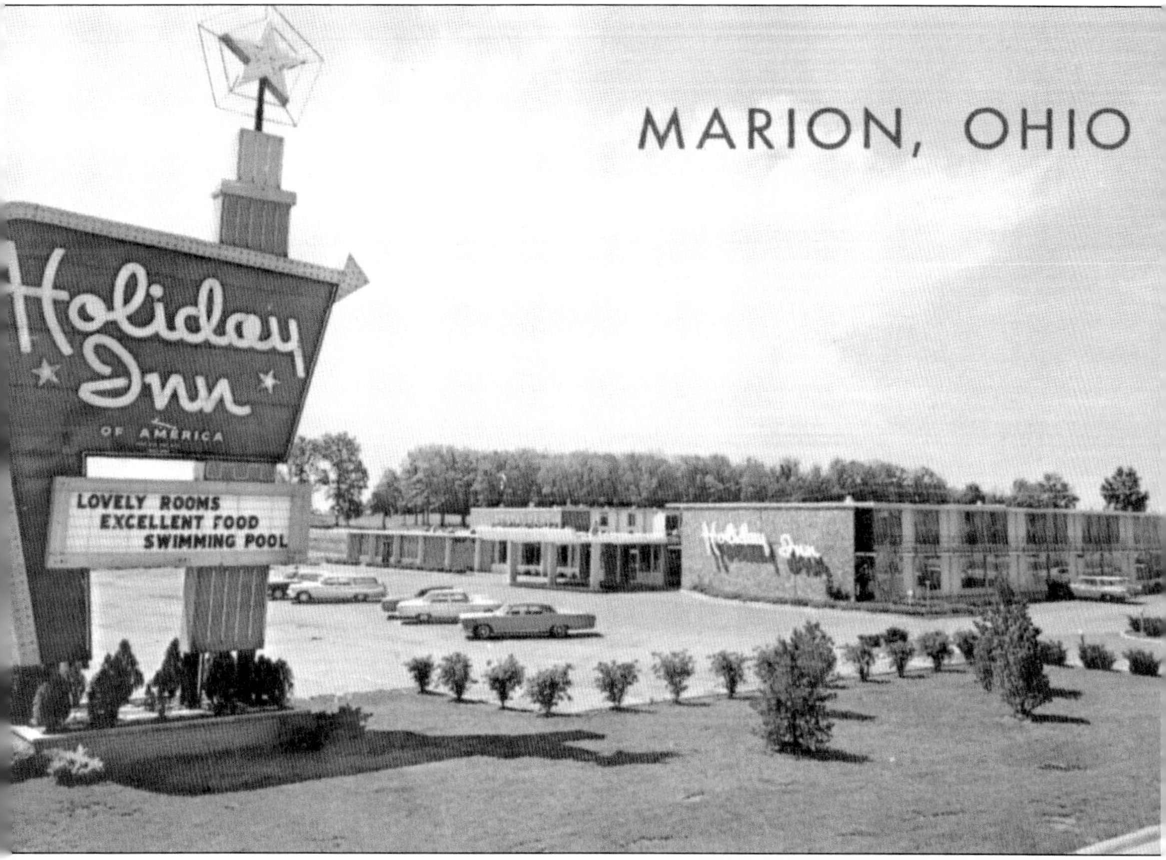

PHOTOCHROME POSTCARD. The iconic arrow points the way to the Holiday Inn Motel and Lounge on Marion's south side. Located on State Route 423 south of the Harding Memorial, it cost approximately $1 million to build in 1962. It was a popular entertainment venue for Marion's young adults as well as those still young at heart. Eventually renamed the Harding Motor Lodge with the Jolly Mushroom Lounge, it was razed in 1994. The site is now a medical office complex. (Author's collection.)

The development of new printing processes in the 1930s led to another change in postcard publishing as paper with higher rag content began to be used. Known as linen postcards, they had a different feel and look than previous versions. The textured surface paper with a cross-hatched surface resembled linen fabric. It allowed the use of brighter dyes for enhanced colors and helped make the cards very inexpensive to produce. Among the most popular cards were those that romanticized common views such as hotels, diners, gas stations, and other commercial structures. Often times undesirable features such as telephone poles, dilapidated structures, and occasionally even cars or people were removed by an air brushing technique. Postcards regained some of their popularity as people purchased and collected them for the varied subject views.

The popularity of the linen card began to decline around 1940 with the development of the color photochrome postcard. These cards featured primarily real photographs, which were easily and cheaply reproduced in bright colors on a shiny card stock, which maintained a very high-quality image. They quickly overshadowed the linen cards and remain the primary type of postcard produced today.

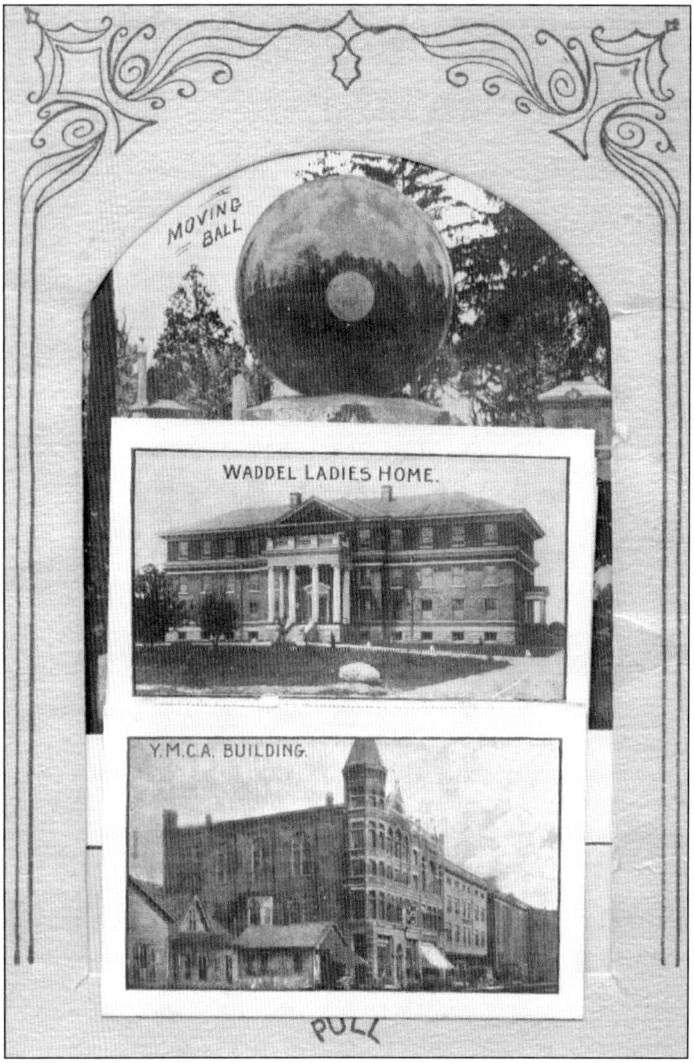

Novelty Postcard. This novelty card features a large image, which was then replaced with several smaller images of Marion locations that flipped over one another when the tab at the bottom was pulled. (Author's collection.)

While most postcards were of one of the standard formats already reviewed, there were numerous other varieties that also proved quite popular. Some examples are applique cards with cloth or some other embellishment attached, embossed cards that feature a raised surface, hold-to-light cards that reveal a scene when the card is held to a light, and novelty cards made from unusual materials like leather or that perform an action such as showing different images when a tab is pulled.

Although the cost of sending one through the mail has certainly risen from the original 1¢ or 2¢ and their value for communicating has been greatly reduced due to advances in technology, postcards still hold a special place for millions of people. Postcard collecting is viewed as the third-most-popular hobby in the world, following only stamp and coin collecting. Whether it is a simple pictorial reminder of a visit to a special location, a cost effective means of advertising for a local business, or the reason for the search for that one elusive card needed to complete a deltiologist's collection, postcards remain an integral part of many people's lives.

Two

Uptown, Downtown, All Around the Town

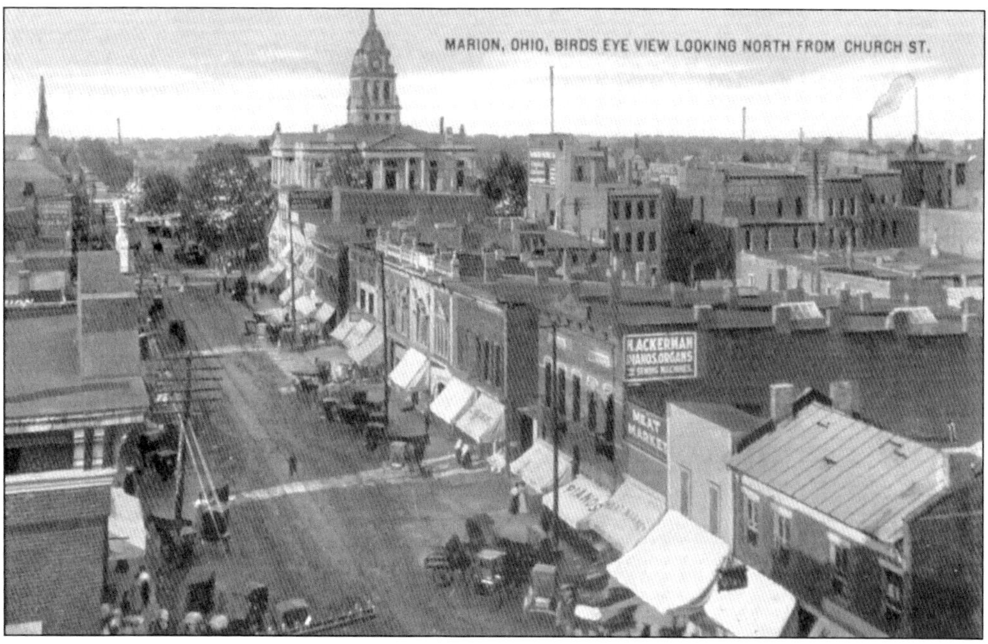

Main Street from Church Street. Shop owners on South Main Street have taken advantage of awnings to protect their storefronts not only from rain but also the late afternoon sun in this c. 1900 view. A favorite activity of youngsters was to grab onto an awning to see how far they could swing. Business must have been brisk judging by the number of buggies parked in front of the stores. (Author's collection.)

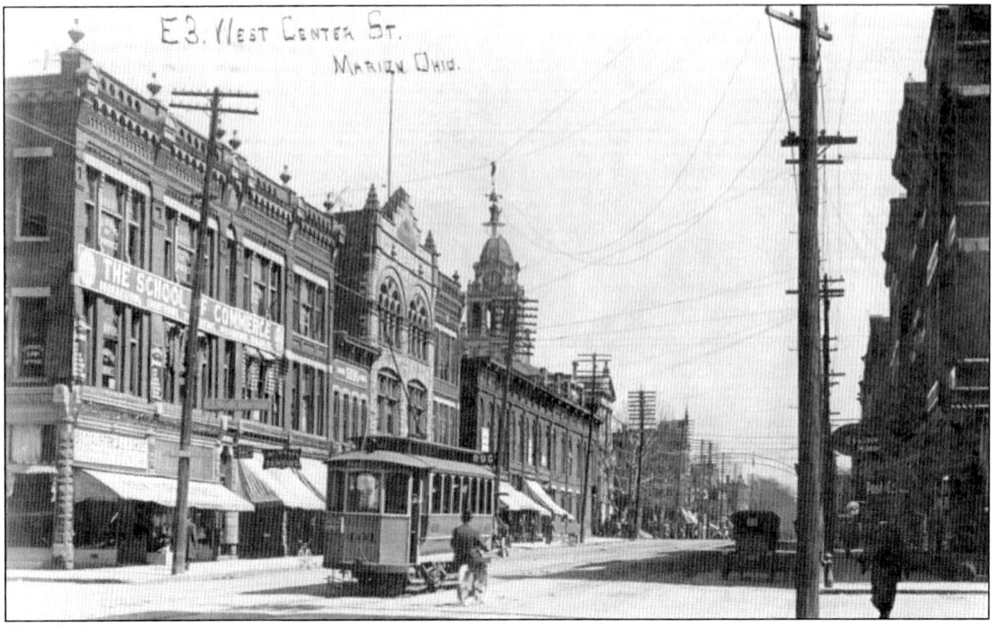

Center Street from Prospect Street. The street trolley passing by the School of Commerce on its way to the Union Depot was just one of the transportation options available for shoppers as they made their way up Center Street. The New York Store provided an enticing opportunity to look for new footwear at the "Big Slaughter Sale of Shoes." (Courtesy of Richard Carey.)

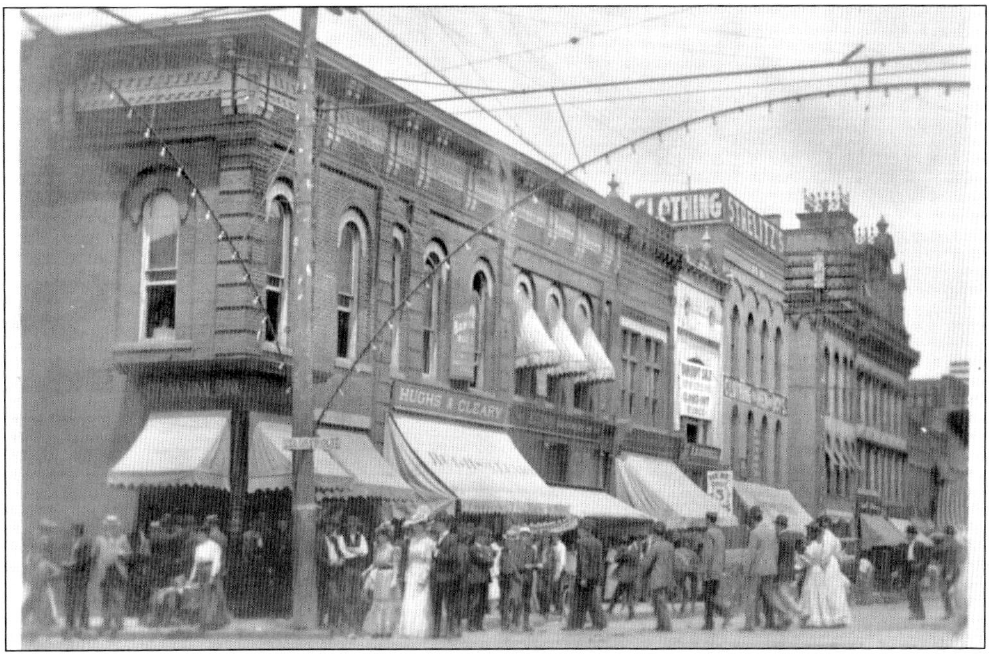

Center and Main Streets. To celebrate the availability of electricity in Marion, the Marion Electric Light Company installed lighted arches in 1898 at the intersection of Center and Main Streets. Perhaps the lights, which lit in a sequential pattern, made shopping easier at Hughs and Cleary Clothes for Men, Kling Hardware, the City National Bank, and Strelitz's Clothing for Men and Boys. (Courtesy of Richard Carey.)

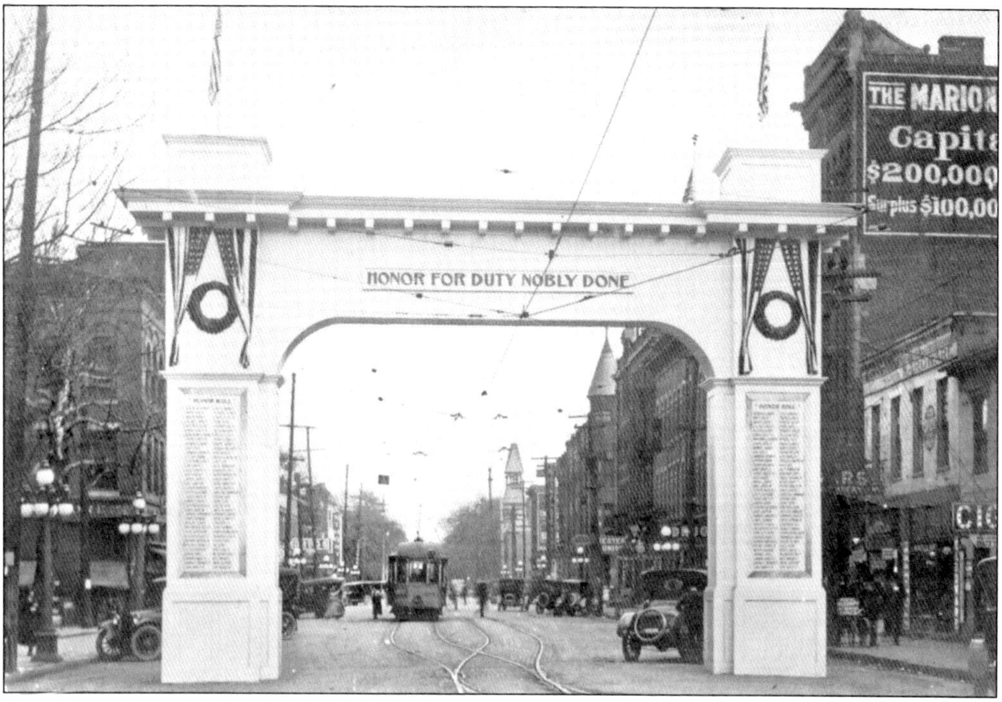

VICTORY ARCH. Marion's Victory Arch, located on Center Street adjacent to the courthouse, honored the soldiers and sailors from Marion County who fought for their nation in what President Wilson referred to as "the war to end all wars." Featuring an honor roll of those who had served, the arch was dedicated on May 27, 1919, when 600 veterans marched through it. The arch was removed later in the same year after causing numerous traffic accidents. (Author's collection.)

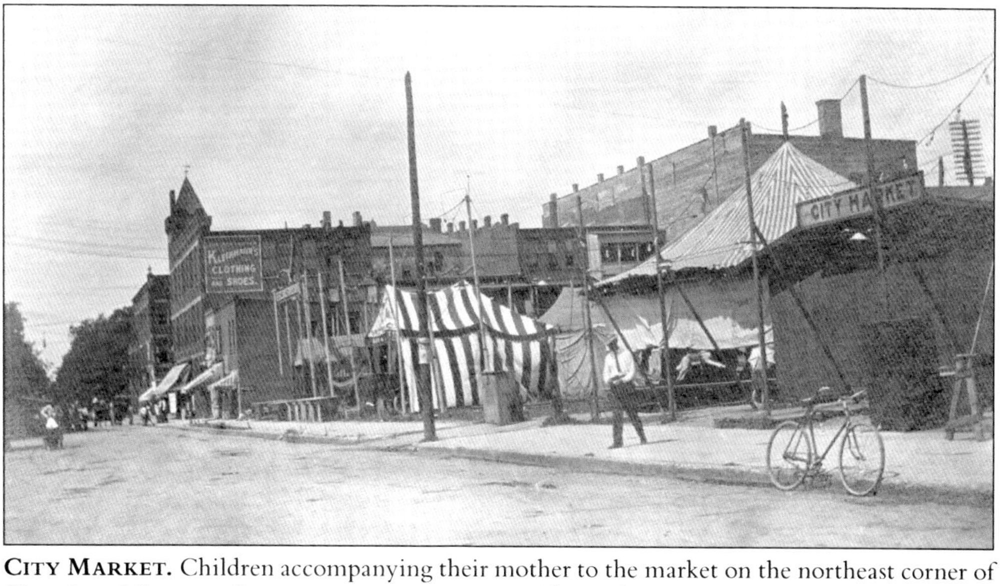

CITY MARKET. Children accompanying their mother to the market on the northeast corner of Church and Prospect Streets were sure to want a ride on the carousel inside the tent. Built in 1857, the market was established to provide a centralized shopping location. The second floor was occasionally used as a music hall until the Wigwam, an entertainment house, opened across the street. (Courtesy of Stuart Koblentz Haley.)

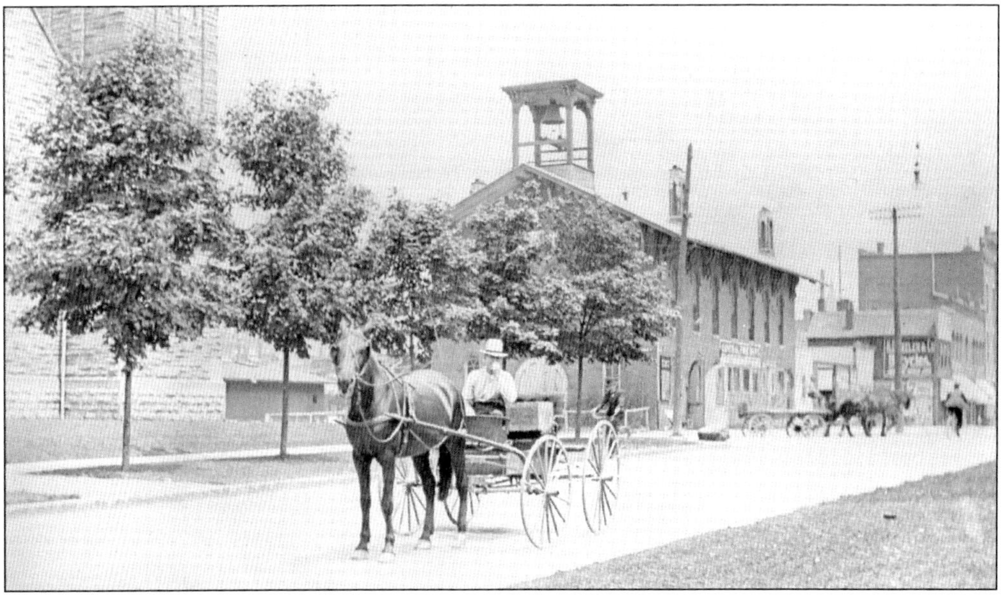

First City Hall. Marion's first city hall was established in the former city market building. It served as home to both the fire and police departments. Citizens charged with crimes such as flying a kite, putting a horse to a mare, or making a fire within 30 feet of a building might spend some time in one of the five cells or the "dark room." The second floor housed the city government offices. (Courtesy of Mike and Linda Perry.)

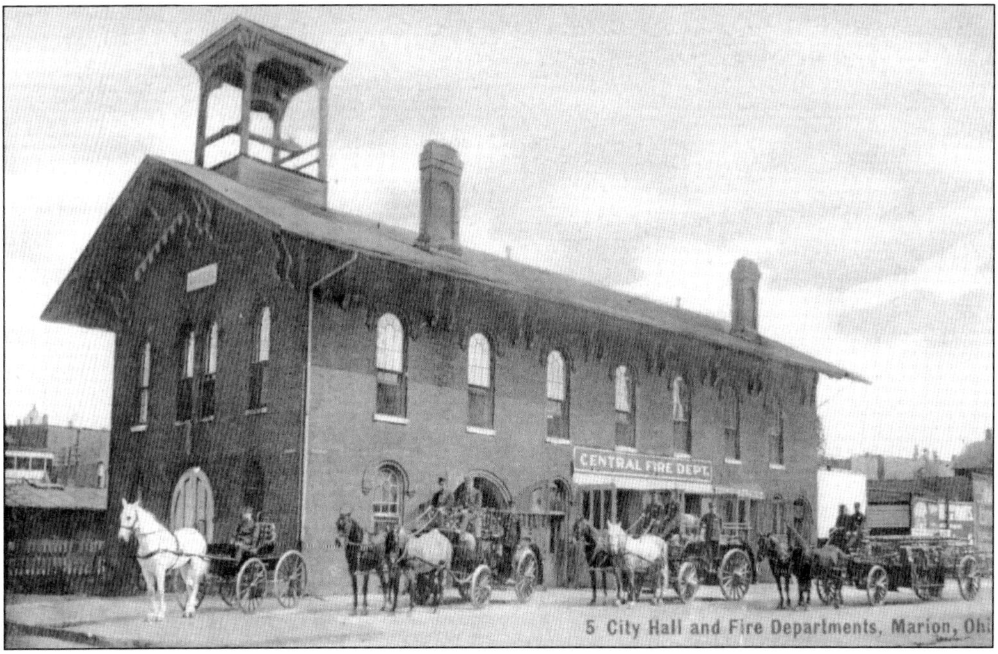

First Fire Department. The Marion Fire Department was created in 1876 after a city ordinance requiring every home to have a leather bucket for fighting fires proved to be inadequate. When a fire was spotted, a bell system signaled which quadrant the fire was in. Chief T.J. McFarland and his horse Old Mack would rush to the scene with the rest of the firefighters following behind. (Author's collection.)

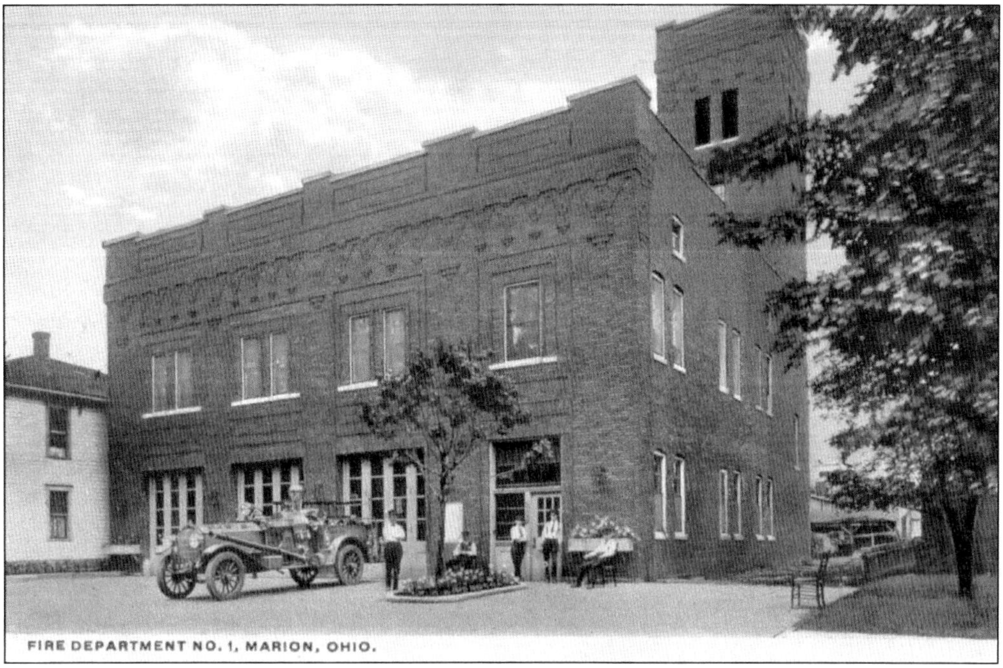

CENTRAL FIRE STATION. With the advent of mechanized equipment came a need for a larger fire station. Built in 1912 at 186 South Prospect Street at a cost of $16,000, Station No. 1 had three large bays and a tower for hanging fire hoses to dry. The station also housed a centralized Gamewell Fire Alarm Telegraph System, with 58 alarm boxes spread throughout Marion. (Author's collection.)

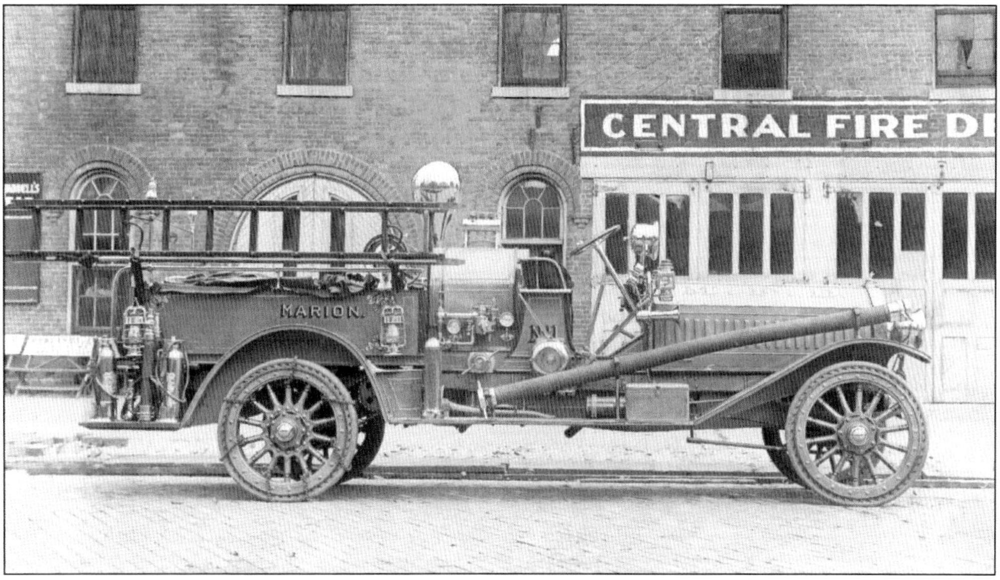

ENGINE NO. 1. Marion City Fire Department's No. 1 fire engine sits in front of the Central Fire Station in this advertising postcard for Bro-Gor Emergency Chains. The Brockett-Gorham Company of Marion manufactured the chains, which "made skidding impossible" and were the only "anti-skid device that will absolutely hold this car" according to Fire Chief McFarland. (Courtesy of Richard Carey.)

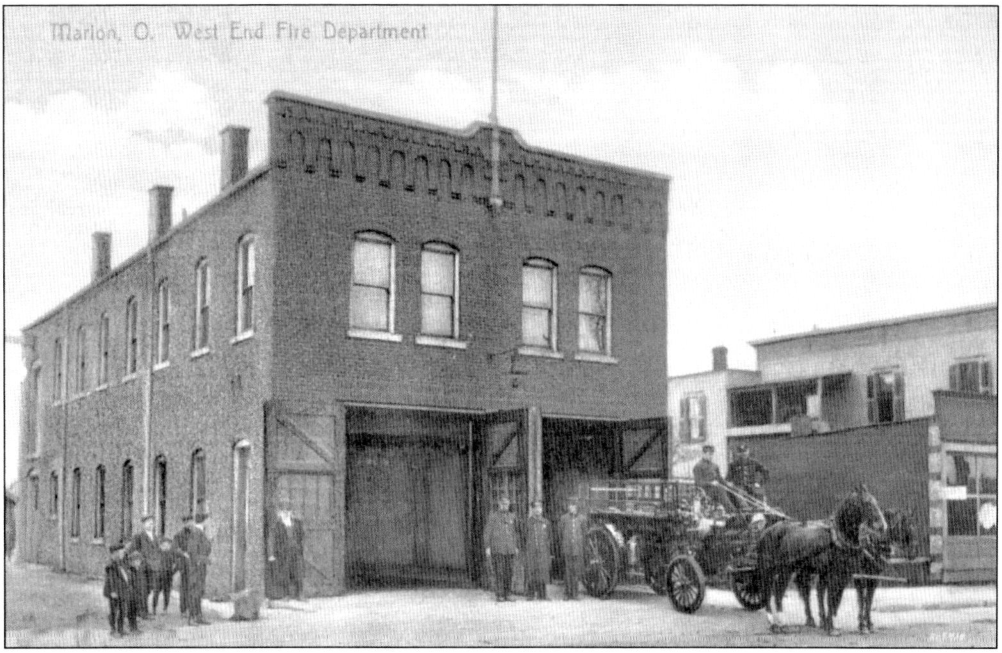

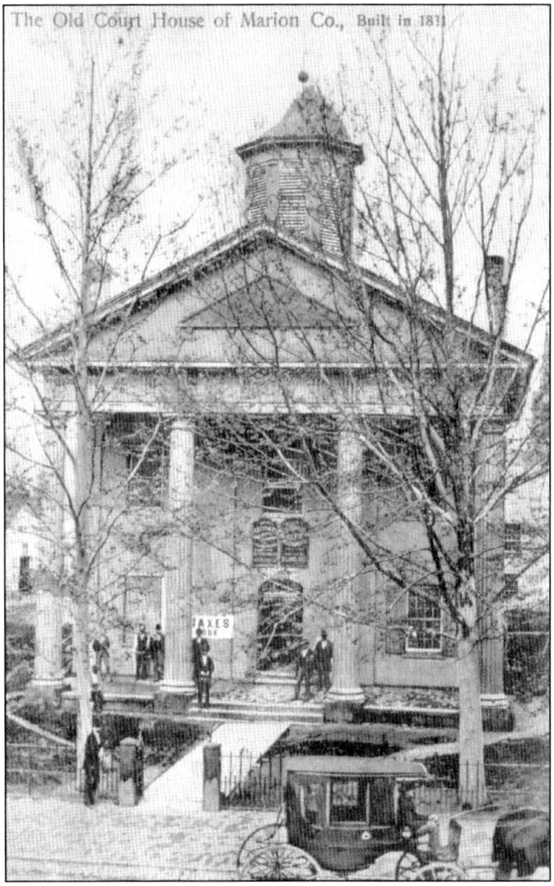

WEST END STATION. As Marion's industry expanded on the west end of town, so did the need for fire protection. Hose Company No. 2 had its home on West Center Street near Davids Street. Four men and a captain provided protection using a Silsby Steamer Fire Engine. The building was later used as a dining hall for Marion Steam Shovel executives. (Author's collection.)

1833 COURTHOUSE. "Taxes Due" reads the sign on the front of Marion's courthouse. The Greek Revival structure was surrounded by 17 sycamore trees, which provided cooling shade and were believed to not attract lightning. The building was erected at a cost of $6,641, an enormous sum for the time. It was torn down in 1883 and replaced with the current structure. (Author's collection.)

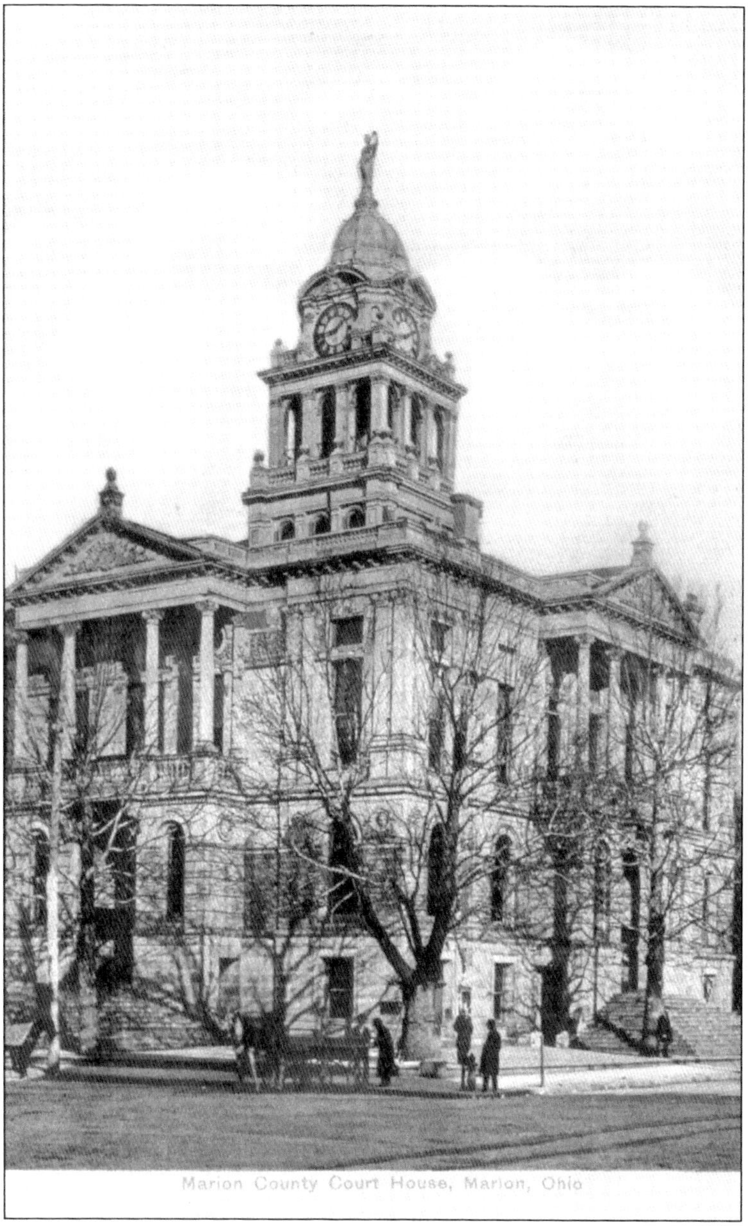

1886 COURTHOUSE. Marion's new courthouse was the pride of the community upon its completion in 1886. Built by Marion contractors Leffler and Bland at a cost of $115,000, it featured an upground basement of Marion limestone and upper floors of Golden Berean sandstone. Two sets of pyramidal steps provided access to the interior with its 15-foot ceilings and walls covered in a variety of murals. Double grand staircases with steps of iron cast in fanciful designs led to the upper floors. A domed rotunda allowed light to enter through a glass ceiling. The exterior had elaborate stone carvings, including two series of faces representing the races of man and the ages of man. Another unusual feature was the four-faced clock with eight-foot-diameter dials, which were originally illuminated by gas jets. High above it all stood a zinc statue, Lady Justice, holding her sword and scales of justice. Removed for repairs in 1952, she disappeared for over 28 years before being returned and put back in her rightful place. (Author's collection.)

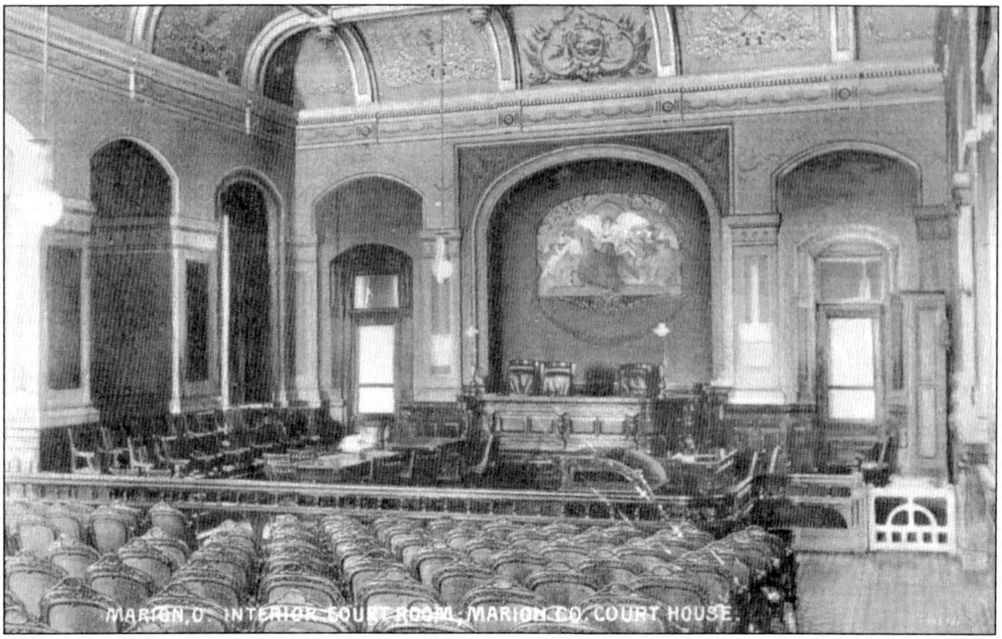

COURTROOM VIEW. People appearing before the judge did so in this beautiful courtroom with walnut and butternut woodwork. Hand-painted murals depicted symbols of Industry, Light, and Commerce. The room was also used for community events such as the 1898 Farmer's Institute, which featured a full-sized replica horse pulling a plow. A mid-1970s renovation significantly altered the building's interior. (Courtesy of Richard Carey.)

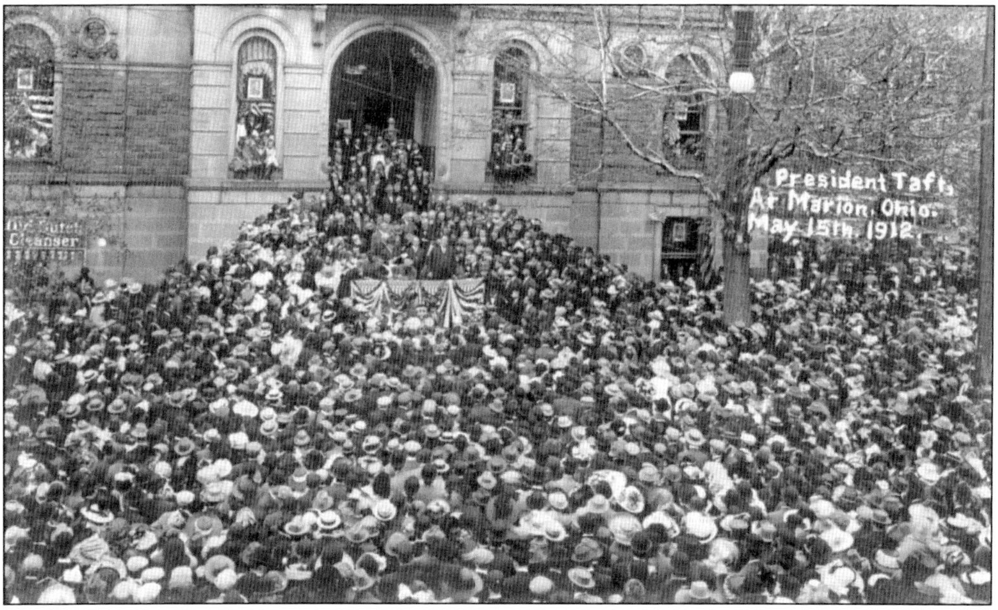

PRESIDENT TAFT VISITS MARION. After traveling from Galion in his private railcar, Pres. William Howard Taft made a speaking stop at the courthouse in Marion during his unsuccessful 1912 campaign for reelection. Taft kept his remarks short as he commented that he was sorry to interfere with the opening day baseball game scheduled for Webb Field on Marion's west side by talking about politics. (Courtesy of Richard Carey.)

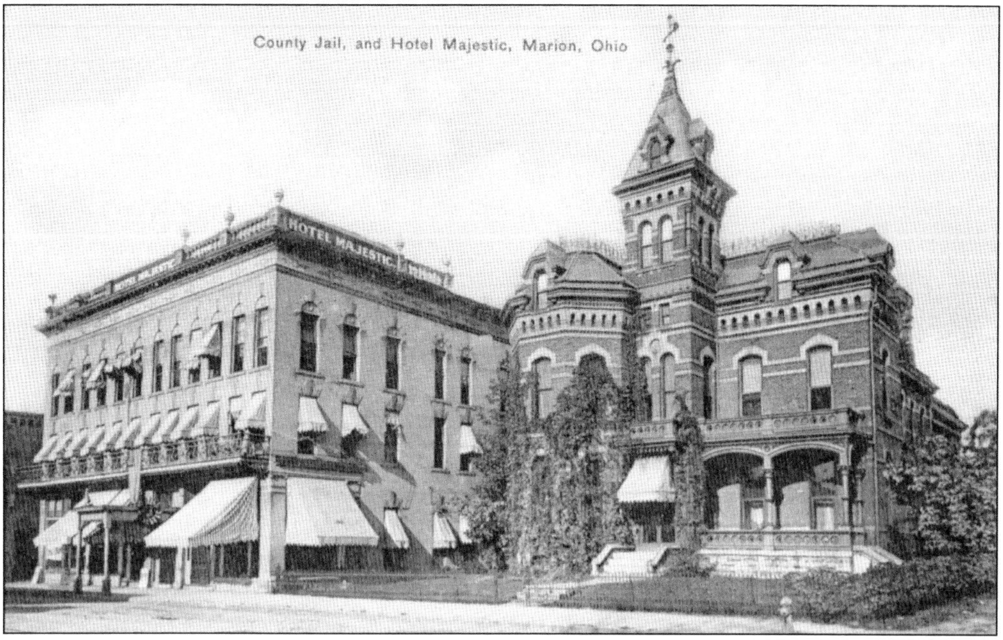

JAIL AND HOTEL. "Guests" in the Marion County Jail—with its 18 cells, including two for women—undoubtedly wished they could change their abode to the Hotel Majestic located next door on North State Street. Built in 1878 at a cost of $28,000, the Victorian building was also the sheriff's residence. The jailor's key weathervane is on display at the Marion County Historical Society. (Author's collection.)

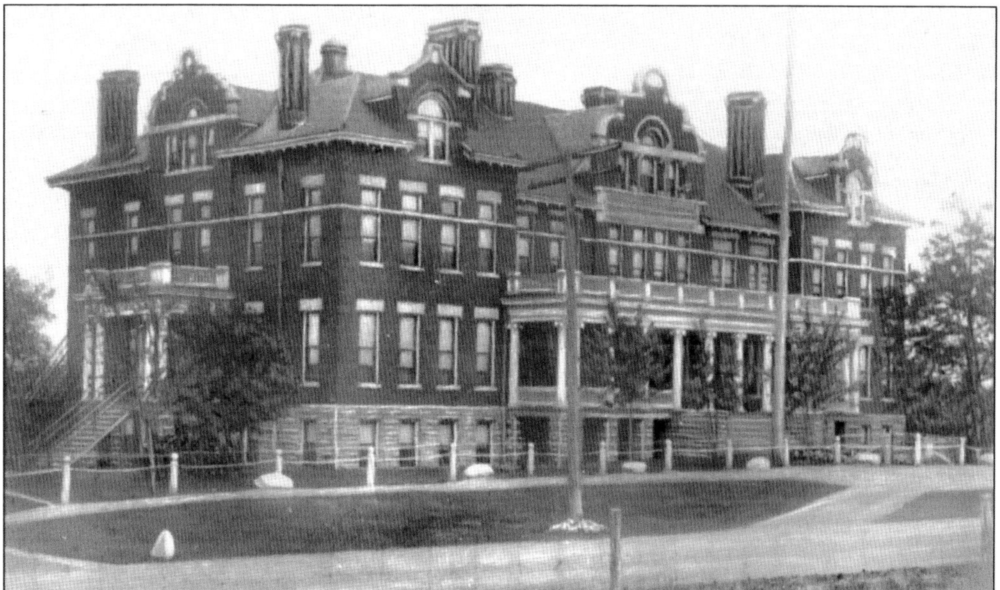

WADDELL'S HOME FOR CHILDREN. Philanthropist Benjamin Waddell built this 52-room home for orphaned children on 60 acres on the Marion and Delaware Pike (State Route 423) in 1901. He deeded it to Marion County with the stipulation that no child would ever be excluded due to color, nationality, or because of the political or religious views of the parents. It was replaced by Waddell Village in 1968. (Courtesy of Mike and Linda Perry.)

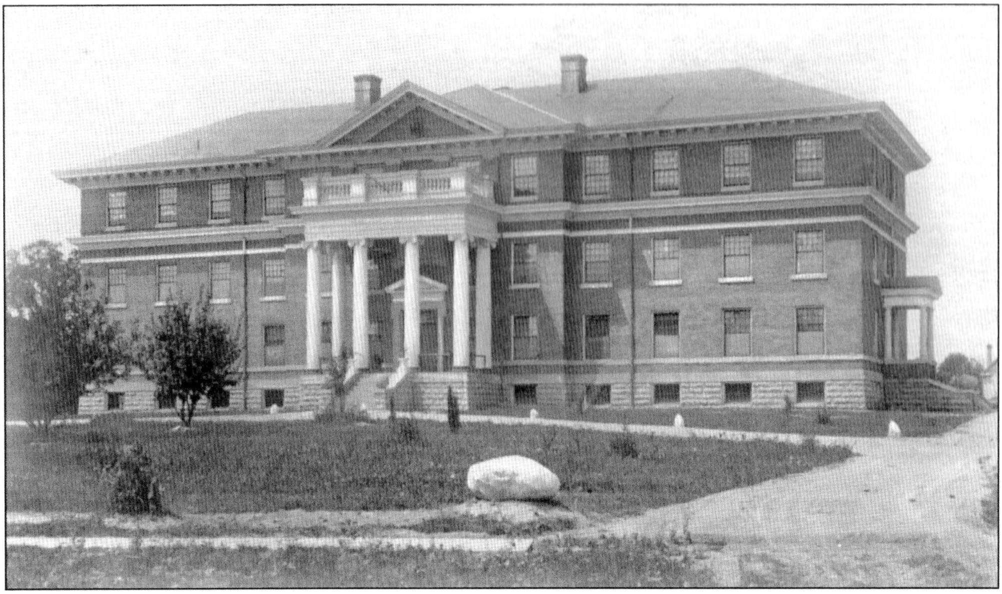

WADDELL'S HOME FOR AGED PEOPLE. In 1905, Benjamin Waddell turned his charitable works to assisting the elderly by building this 70-room home on Delaware Avenue. He also endowed the Old Ladies Home Association to maintain the facility. In 1922, the building became Marion City Hospital. A large wing was added during World War II. It later served as Marion City Hall and is now office and retail spaces. (Author's collection.)

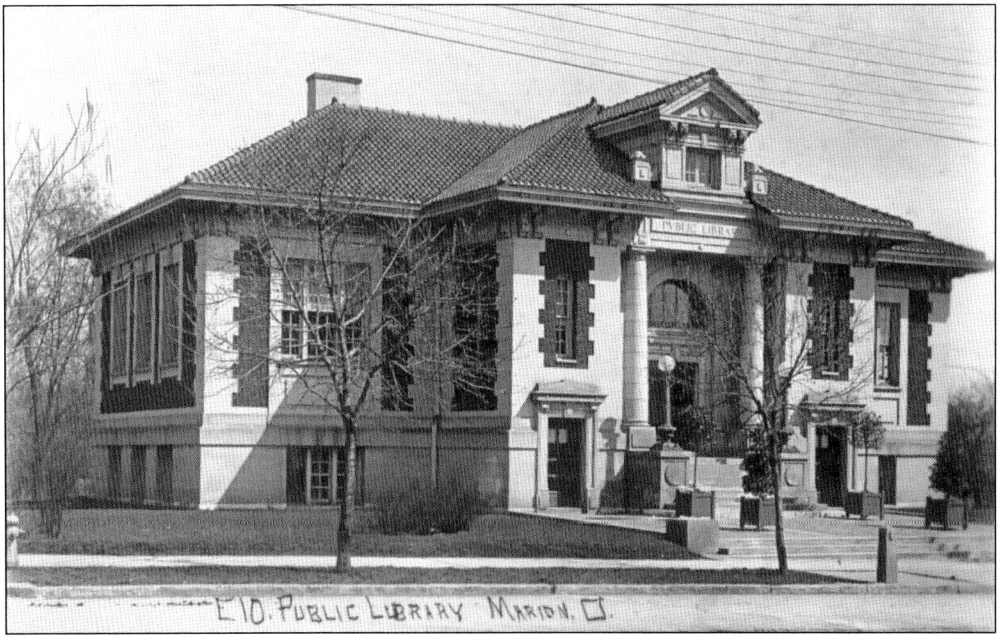

CARNEGIE LIBRARY. Marion industrialist Edward Huber established the first free public library in Marion with his Mechanics Library in 1886. In 1905, steel magnate Andrew Carnegie donated $30,000 to build this Beaux Arts–style library with its stone piazza in Ludlow Park on South Main Street across from Dr. Sawyer's Sanatorium. Closed in 1978, the former library is now used by Trinity Baptist Church. (Courtesy of Bob Turner.)

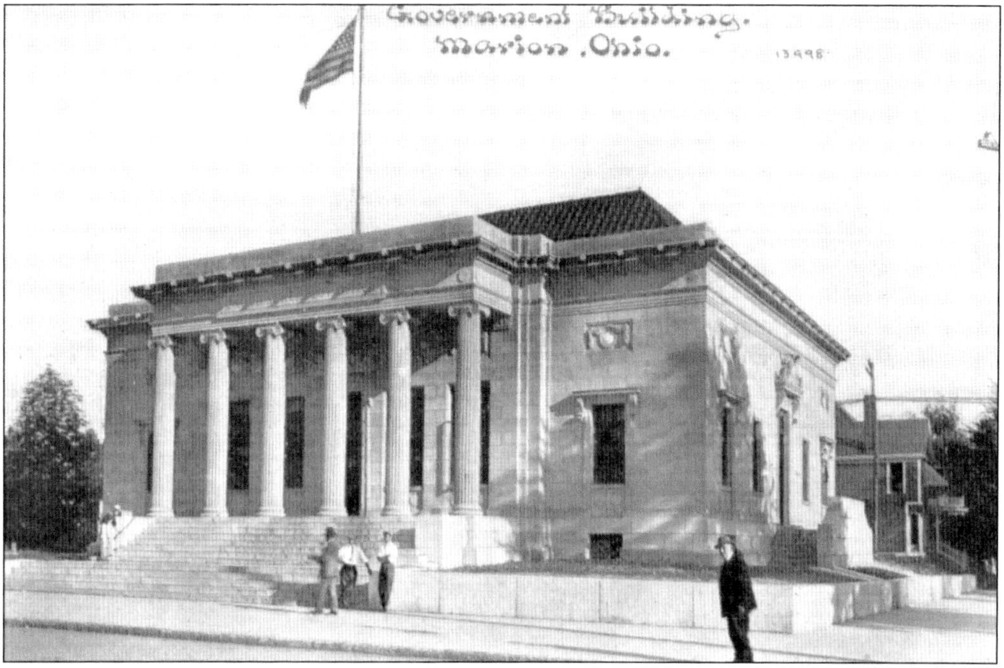

Post Office. This 1910 Beaux Arts–style building, complete with columned porticos and decorative garland, served as Marion's central post office for over 75 years. Interior features included a large skylight and hidden observation platforms for postal inspectors. An addition to the south side in 1937 nearly doubled the original building's size. Current occupants are the Marion County Historical Society and the Wyandot Popcorn Museum. (Courtesy of Marion County Historical Society.)

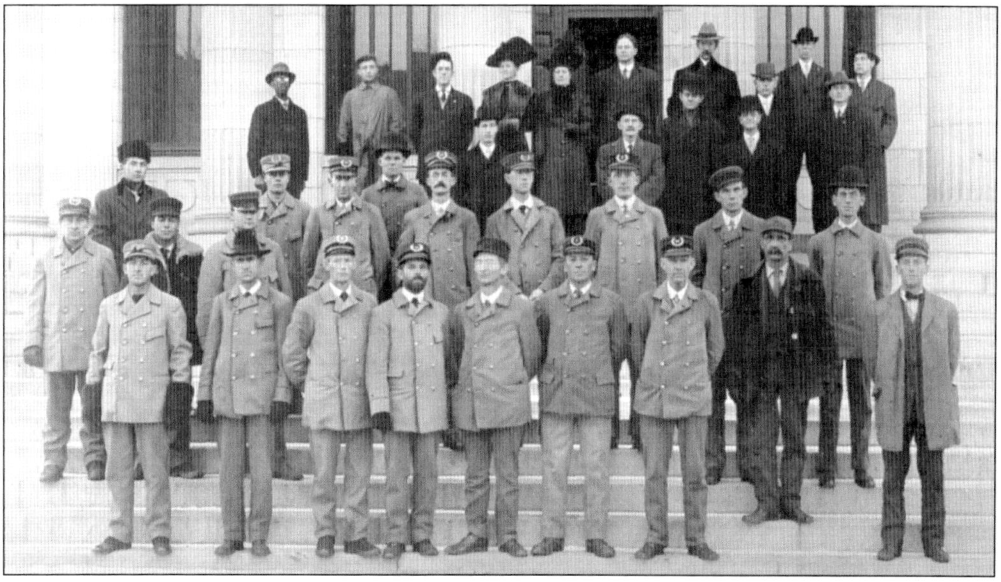

Opening Day. Postal employees celebrate the grand opening of their new $75,000 home on December 26, 1910, with this group photograph. The building was designed by James Taylor Knox, who was supervising architect of the Department of the Treasury from 1897 to 1912. Postmaster M.B. Dickerson oversaw 10 clerks, 8 rural-route carriers, and 13 city carriers, as well as 4 other employees. (Courtesy of Marion County Historical Society.)

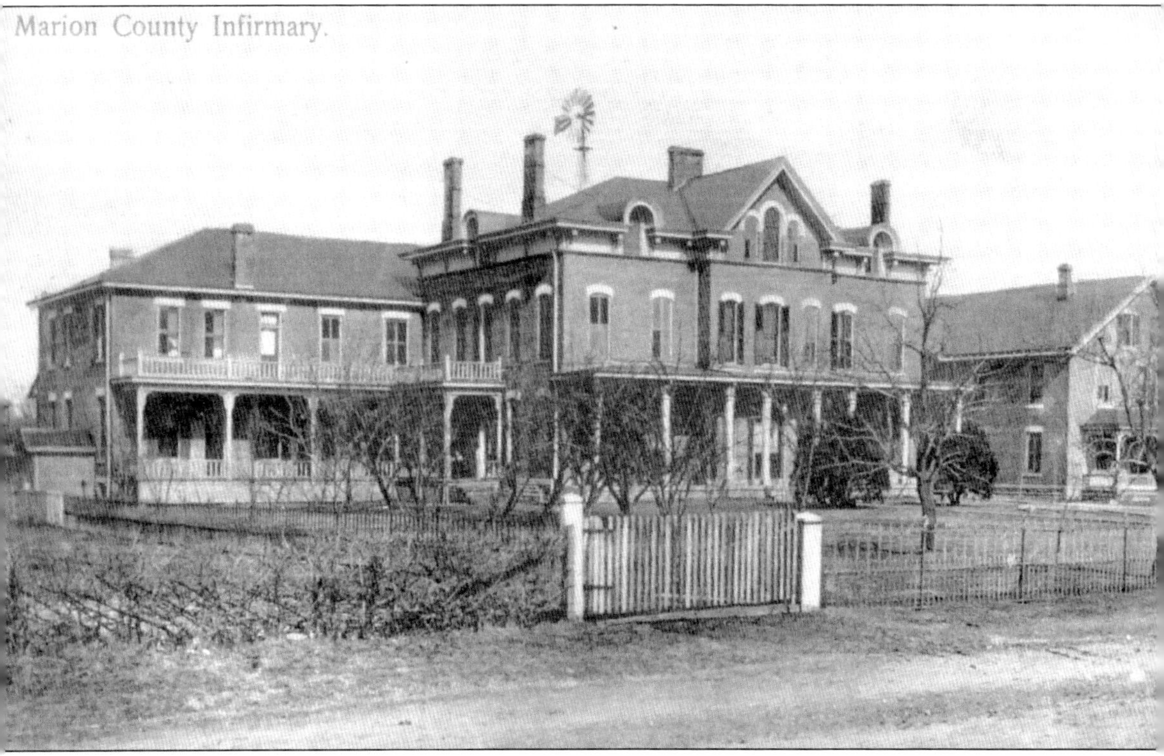

MARION COUNTY INFIRMARY. Marion County's paupers were taken care of by their respective townships until 1852, when the county established the Marion County Poorhouse just north of the city near Linn-Hipsher Road. Teachers, preachers, ex-soldiers, and schoolchildren could live there at no cost. Others were required to pay a fee or work for their room and board. In 1869, the county purchased 230 acres on Claridon Road east of the city of Marion and erected the Marion County Infirmary. Featuring several buildings with accommodations for 125 residents as well as barns and a small hospital building, it operated as a farm, with residents working to help with the costs of their housing and care. Around 1929, the name was changed to the Marion County Home. Eventually, 180 acres were sold to The Ohio State University for development of the Marion Campus. A new facility named East Lawn Manor was opened in 1971 and the older buildings were demolished. East Lawn met the same fate in 2005, with the area now used for commercial purposes. (Author's collection.)

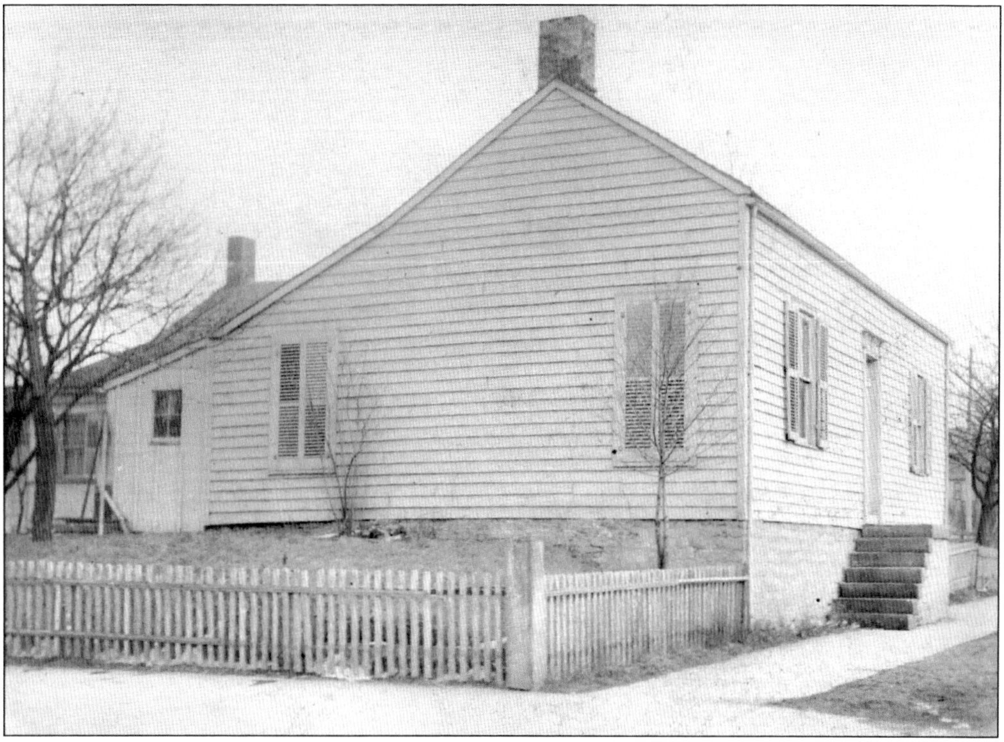

Lewis Raichley Home. This saltbox house on the northeast corner of Church and State Streets was a classic example of 1820s-era homes in Marion. Front yards were considered luxuries for homeowners, as evidenced by the doorway being literally next to the sidewalk. Raichley willed the property to the Marion Masons for a new lodge, which was never built. Huntington Bank now occupies the lot. (Courtesy of Stuart Koblentz Haley.)

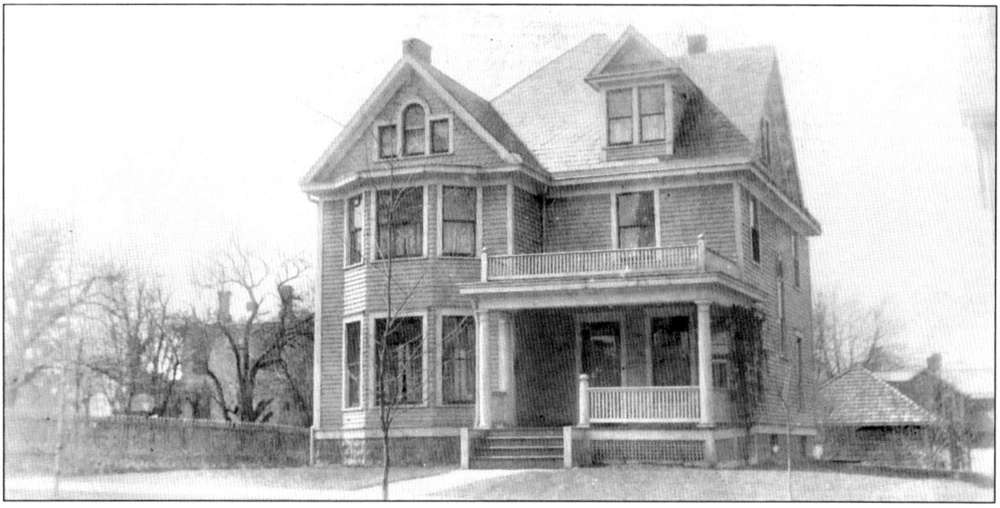

View from Gospel Hill. Once called Berry's Hill, the area later became known as Gospel Hill due to the large number of ministers living there in the early 1900s. The Italianate brick building (seen in the background) on South State Street was later used by J.H. Maish Advertising and Folks Printing. It was eventually razed, and the property is now the site of Rotary Towers. (Courtesy of Stuart Koblentz Haley.)

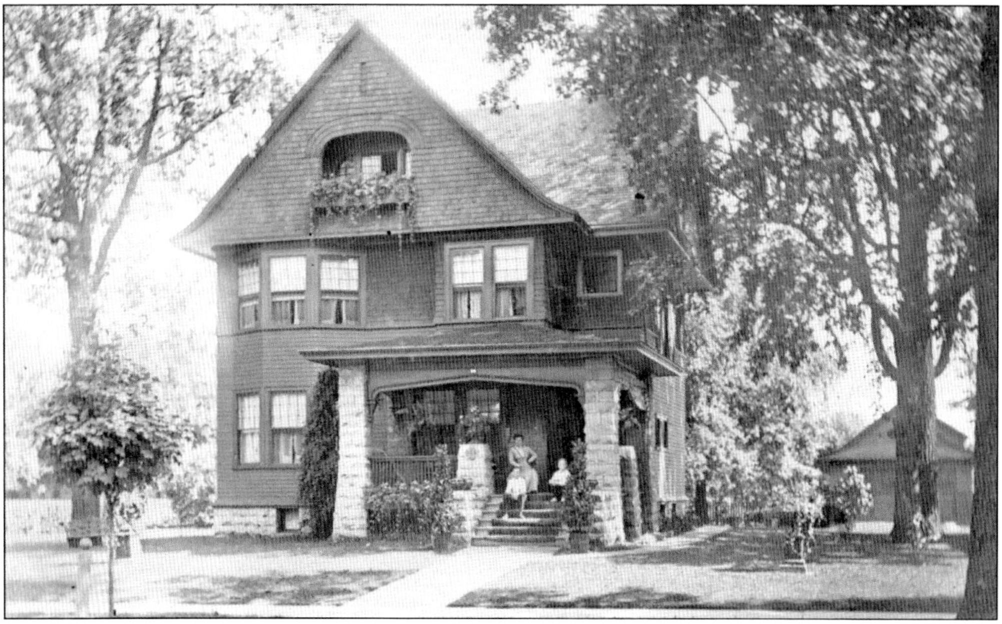

PRENDERGAST HOME. Resplendent with its cut limestone pillars and recessed window box, the Prendergast residence on Silver Street was a visible reminder of the success of the family's lumber company located on Oak Street. The sign on the porch signaled the ice company to include this residence on its delivery rounds. A piece of ice might be chipped off as a treat for the children. (Courtesy of Richard Carey.)

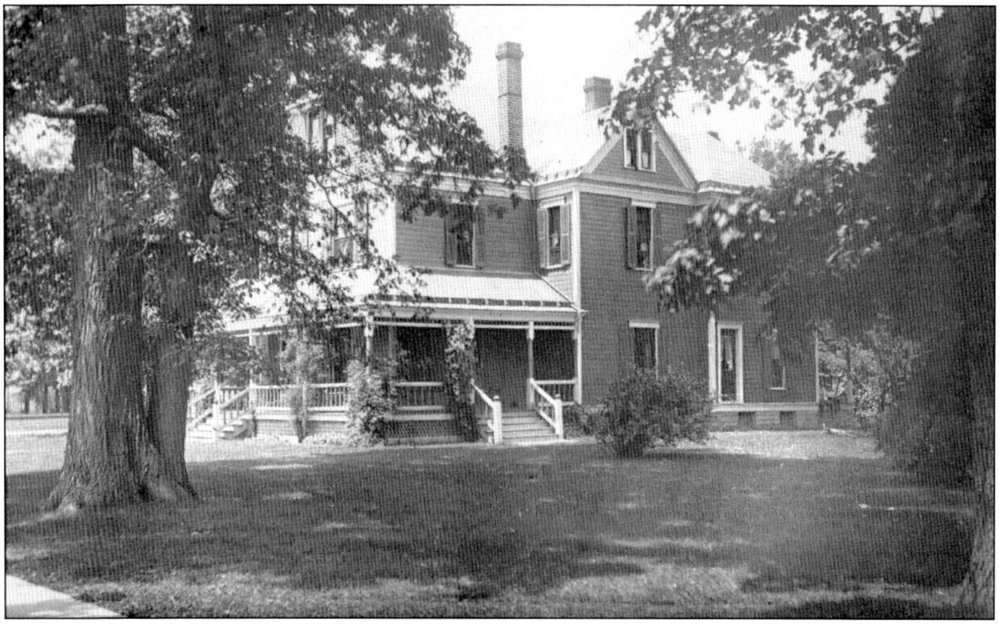

CHERRY HILL FARM. Eli Bush, a successful real estate developer who made his mark by building low-cost housing, was able to enjoy the fruits of his success at his 25-acre farm and residence on East Center Street at True Avenue. The farm was noted for its cherry, apple, and pear orchards. The home still stands but has been drastically altered, with the porches removed. (Courtesy of Stuart Koblentz Haley.)

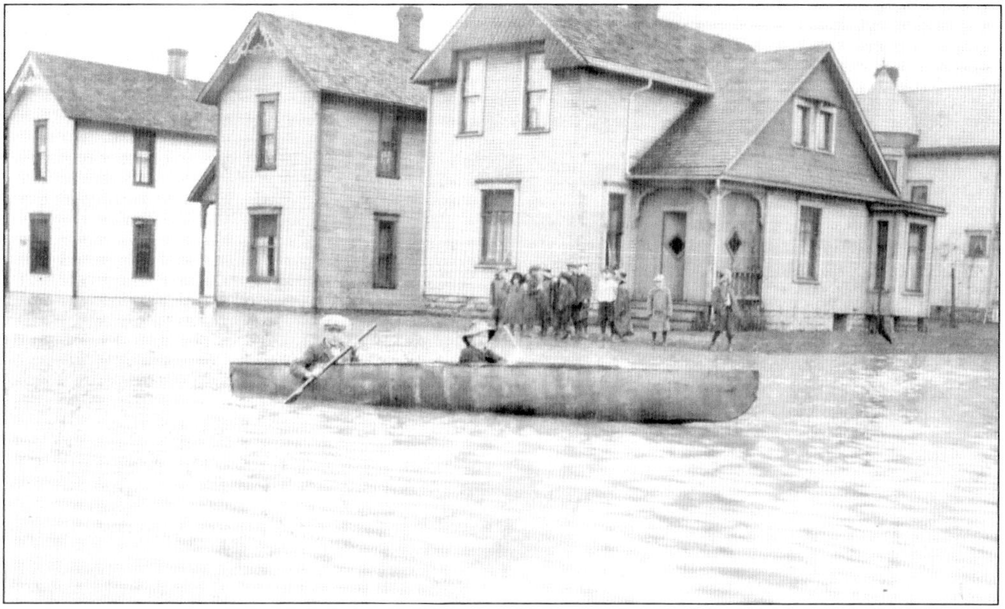

1913 FLOOD. These two young men are the envy of their friends, who are stranded in the background, as they paddle down a Marion street swollen from the 1913 flood. On March 23, rain fell on Marion for 36 straight hours, causing streets to turn into rivers and making boats the best means of transportation for many areas of the city. (Author's collection.)

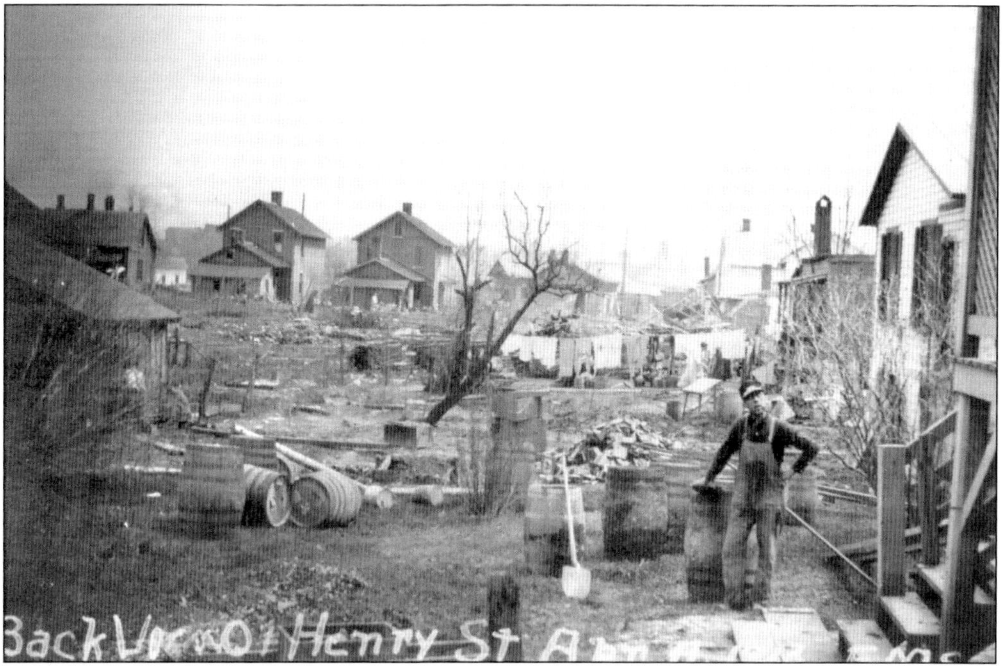

BACKYARD MESS. Looking over the devastation in the backyard of his Henry Street residence in southwest Marion, this homeowner contemplates the job ahead in cleaning up after the 1913 floodwaters had receded. The lack of a waterway through the city saved Marion from much of the devastation other communities, such as LaRue and Prospect, endured. (Courtesy of Richard Carey.)

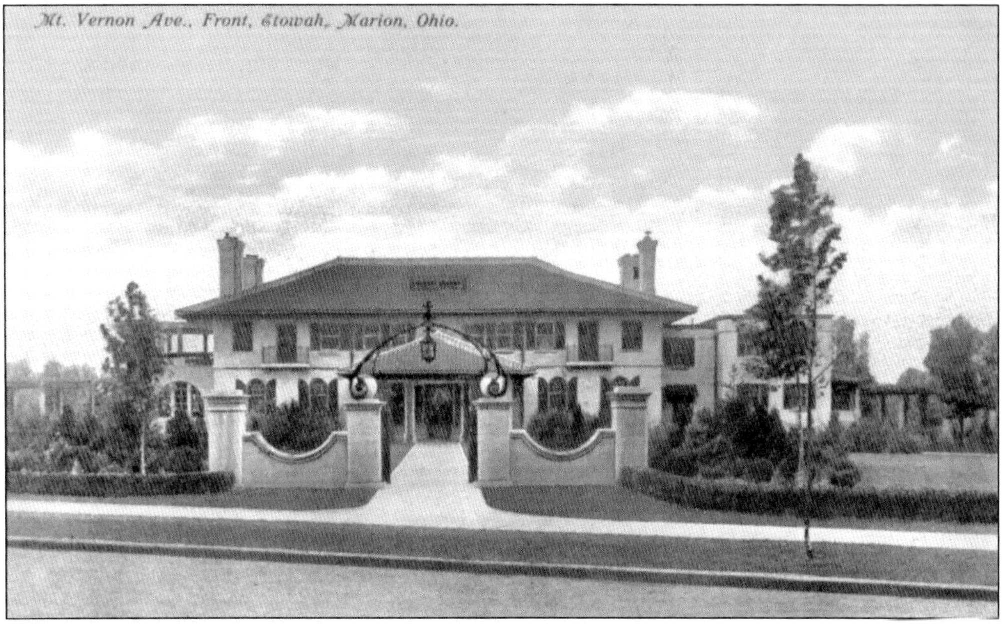

KING'S MANSION. Marion Steam Shovel president George W. King built his Mediterranean-style, 55-room home on Mount Vernon Avenue in 1908. King's daughter Ava married W. Hoover Brown in 1923 and moved into the home. After some renovations, her brother Ray King and his family joined them. The property was purchased in 1948 by Central Christian Church and is used as its worship center. (Author's collection.)

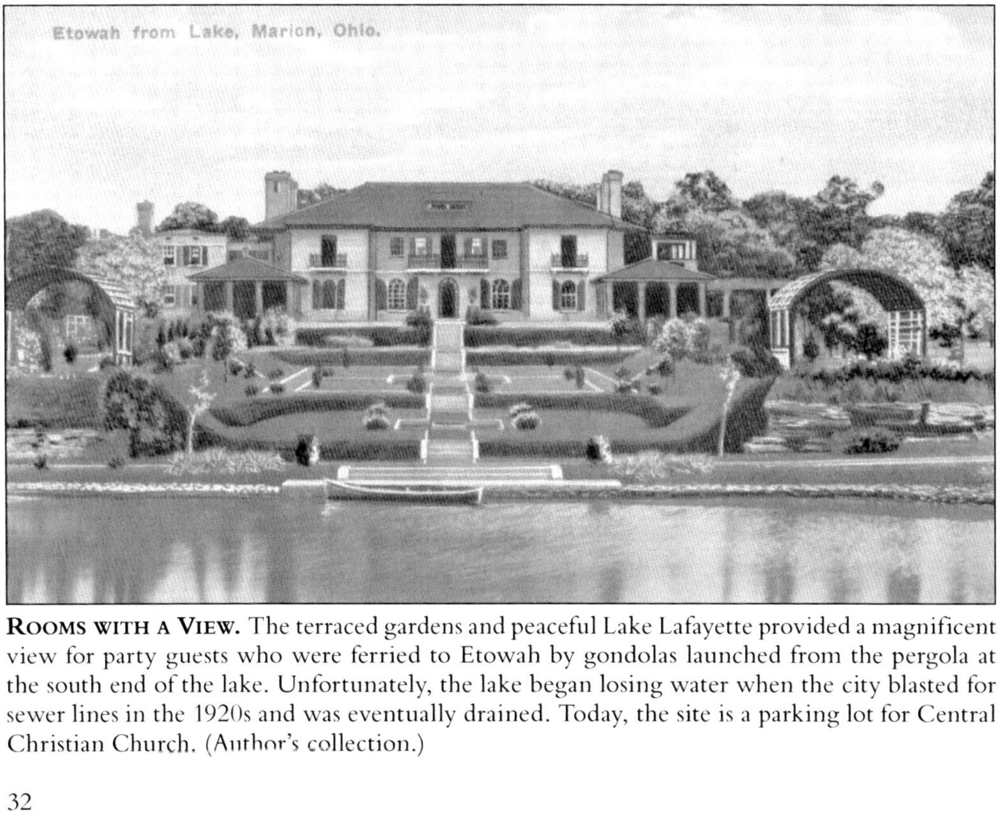

ROOMS WITH A VIEW. The terraced gardens and peaceful Lake Lafayette provided a magnificent view for party guests who were ferried to Etowah by gondolas launched from the pergola at the south end of the lake. Unfortunately, the lake began losing water when the city blasted for sewer lines in the 1920s and was eventually drained. Today, the site is a parking lot for Central Christian Church. (Author's collection.)

THE REPUBLICAN CHOICE. Warren G. Harding rose from being the owner of a struggling, small-town Republican-view newspaper in a predominantly Democratic-leaning town to serve two terms in the Ohio Senate followed by a term as Ohio's lieutenant governor. In spite of the obvious qualifications stated on this advertising postcard, he was not successful in his run for governor in 1910. (Courtesy of Richard Carey.)

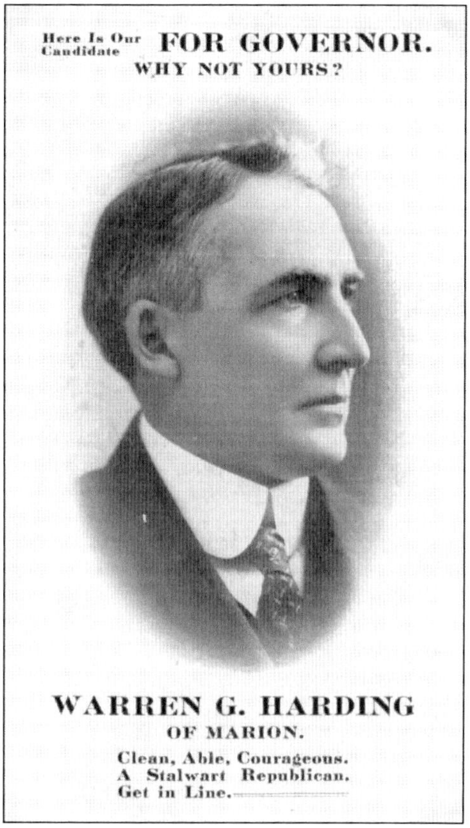

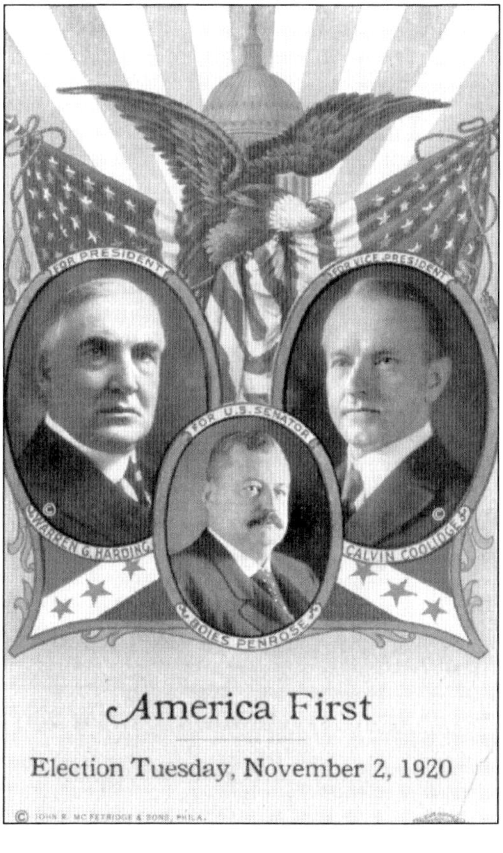

SOMETIMES THE DARK HORSE WINS. Going into the 1920 Republican presidential convention as a dark horse candidate, Warren G. Harding emerged as the party's nominee on the 10th ballot. Paired with running mate Calvin Coolidge, Harding campaigned for a "Return to Normalcy" after the tumult of World War I. The American people supported his agenda as they elected Harding in a landslide victory. (Courtesy of Richard Carey.)

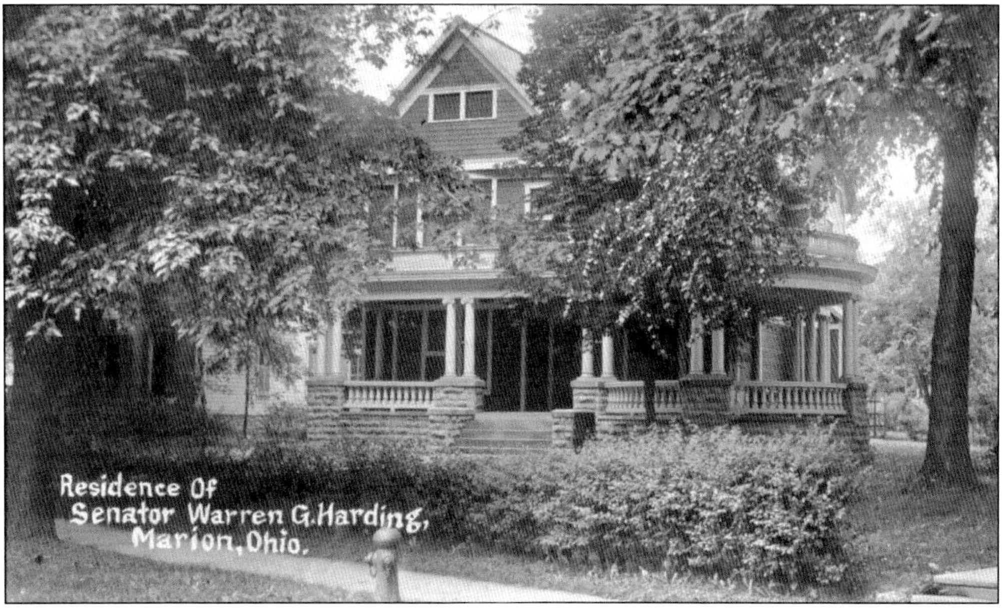

Front Porch Campaign. The home Warren G. Harding built for his new bride in 1891 eventually became the center of attention for the entire nation. In his 1920 race for president, Harding campaigned primarily from the large front porch he had added to the residence. Thousands of people visited Marion to hear his orations. After his election, Harding moved to Washington, DC, never to return to his Marion home. (Courtesy of Richard Carey.)

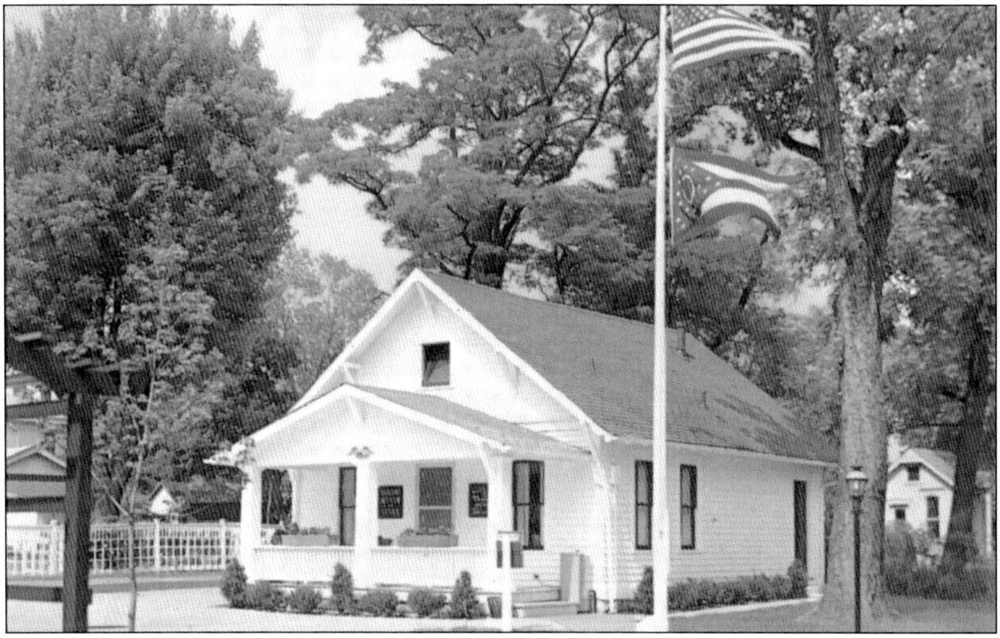

Press Palace. As a former newspaperman, Warren G. Harding knew the value of positive press. Harding made friends with members of the press corps who came to Marion to cover his campaign by providing them with their own sanctuary located behind his home. After Harding died in office, the press office was preserved as part of the Harding Home and Museum. (Author's collection.)

Three

THE BUSINESS OF BUSINESS

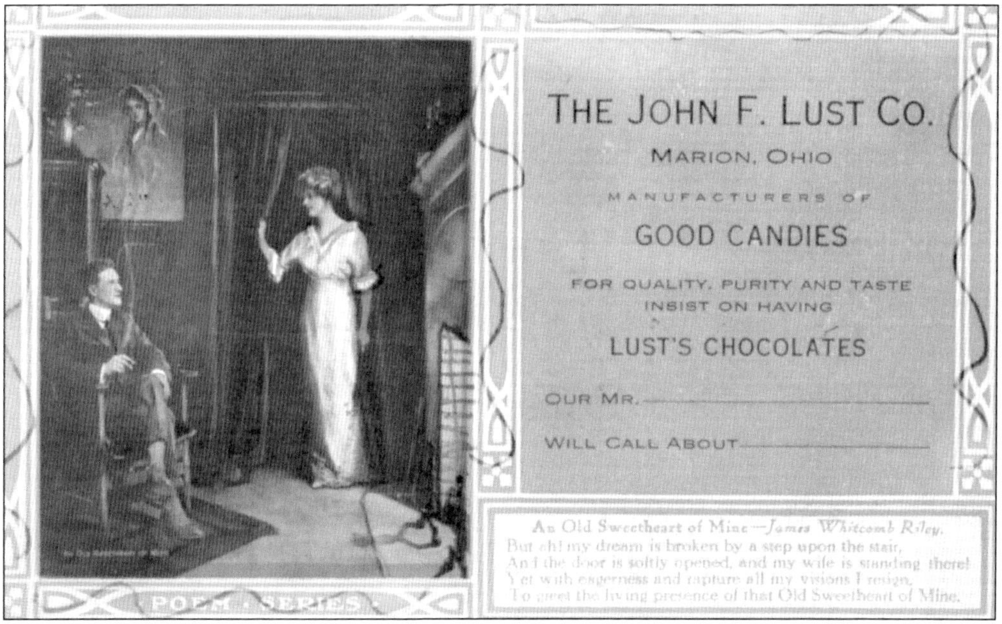

LUST CANDY MANUFACTURING. Advertising cards attempted to do more than just provide information about the company's product, as shown by this early 1900s card for the John F. Lust Candy Company. The card was mailed to a potential customer with the hope that a time could be arranged for a sales presentation. Lust's was located on North Main Street close to the railroad tracks and was noted for its excellent chocolate. (Courtesy of Richard Carey.)

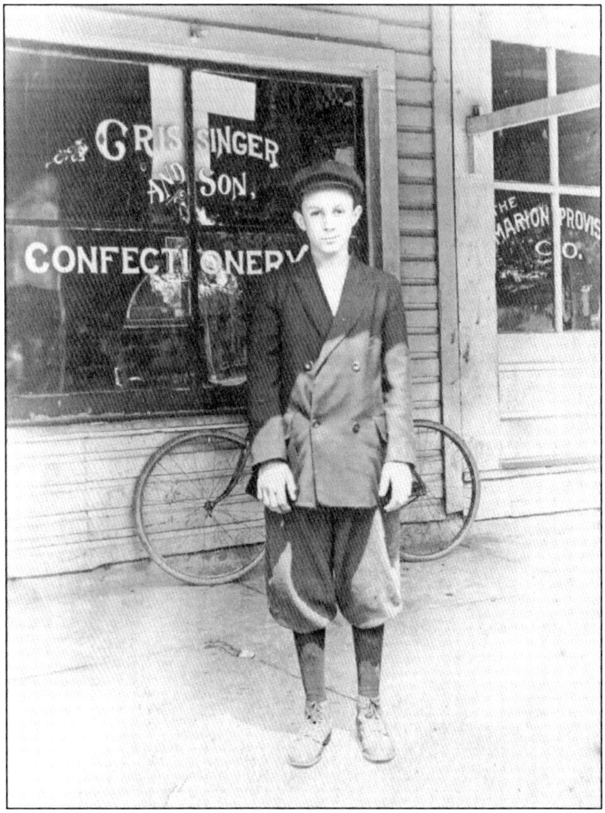

CRISSINGER AND SON CONFECTIONERY. The J.F. Crissinger and Son Confectionery offered a wide variety of sweet treats at its 812 East Center Street location. Many turn-of-the-century businesses offered delivery service as a means of increasing sales. This young man, with his bicycle at the ready, appears to be waiting for his next assignment. (Courtesy of Mike and Linda Perry.)

MARION PROVISION COMPANY. Offering groceries and fresh-cut meats, the Marion Provision Company was a business on the move as it relocated at least four times in a span of less than 10 years. Posters for relief efforts for the victims of the 1908 Sicilian earthquake and tsunami are posted on the wall of its East Center Street location. (Courtesy of Mike and Linda Perry.)

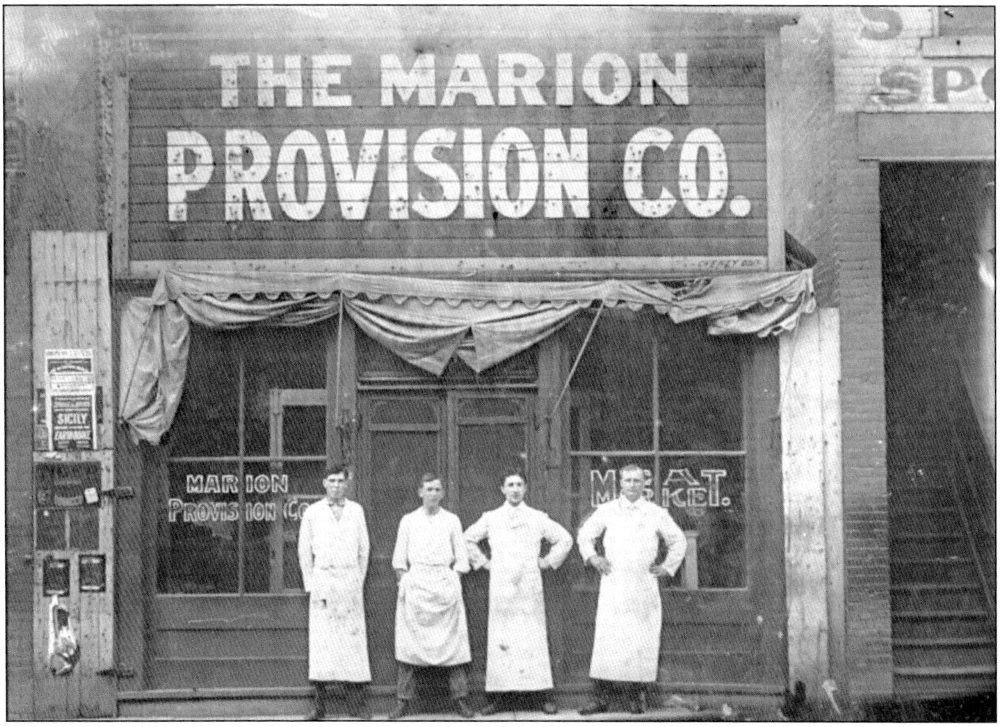

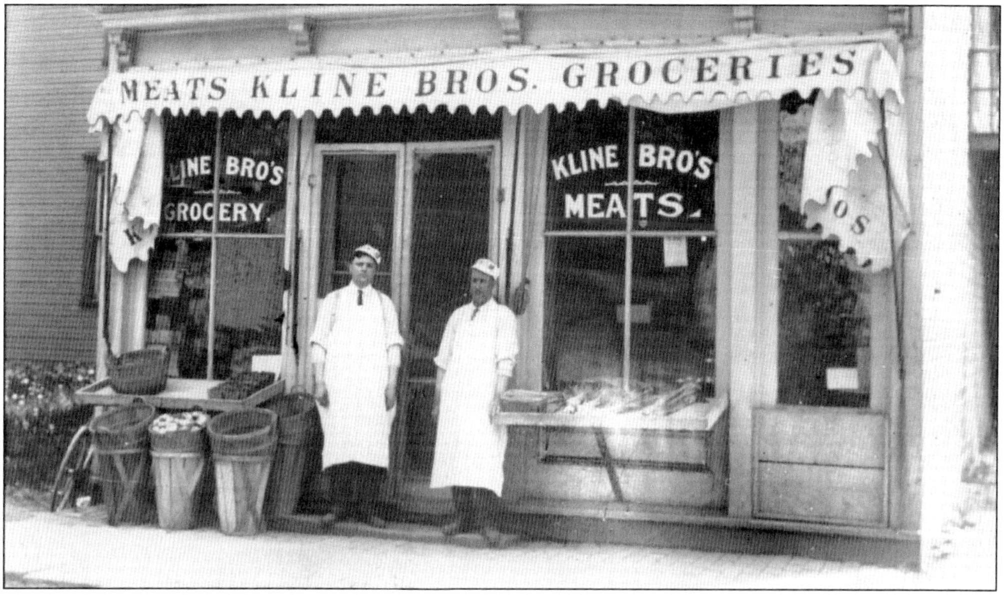

KLINE BROTHERS. Meat and grocery markets such as Kline Brothers were once found in every neighborhood in Marion. Even chain grocery stores were located close to their customers, with Kroger having 14 stores in Marion in 1929. Store names could sometimes be confusing, as both the Clean Cut Meat Market and the Klean Kut Meat Market called East Center Street home. (Courtesy of Mike and Linda Perry.)

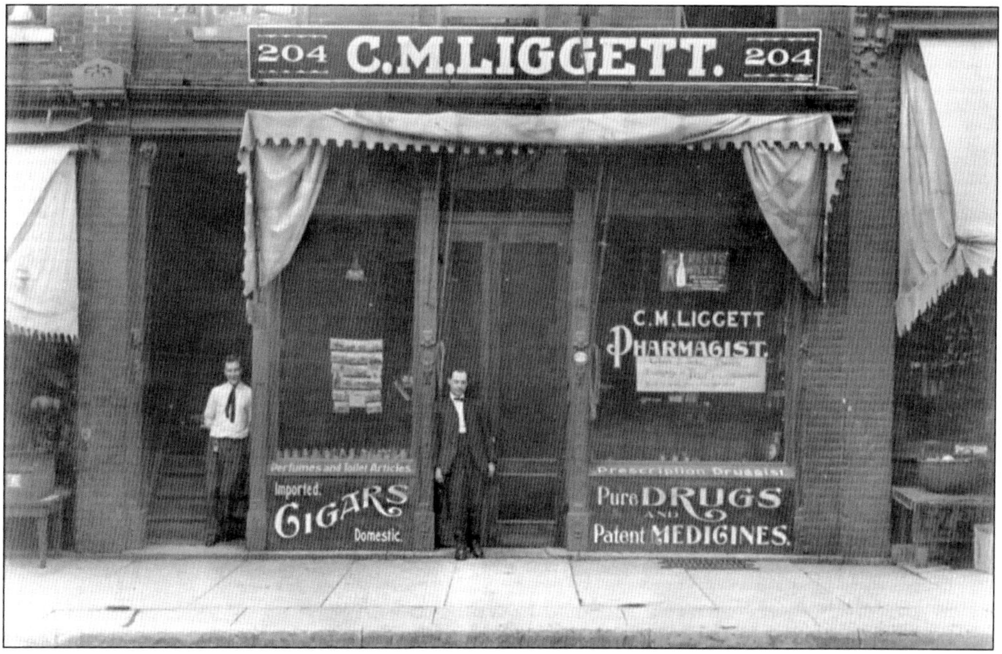

C.M. LIGGETT PHARMACIST. "Pure Drugs and Patent Medicines" were only two of the choices available in Liggett's Pharmacy at 204 East Center Street. Pluto Water is also featured in the window display. A natural water with strong laxative tendencies, Pluto Water's slogan was "When Nature Won't, Pluto Will." Apparently it worked, as 450 railroad cars were required to transport the bottler's output in 1919. (Courtesy of Ellis and Marjorie Hudson.)

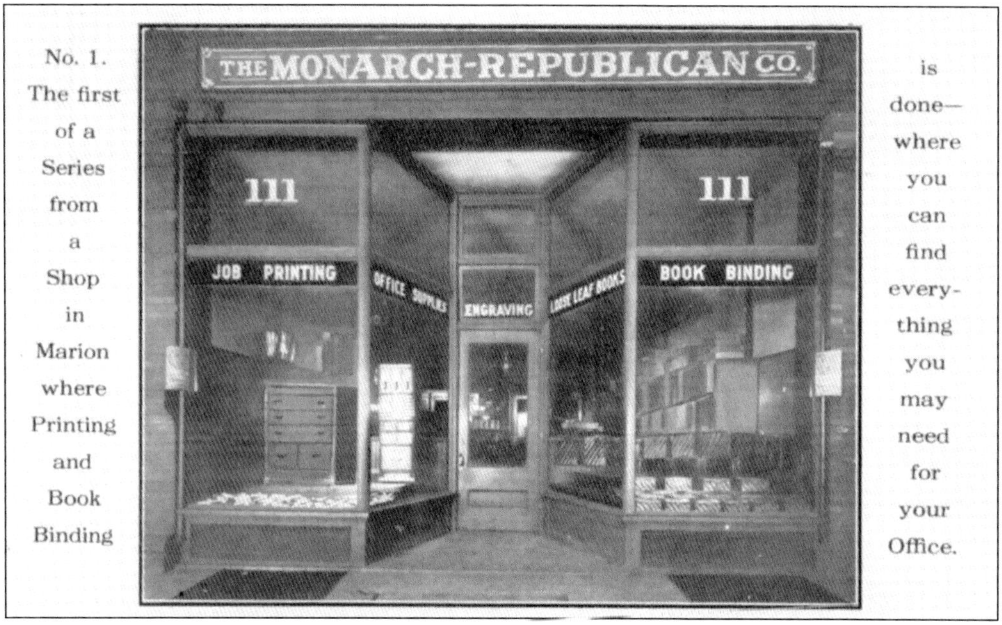

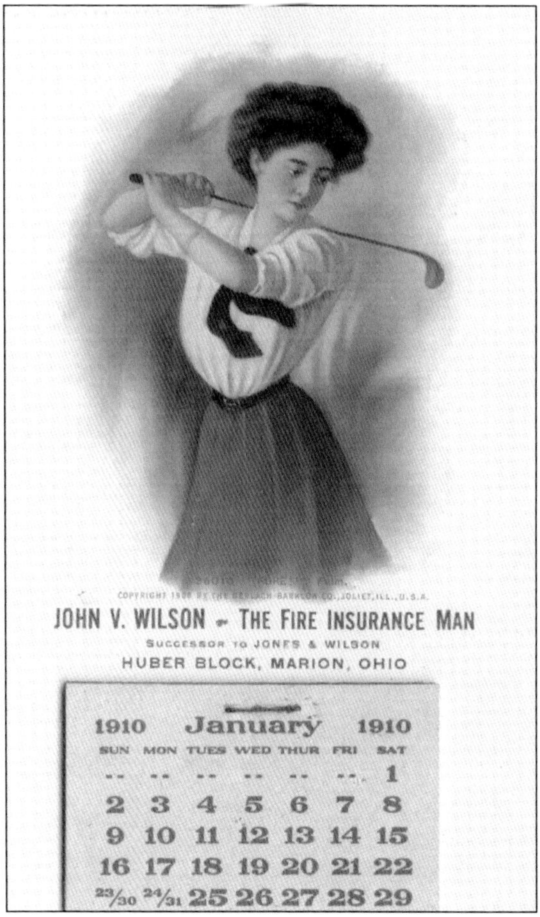

MONARCH-REPUBLICAN PRINTING. Many printing companies offered services in addition to typesetting and printing. The Monarch-Republican Company, located at 111 West Church Street, provided bookbinding in addition to printing. Bookbinding was used to maintain public records such as court documents, turnpike bonds, and tax receipts, among other purposes. The company also provided engraving for letterheads and books, a time-consuming process requiring specialized skills. (Courtesy of Michael Crane.)

JOHN WILSON INSURANCE. In the days before refrigerator magnets, some businesses utilized specialized postcard mailers in an effort to keep their name in front of customers. John Wilson, known as "The Fire Insurance Man," hoped the image of an attractive lady golfer on a monthly calendar would generate business for his company, which was located in the Huber Building on West Center Street. (Courtesy of Mike and Linda Perry.)

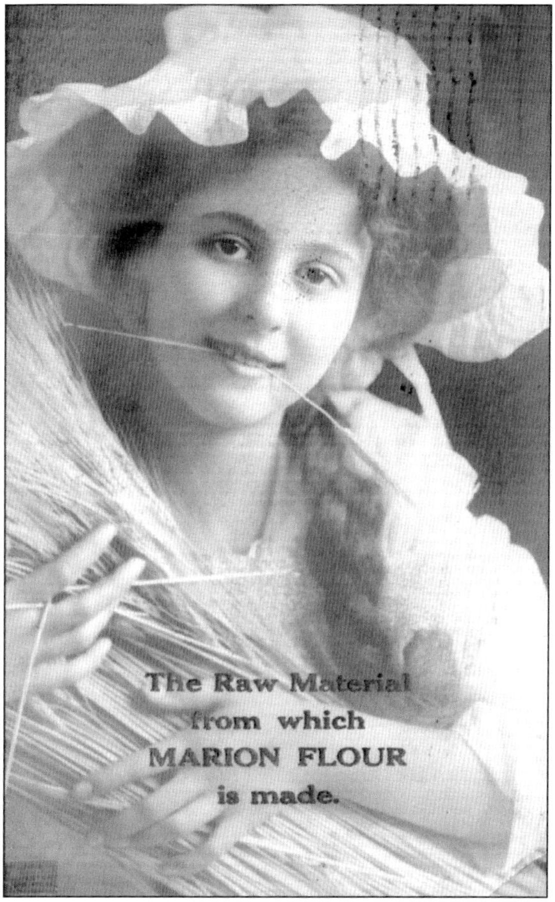

MARION NATIONAL GRAIN MILL. After their mill in Prospect burned in 1908, the owners relocated to Marion. Flour was ground for the Clover Leaf, Carnation, and Pride of Marion labels in the mill on the corner of Prospect and Mill Streets. This postcard confirms that the adage "sex sells" was true even in the early 1900s. (Courtesy of Mike and Linda Perry.)

MARION PAINT COMPANY. The Marion Paint Company utilized mobile advertising to promote its Dean and Barry Paints and other products. Located on East Center Street, the company is believed to be the predecessor of Young's Paints, a longtime Marion business. (Courtesy of Richard Carey.)

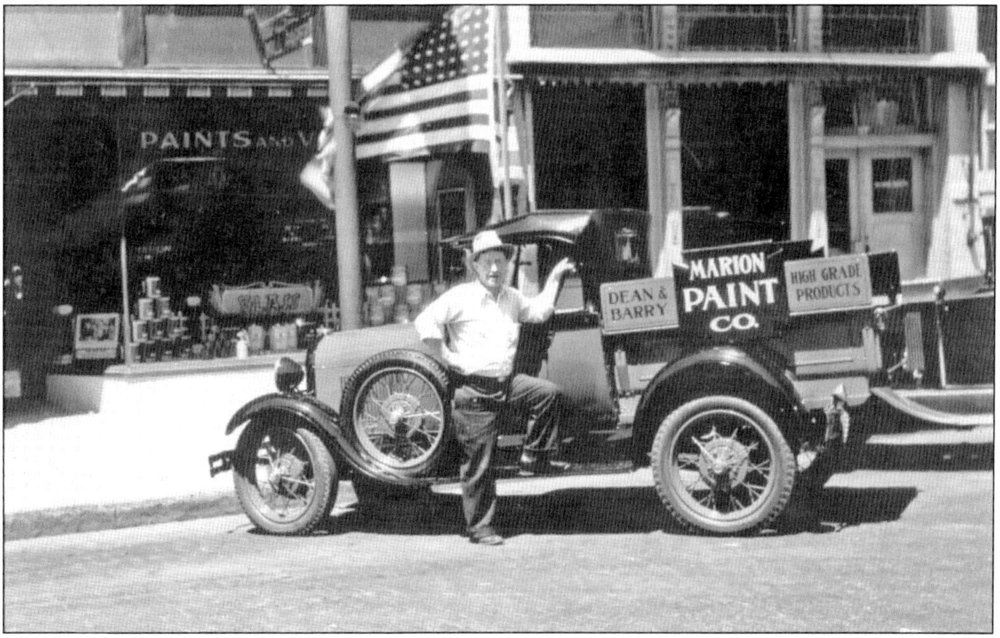

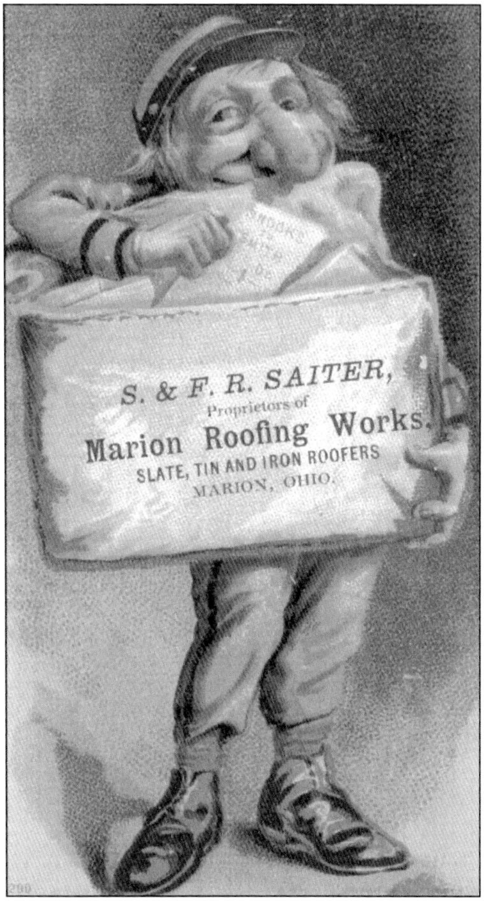

MARION ROOFING WORKS. Coffins were the main product made by Samuel and Frank R. Saiter when they first opened their business in 1865. By 1897, they were providing "everything for the roof and kitchen" from their store at 131 South Main Street. Products offered included stoves, furnaces, mantles, grates, and the standard roofing materials of the day, including slate, tin, and iron. Which brother the card represents is unclear. (Courtesy of Richard Carey.)

SAM H. KELLER COMPANY. Tinsmiths, such as those employed by the Keller Company, learned their trade through apprenticeship programs. Most apprentices served four to six years as trainees before qualifying as journeymen. Furnace installation required tinsmithing skills to build and install the ductwork. After a cold ride in the Keller Company's wagon, a warm furnace would have been greatly appreciated. (Courtesy of Richard Carey.)

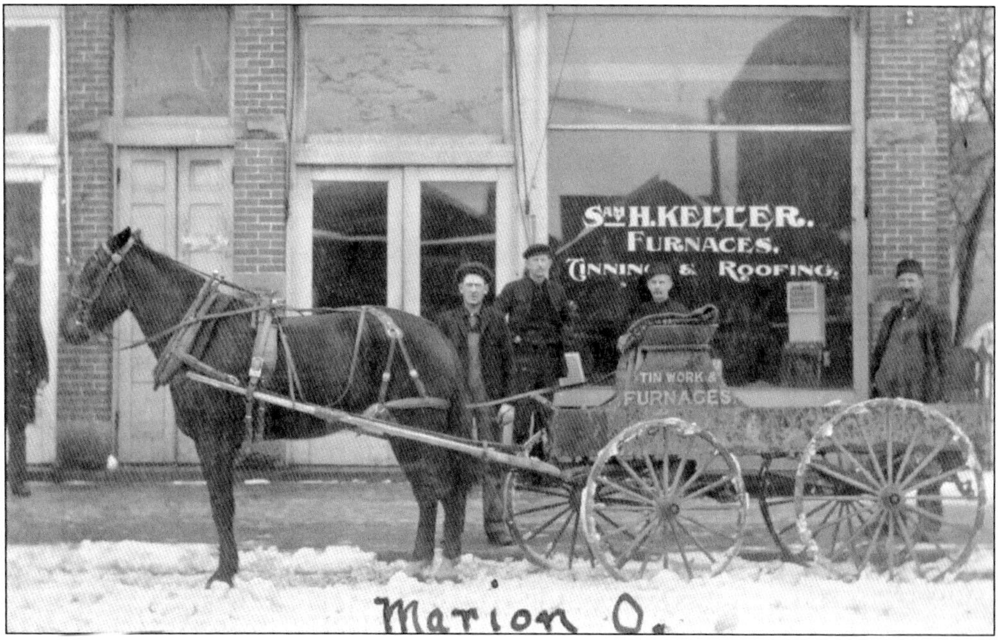

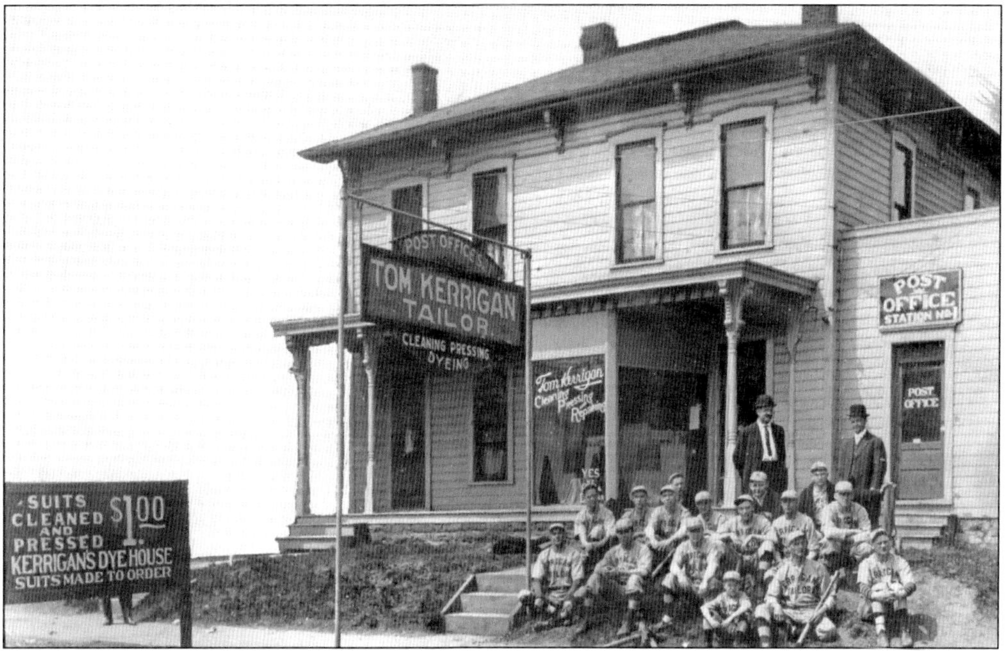

KERRIGAN TAILORS. The Kerrigan Tailor Shop located on West Center Street was known for more than providing a cleaned-and-pressed suit for a dollar. The baseball team sponsored by Kerrigan was widely regarded as one of the top teams in the Marion area. Looking to maximize his building's earning potential, Kerrigan also leased space to the post office. (Courtesy of Richard Carey.)

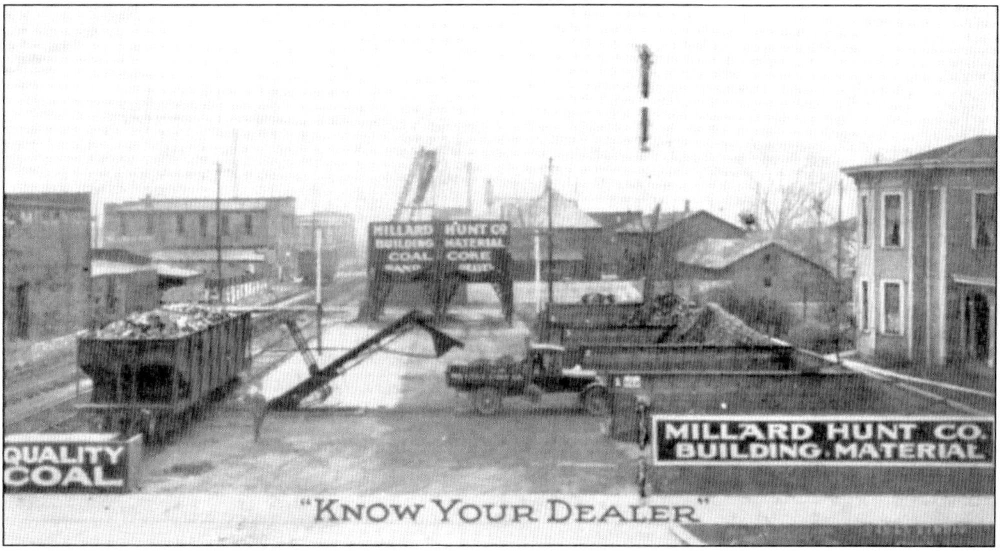

MILLARD HUNT COMPANY. A railcar of coal waits to be unloaded for the Millard Hunt Company at its North Prospect Street location adjacent to the railroad. Sales of building supplies provided a brisk business around 1900 due to the rapid growth of Marion's housing and industries. (Courtesy of Bob Turner.)

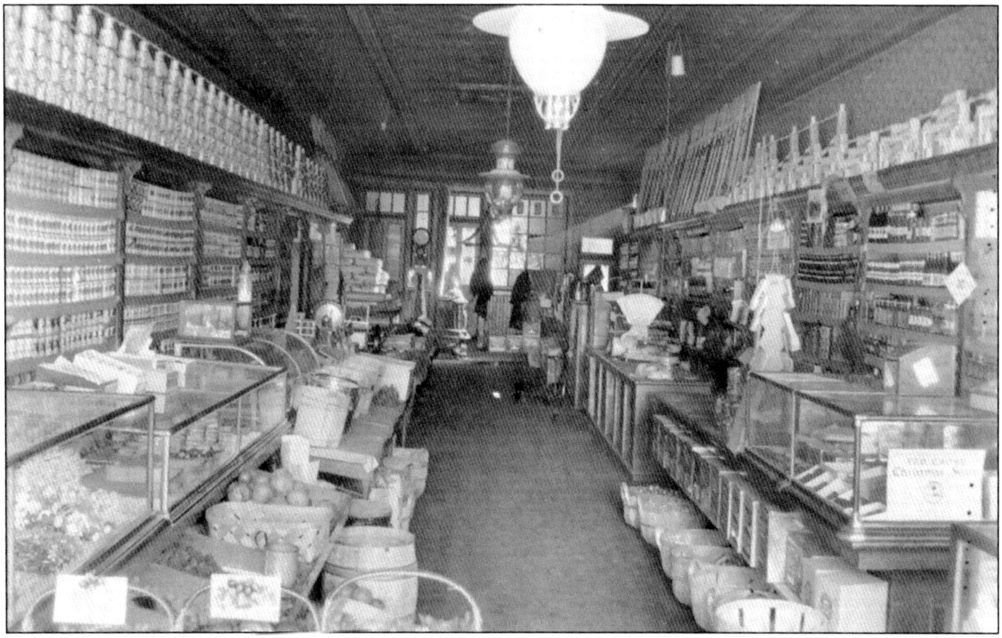

D.A. TERRY STORE. Row upon row of canned produce along with baskets of fresh fruit and vegetables were all available for purchase at D.A. Terry's grocery store located at 138 North State Street. Special treats were kept inside the protective glass display cases, which also displayed posters asking for support of the Red Cross Christmas Seals. (Courtesy of Richard Carey.)

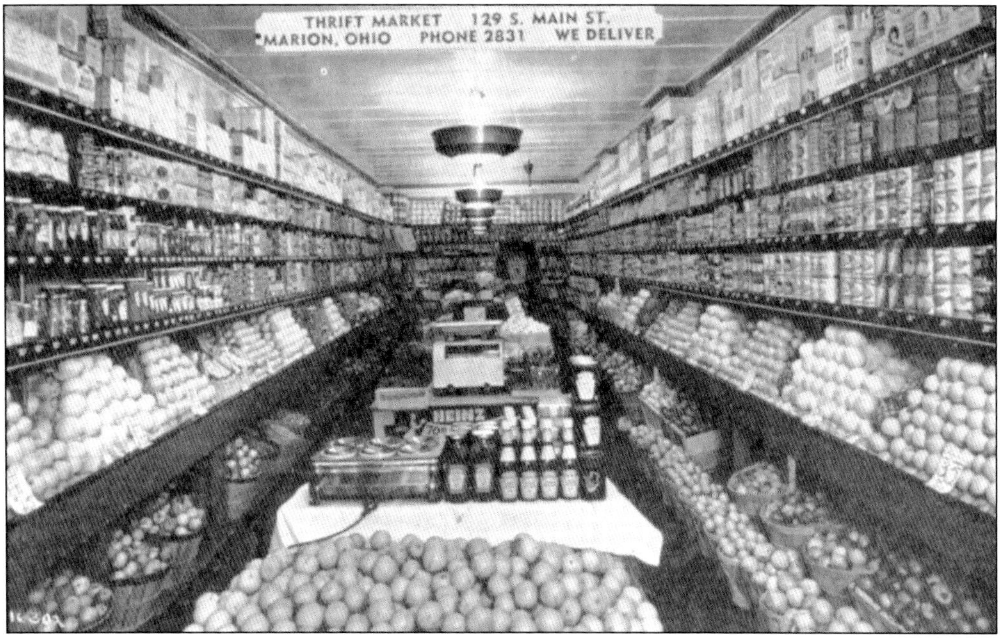

THRIFT MARKET. Fresh produce was certainly in good supply at the Thrift Market. During World War II, the market supported the armed forces by reminding customers, "Don't forget the boys in service! Send a bushel of apples to the Marion Canteen today. In fact, we'll sell you anything in our store at cost and deliver it free to the Marion Canteen!" (Courtesy of Mike and Linda Perry.)

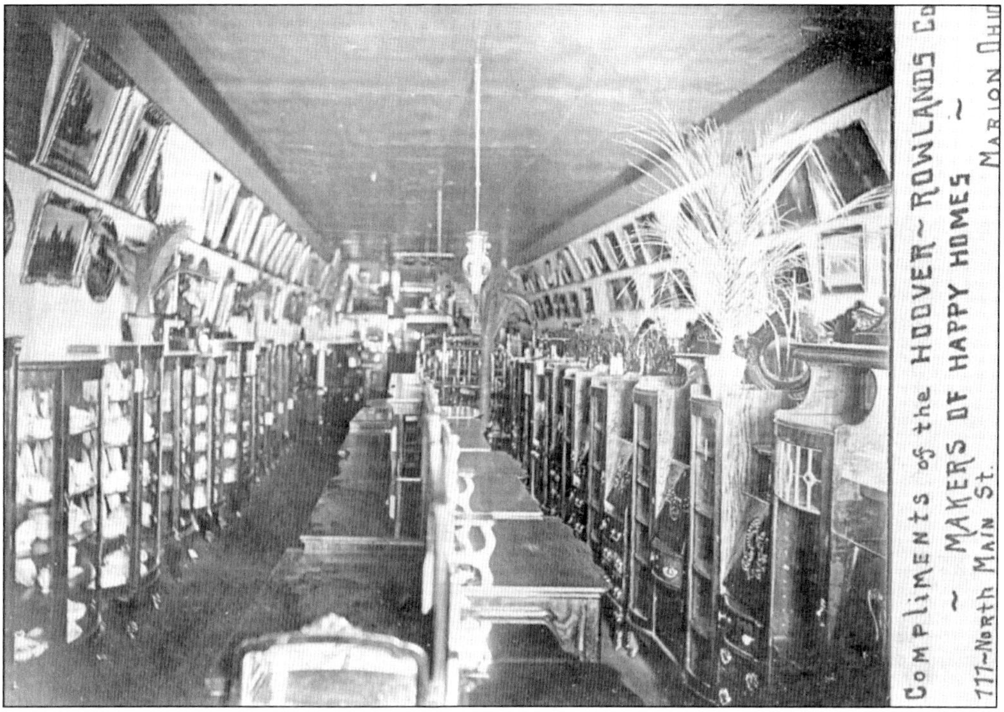

HOOVER-ROWLANDS COMPANY. Golden oak furniture along with china and home decorations fill the aisles at Hoover-Rowlands in this c. 1910 view. Golden oak enjoyed immense popularity from 1880 to 1920, as walnut furniture had become very expensive due to a shortage of walnut lumber. Hoover-Rowlands was purchased by Schaffner Furniture in 1926. The two stores then combined under the Schaffner name at 182 South Main Street. (Author's collection.)

MARKERT'S CHINA STORE. Customers shopping at Markert's China on West Center Street had a wide variety to choose from at "The Only Exclusive China Store in Marion County." Being built on a deep lot with small street frontage, Markert's narrow aisles were typical of many downtown Marion buildings. (Author's collection.)

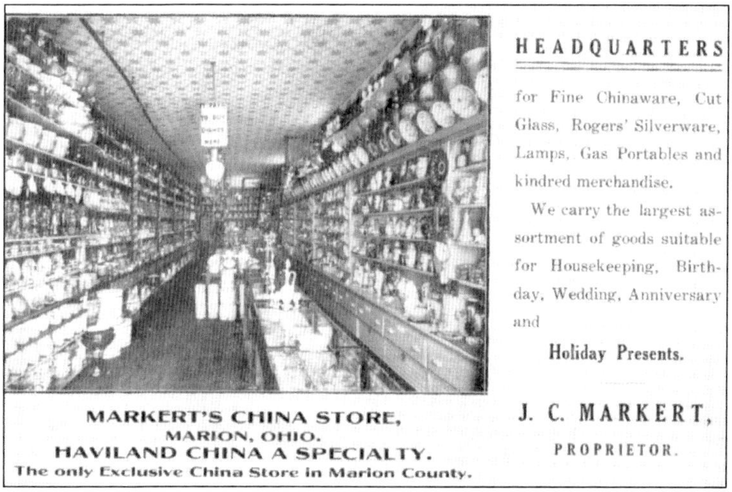

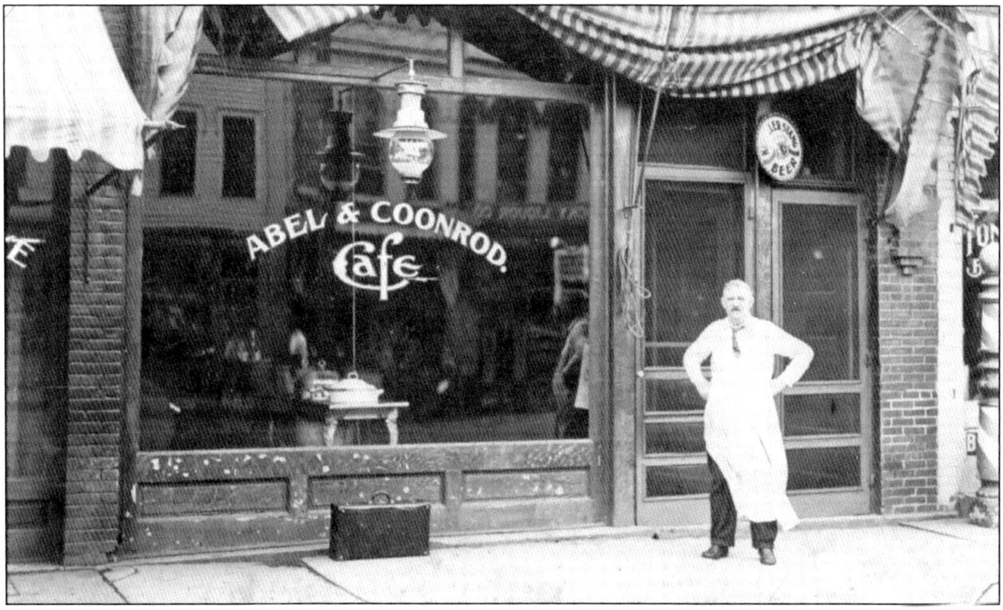

ABEL & COONROD CAFÉ. Customers visiting the Abel & Coonrod Café at 124 West Center Street could enjoy a frothy glass of Kuebler Stang Beer brewed with water from the Crystal Rock Spring in Sandusky, Ohio. If time permitted, tonsorial services were available at the barbershop next door. The purpose of the briefcase sitting on the sidewalk can only be surmised. (Courtesy of Richard Carey.)

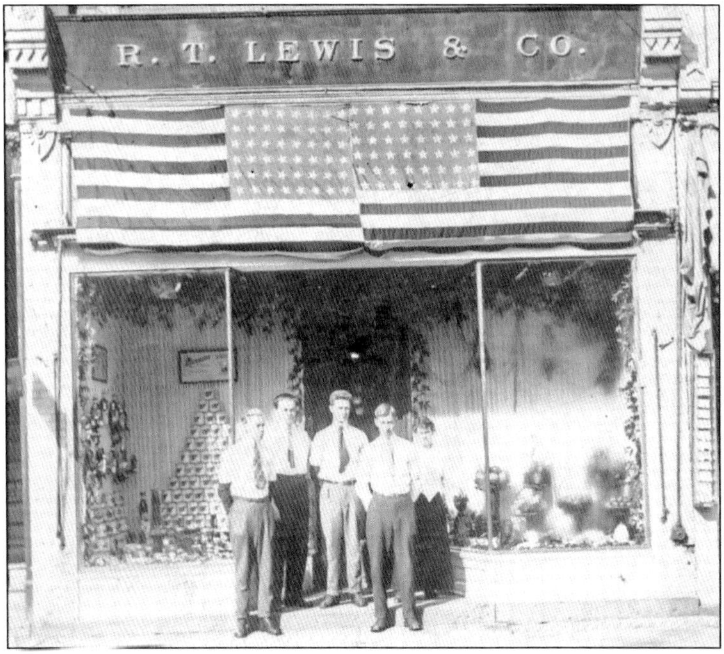

R.T. LEWIS & COMPANY. The first motortruck delivery service of groceries in Marion was offered by R.T. Lewis from his store on North Main Street across from the courthouse. Lewis became a very successful businessman and realtor who developed the Vernon Heights subdivision. Married to Abigail "Daisy" Harding, sister of Warren G. Harding, he was well known for his philanthropic and community service efforts. (Courtesy of Shelby Needham.)

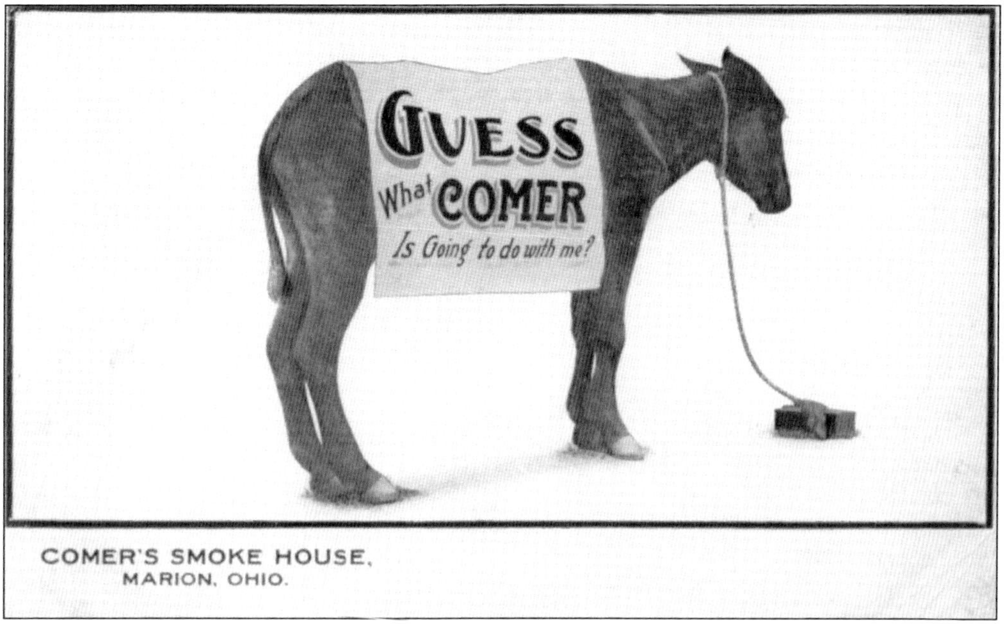

COMER'S SMOKE HOUSE. Orin John Comer was an innovative businessman with a knack for advertising. His use of mules in ads included having one push (instead of pull) a cart while another carried a large bass drum as part of Comer's Smoke House Band. His store at 105 East Center Street advertised "the courthouse is still across from us" and had a large cigar displayed on an outside wall. (Courtesy of Richard Carey.)

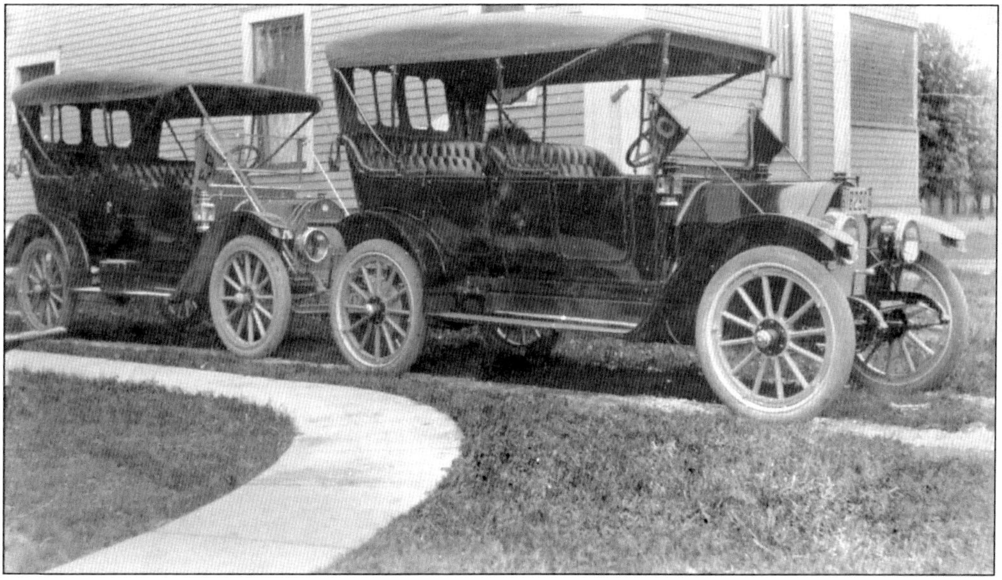

REO MOTORCAR. One of the earliest car companies was started by Ransom Eli Olds in Lansing, Michigan, in 1904. The cars became noted for their reliability, with one making the first trans-Canadian journey in 1912. REO trucks, named Speed Wagons, proved to be more popular than the cars. Truck configurations included tow and fire trucks. REOs were sold in Marion by Hoch Motor Sales on South Prospect Street. (Courtesy of Richard Carey.)

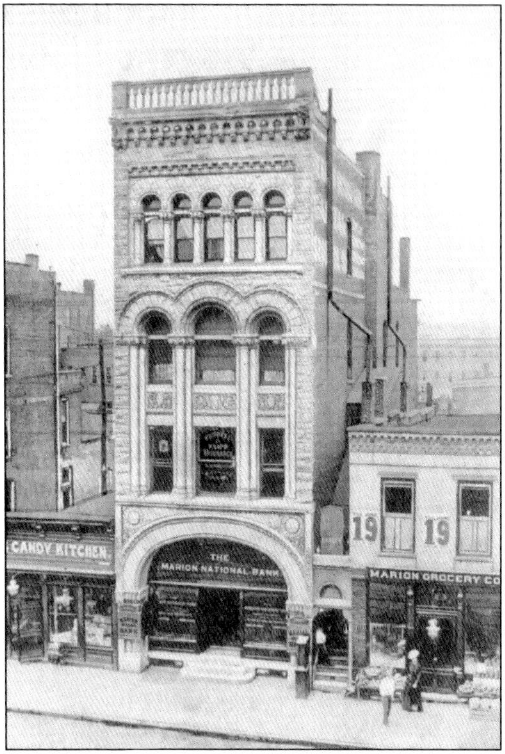

MARION NATIONAL BANK. The most elaborately designed building in Marion stood directly across from the county courthouse on Center Street and served as the home of the Marion National Bank. The bank originally opened in 1851 as the Farmer's & Mechanics Bank before being reorganized in 1865 as the First National Bank of Marion. The building was eventually razed to make way for a parking lot. (Author's collection.)

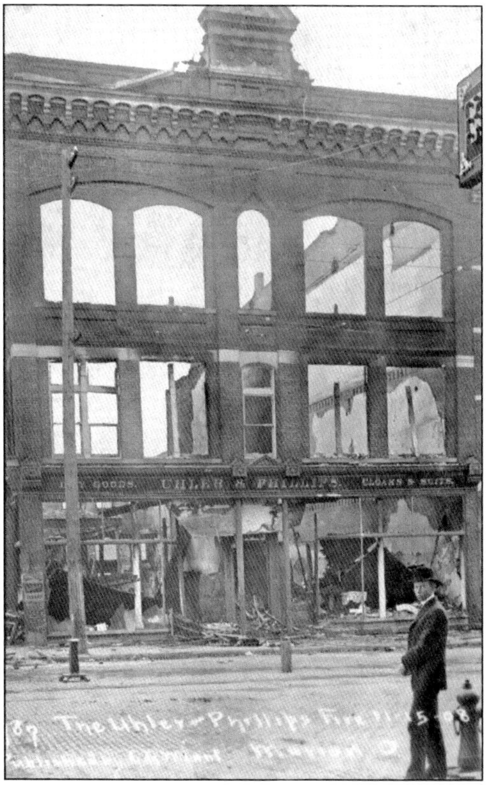

UHLER-PHILLIPS FIRE. In 1891, E.K. Uhler and J.E. Phillips formed a partnership and opened a dry goods business on West Center Street. The business grew rapidly until 1908, when a fire destroyed the building and the company's entire inventory. Instead of rebuilding, Uhler & Phillips purchased the home furnishings inventory of the C.W. McLain Company and moved into McLain's former location in the Huber Building. (Author's collection.)

HUBER BUILDING. Edward Huber's impact on Marion extended beyond manufacturing as he also built one of the largest retail buildings in the city. Completed in 1903 at the northwest corner of Center and Prospect Streets, the 54,000-square-foot structure featured two elevators, a rooftop garden, and a light court for interior rooms. Uhler-Phillips Department Store was a primary tenant for 60 years. (Courtesy of Marion County Historical Society.)

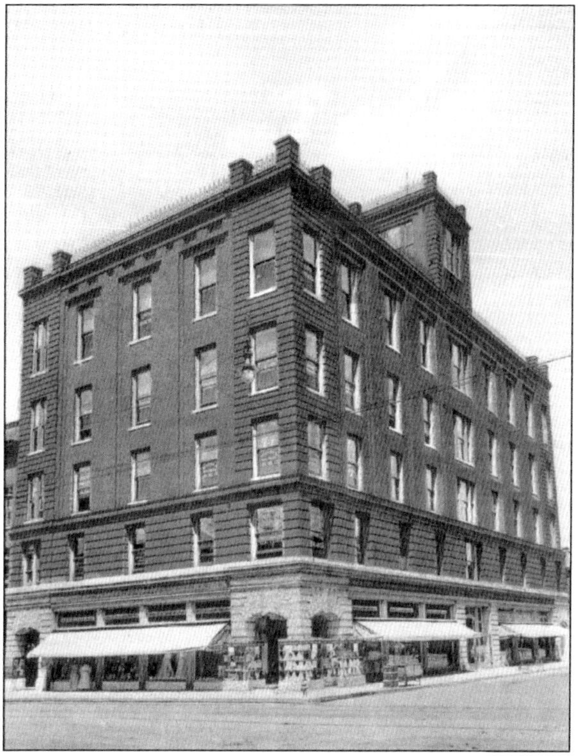

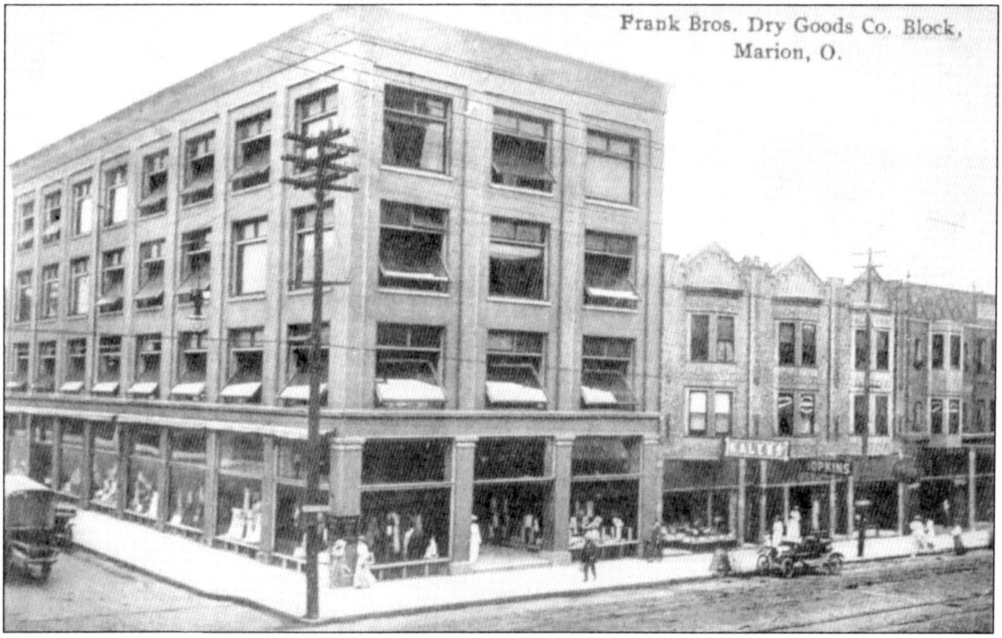

FRANK BROTHERS BUILDING. D.A. and G.E. Frank celebrated the opening of their dry goods store at the southwest corner of Center and Prospect Streets on March 24, 1908, with music provided by Dowler's Orchestra. Built of buff-colored Pennsylvania brick, the building featured massive awning-style glass windows on the upper floors. Frank Brothers closed in 1979, and the site became the home of Bank One. (Courtesy of Mike and Linda Perry.)

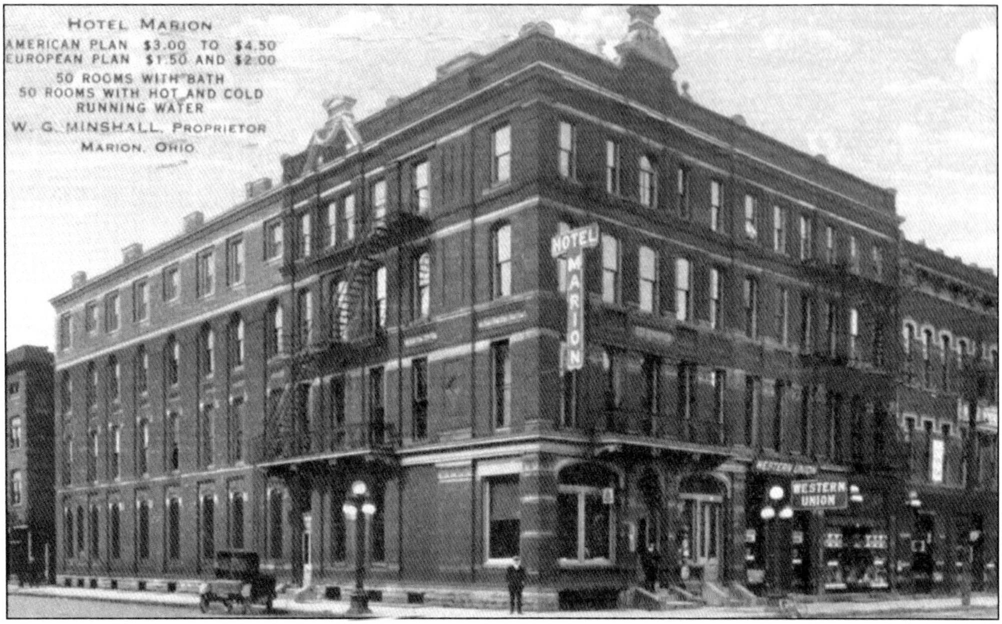

HOTEL MARION. Opened for business in 1883 at the southwest corner of Center and State Streets, the hostelry was the first choice of many performers appearing in local theaters such as the Grand Opera House located just down the street. Guests could choose from the American plan, which included all meals, or the less expensive European plan. The building was eventually razed, and the site is now a parking lot. (Author's collection.)

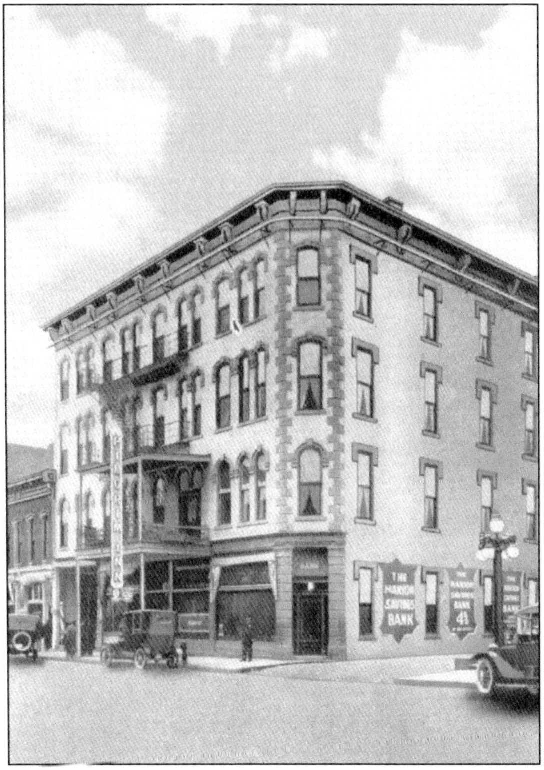

PILGRIM INN. The Pilgrim Inn featured an ingenious method to deliver luggage to guest rooms in its building just north of the courthouse. Utilizing an iron railing at the top of the building equipped with a rope and pulley system, bellboys could move luggage into rooms through the windows. Opened as the Kerr Hotel, it was also the Milner Hotel and finally the Taft Hotel before being razed in the early 1960s. (Author's collection.)

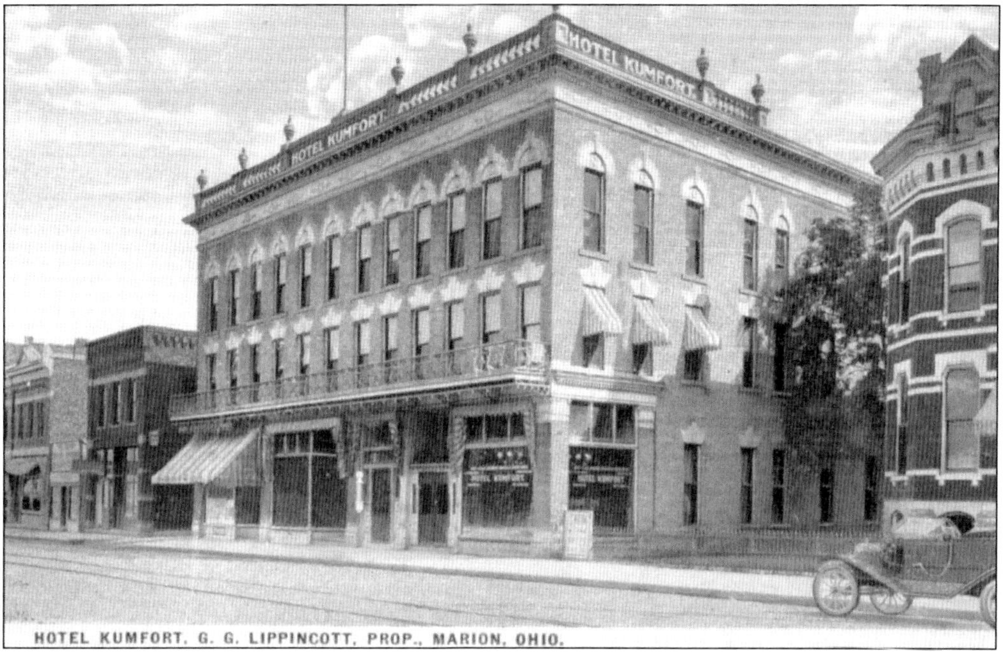

HOTEL KUMFORT. The title "a building of many names" would seem to be appropriate for what was originally built as the Reber House Hotel in 1901. Located on North State Street adjacent to the Marion County Jail (partially visible to the right), it also served as the Marion City and County Hospital from 1904 to 1906 before becoming the Hotel Majestic, Hotel Kumfort, and Snyder Hotel. (Author's collection.)

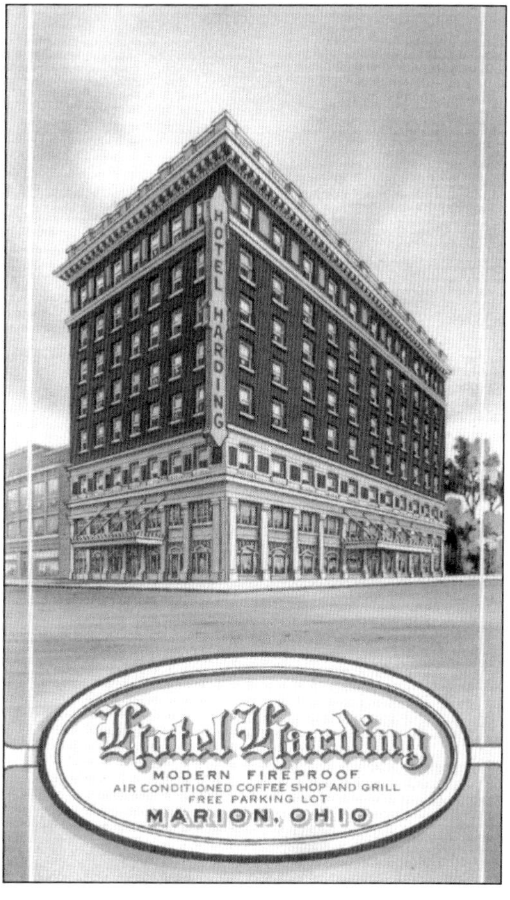

HARDING HOTEL. The Harding Hotel opened in 1924 with "every room an outside room with circulating ice water and soft water for your bath and toilet." It featured retail stores and a popular restaurant, with notable guests including John Dillinger, Will Rogers, and Ethel Barrymore. While going through a series of owners, the building slowly deteriorated before closing in 1975. It reopened in 1997 as a 67-unit senior housing facility. (Author's collection.)

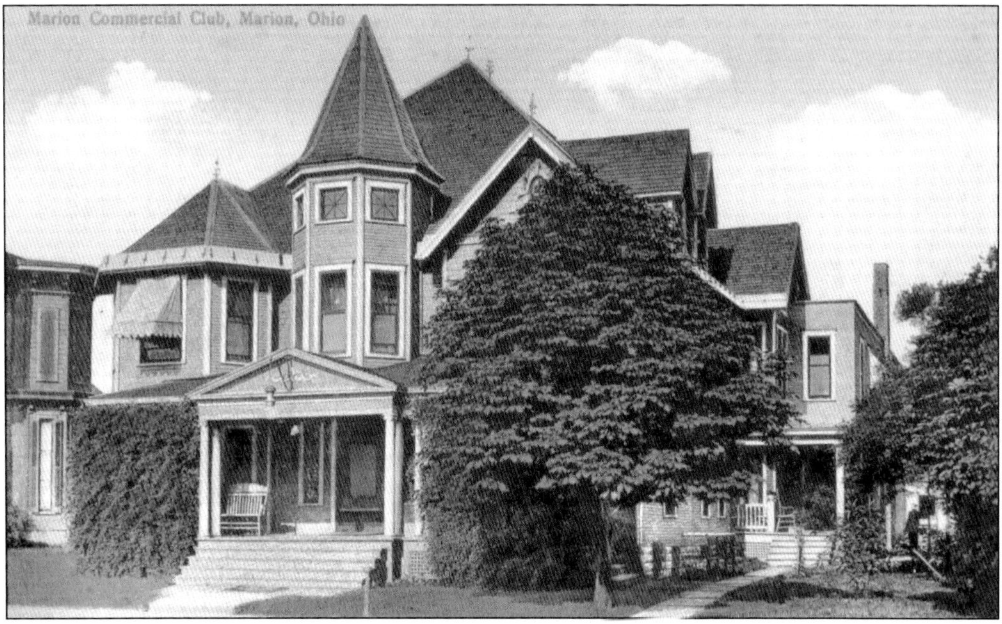

MARION COMMERCIAL CLUB. Started in 1901, the Commercial Club had the goal of promoting the business and industrial interests of Marion. Located on South Prospect Street at the site of the former Rhu Sanatorium, it was renamed the Marion Club in 1910 and served as essentially a fraternal chamber of commerce. The site eventually became home to the Sutton and Lightner Department Store. (Courtesy of Marion County Historical Society.)

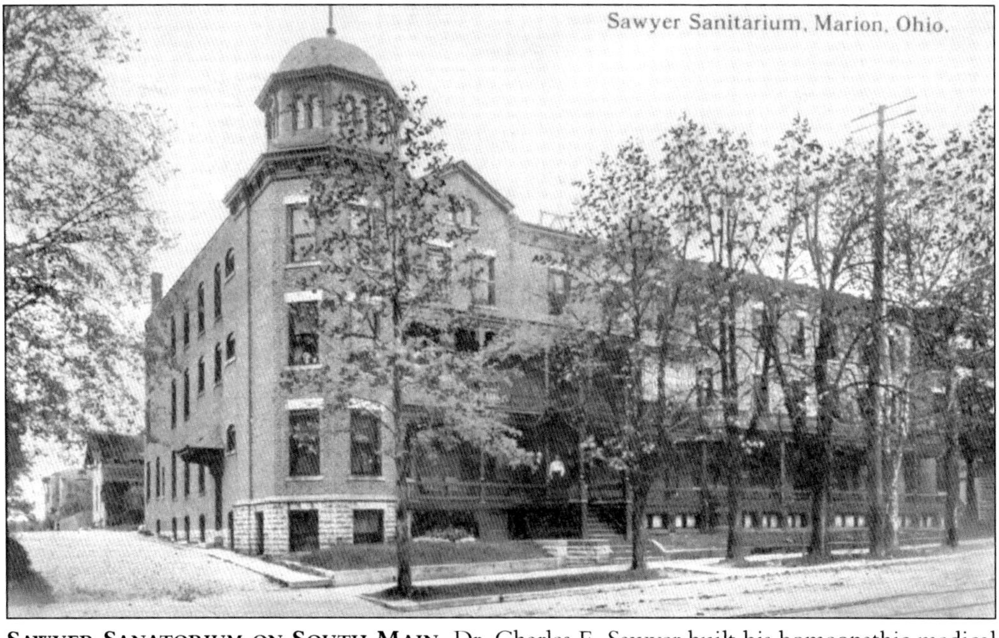

SAWYER SANATORIUM ON SOUTH MAIN. Dr. Charles E. Sawyer built his homeopathic medical showplace starting in 1891 at 235 South Main Street. It featured "homelike surroundings" with treatment for "all forms of chronic diseases, cripples and deformities" using "X-ray, hydropathic and electropathic equipment." Dr. Sawyer eventually expanded his practice to a new facility on White Oaks Road, with this building now serving as an apartment complex. (Author's collection.)

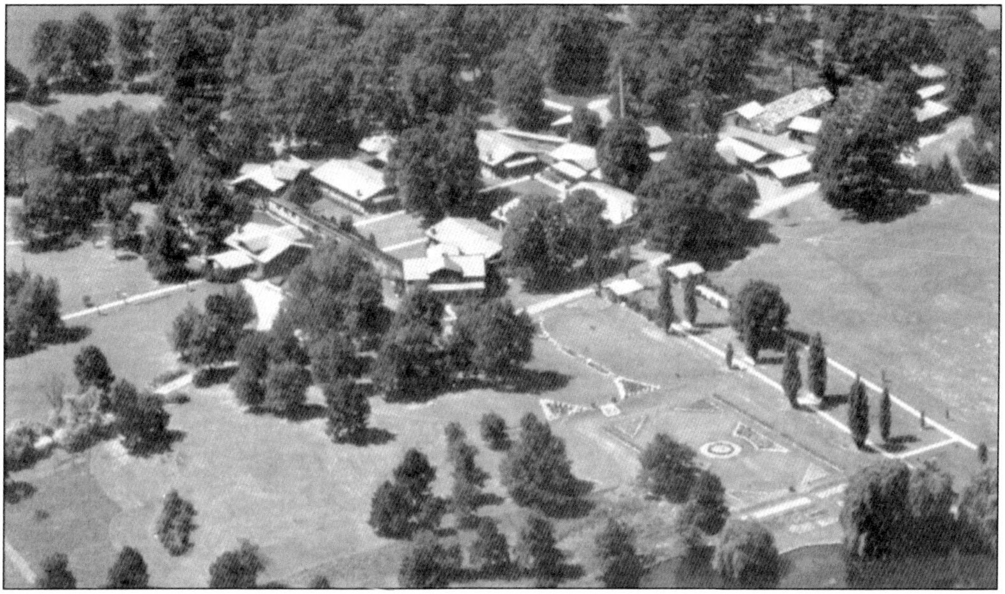

SAWYER SANATORIUM AT WHITE OAKS. Opened in 1910 on 59 acres of Dr. Sawyer's White Oaks Farm, the sanatorium featured a tranquil forest and scenic gardens that led to a lake. Fresh flowers were grown in the farm's own greenhouse. Medical care for individuals suffering from "diseases of later life including geriatrics" was provided, while cases of "pulmonary tuberculosis, contagious disease, or drug or alcohol addiction" were turned away. (Author's collection.)

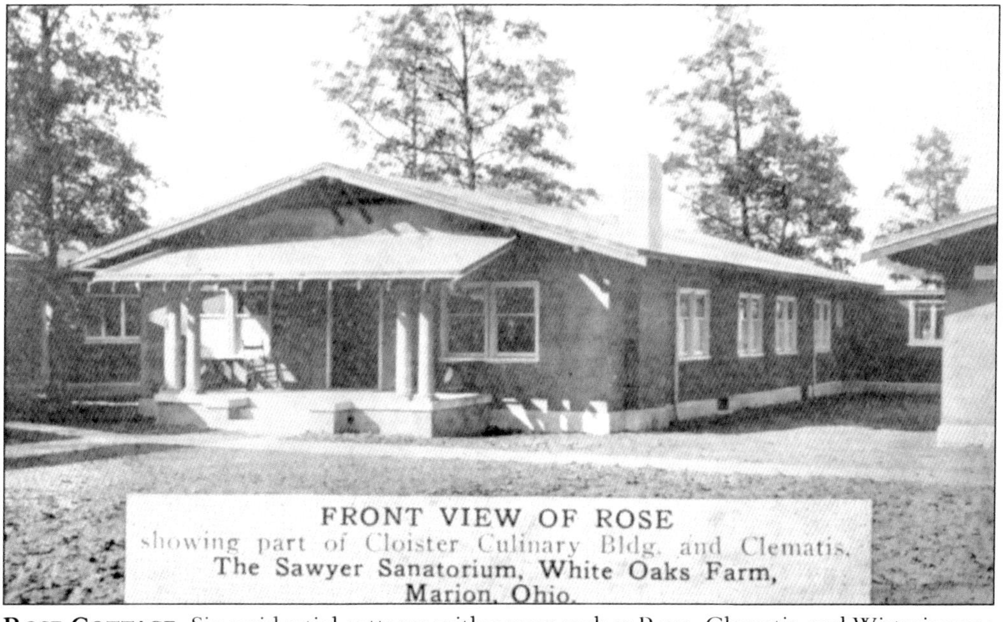

ROSE COTTAGE. Six residential cottages with names such as Rose, Clematis, and Wisteria were part of a 15-building cloister joined by an enclosed walkway. The cottages provided each patient with a separate outside room equipped with hot water heat, an electric fan, and signaling devices that could be used to call for assistance. (Author's collection.)

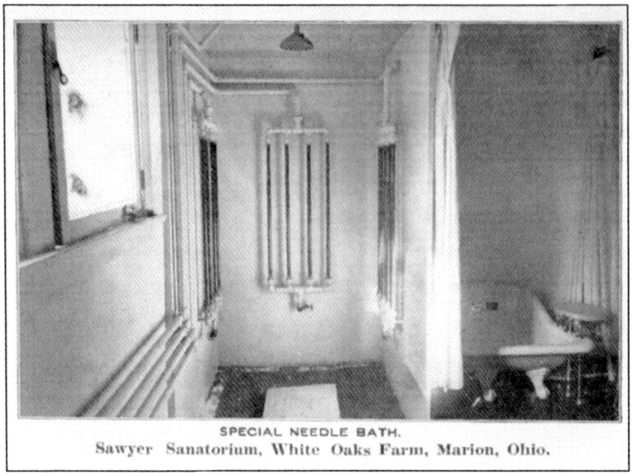

HYDROPATHIC CARE. Homeopathic medicine was very popular in the United States in the early 20th century, with more than 15,000 practitioners in 1900. While later research found that most homeopathic treatment was ineffective, it usually did little harm as opposed to some traditional medical practices of the time, which could actually endanger the patient. Water was utilized in various hydropathic modalities, such as this needle bath. (Author's collection.)

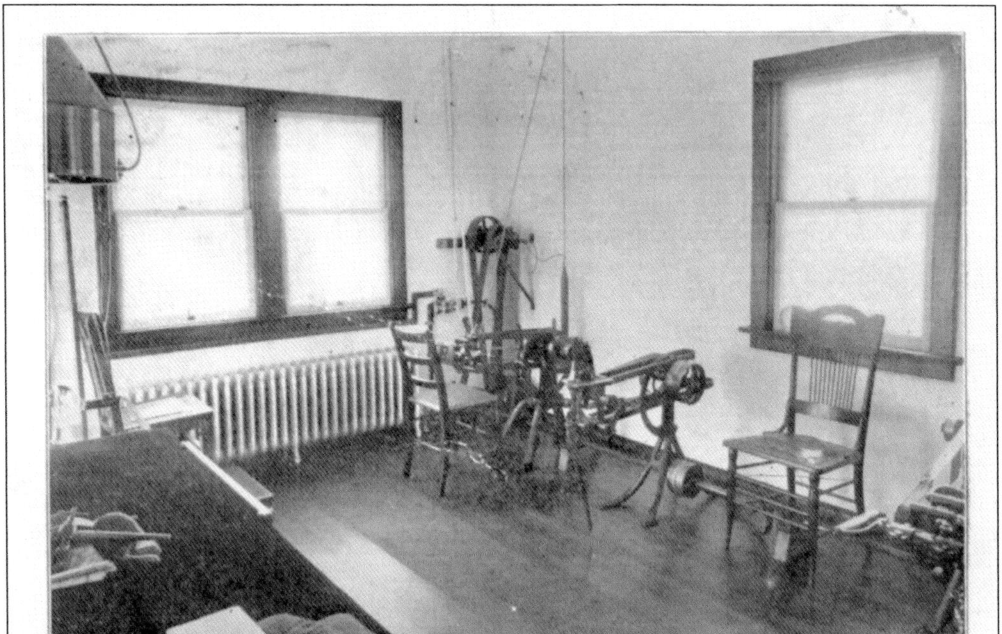

MECHANICAL MASSAGE. Physical activity and movement were cornerstones of Dr. Sawyer's philosophy of treatment. Machines designed to assist in that process were available in a variety of configurations. Walking paths in the elaborate gardens encouraged patients to gain the benefits of outdoor exercise. Occupational therapies designed to enhance concentration and dexterity, such as basket weaving, were also available. (Author's collection.)

Four

MADE IN MARION

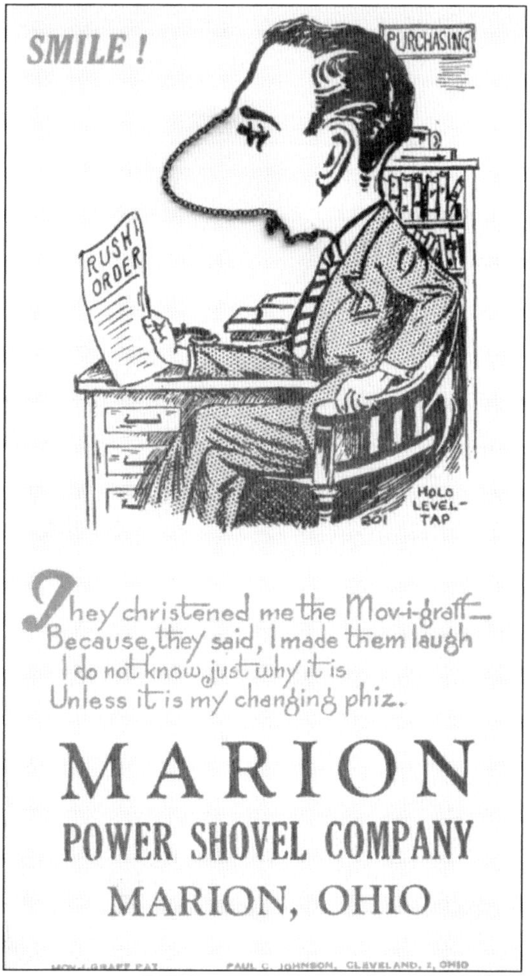

SHOVEL SALESMAN. This Mov-i-graff postcard featured a Marion Power Shovel salesman whose facial features, as outlined by a small chain, were determined by tapping or jiggling the card. Since he appears to have just received a rush order, he probably would be wearing a big smile. How this card could have been mailed without the chain being broken remains a mystery. (Author's collection.)

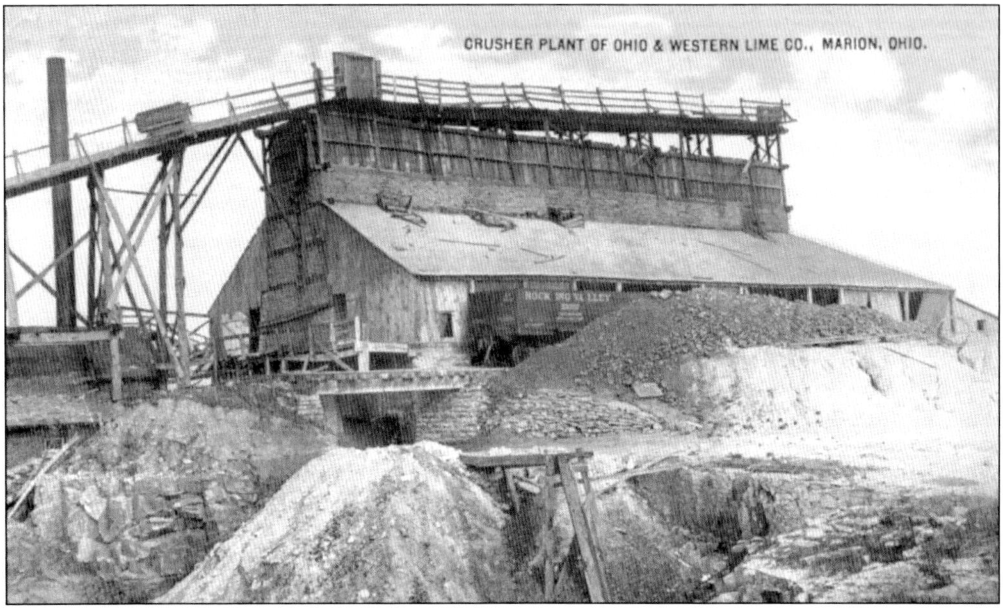

LIMESTONE PLANT. Marion was once known as Lime City, due to its numerous limestone quarries. Much of the stone was so-called blue limestone, which was highly sought after for construction purposes, including building foundations and street curbs. Stone of lesser quality was burned in large kilns to make powdered lime for use as a soil additive and in mortar. (Courtesy of Mike and Linda Perry.)

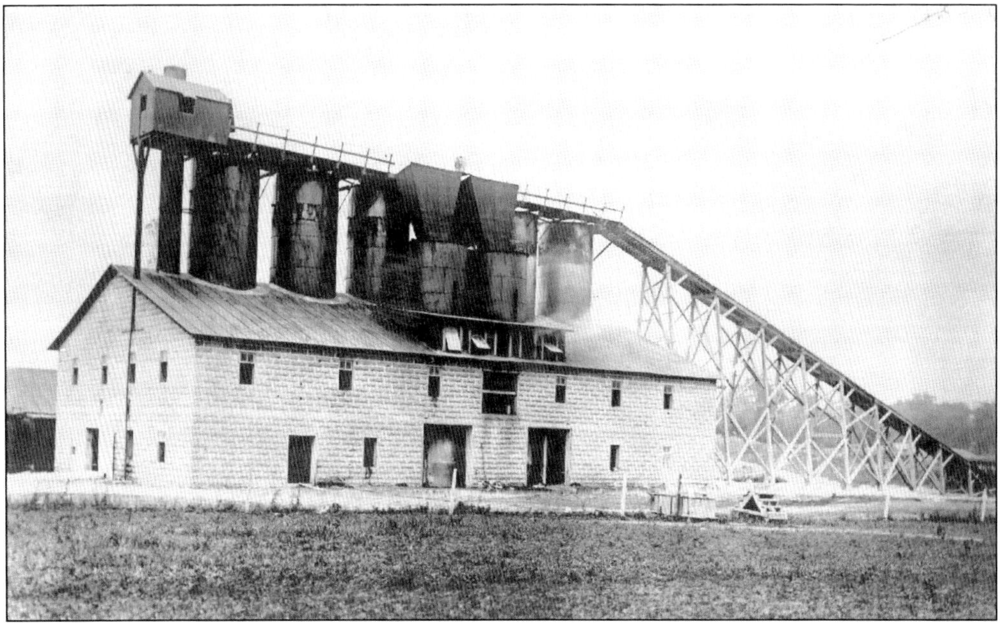

OWEN'S QUARRY. John Owens, a native of Wales, developed this limestone quarry and crusher plant in southern Marion County and also a town to go with it. The village of Owens featured a school, opera house, general store, hotel, post office, and train station in addition to the homes of the quarry employees. The opera house is one of the few surviving buildings. (Courtesy of Richard Carey.)

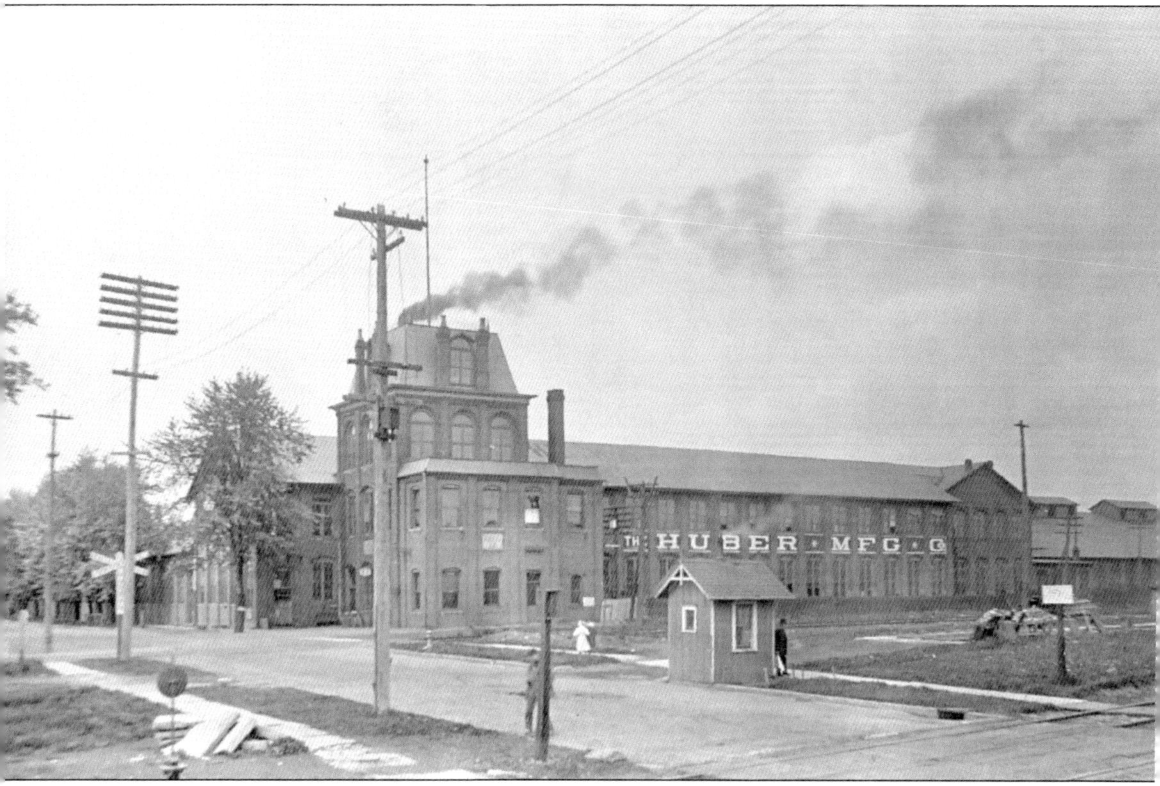

HUBER MANUFACTURING. Edward Huber moved to Marion in 1865 to manufacture his invention of a revolving hay rake. He rented space in the former Centenary Methodist Church until his business had grown sufficiently and allowed him to move to this new factory located on North Greenwood Street. Huber's product line soon grew to include portable steam engines, road scrapers and rollers, and a variety of farm machinery, including threshers. Huber was a successful businessman as well as an inventor. He teamed with Henry Barnhart to design the first steam shovel built by what eventually became the Marion Steam Shovel Company. He assisted other inventors by financing their patents in return for a substantial share of the revenues if they were a success. During World War II, Huber Manufacturing focused on manufacturing road building equipment. When the war ended, the company was never able to regain a strong position in the agricultural equipment field. The factory was sold in the 1970s, with the company moving to South Carolina. (Author's collection.)

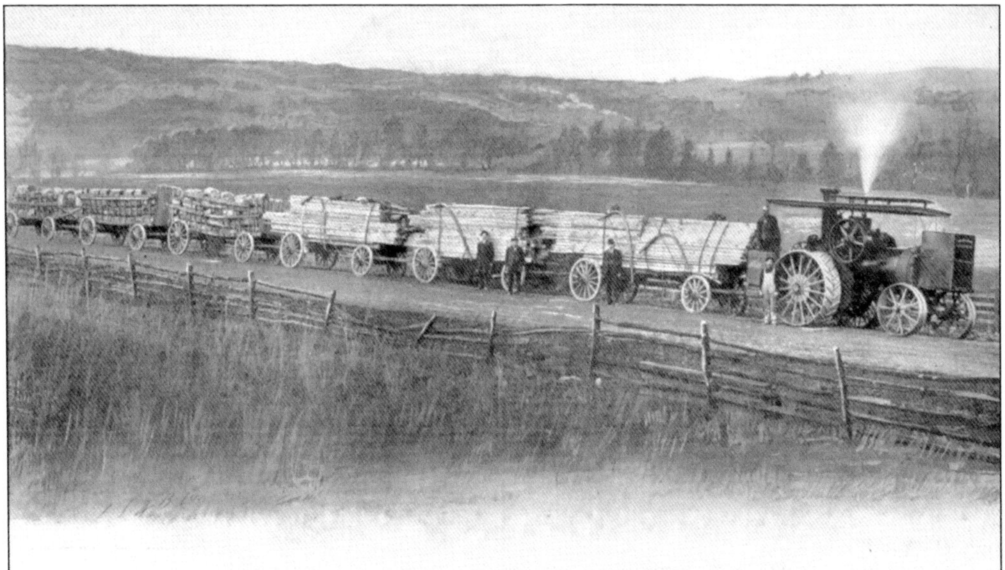

The 25 Horse Power Huber Contractor Engine.

HUBER STEAM ENGINE. The Huber 25-horsepower Contractor Engine demonstrated how a relatively low amount of horsepower, when coupled with enough weight and torque, can move substantial loads. Six wagonloads of lumber and barrels with a combined weight of over 39 tons were pulled over 18 miles up grades of 12–15 percent by this mechanical workhorse. (Courtesy of Bob Turner.)

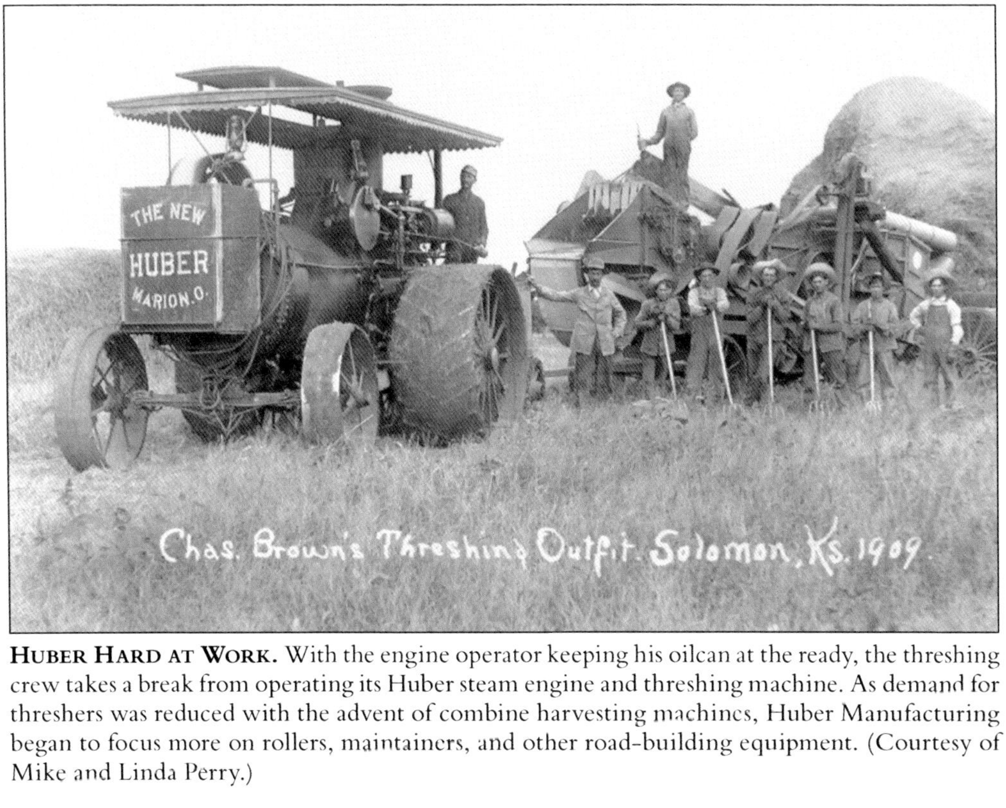

HUBER HARD AT WORK. With the engine operator keeping his oilcan at the ready, the threshing crew takes a break from operating its Huber steam engine and threshing machine. As demand for threshers was reduced with the advent of combine harvesting machines, Huber Manufacturing began to focus more on rollers, maintainers, and other road-building equipment. (Courtesy of Mike and Linda Perry.)

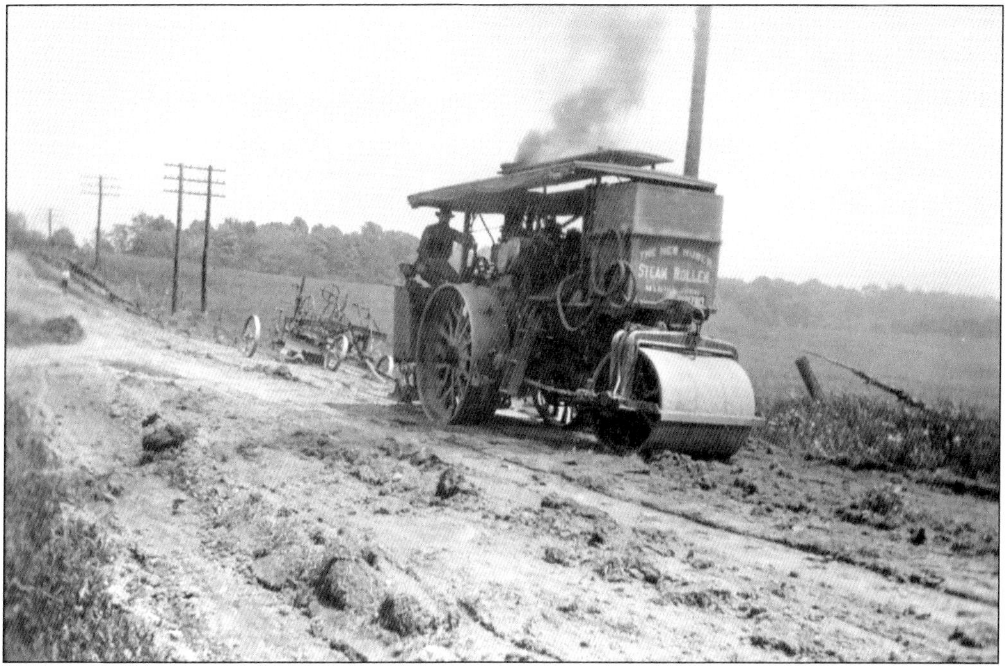

Huber Road Roller and Scraper. Constructing new roads was a challenge for early road-building equipment such as this Huber steam roller and blade scraper. While the roller's weight made it perfect for compacting the soil, it could also be a problem if conditions were less than ideal, as it would quickly become bogged down and could only be extracted with great difficulty. (Courtesy of Mike and Linda Perry.)

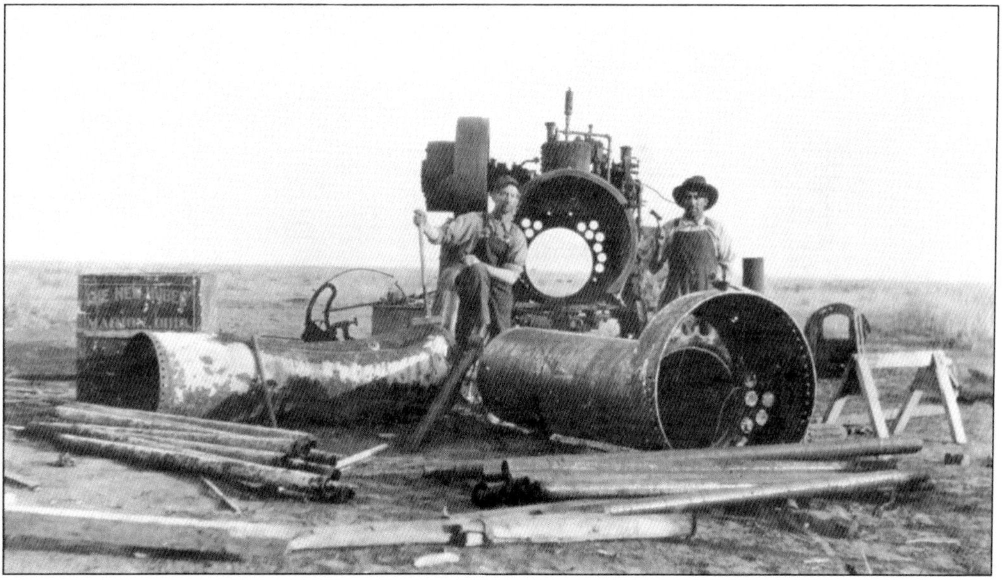

Just Some Minor Repairs. While Hubers were very well built, they were not indestructible, as evidenced by this 1916 view of a steam engine in Farwell, Texas. The card's message reads, "She kinda sorter blowed up." Apparently, the incident was not overly drastic, as the sender also writes about how many squirrels he had killed that "make fine chewing." (Courtesy of Mike and Linda Perry.)

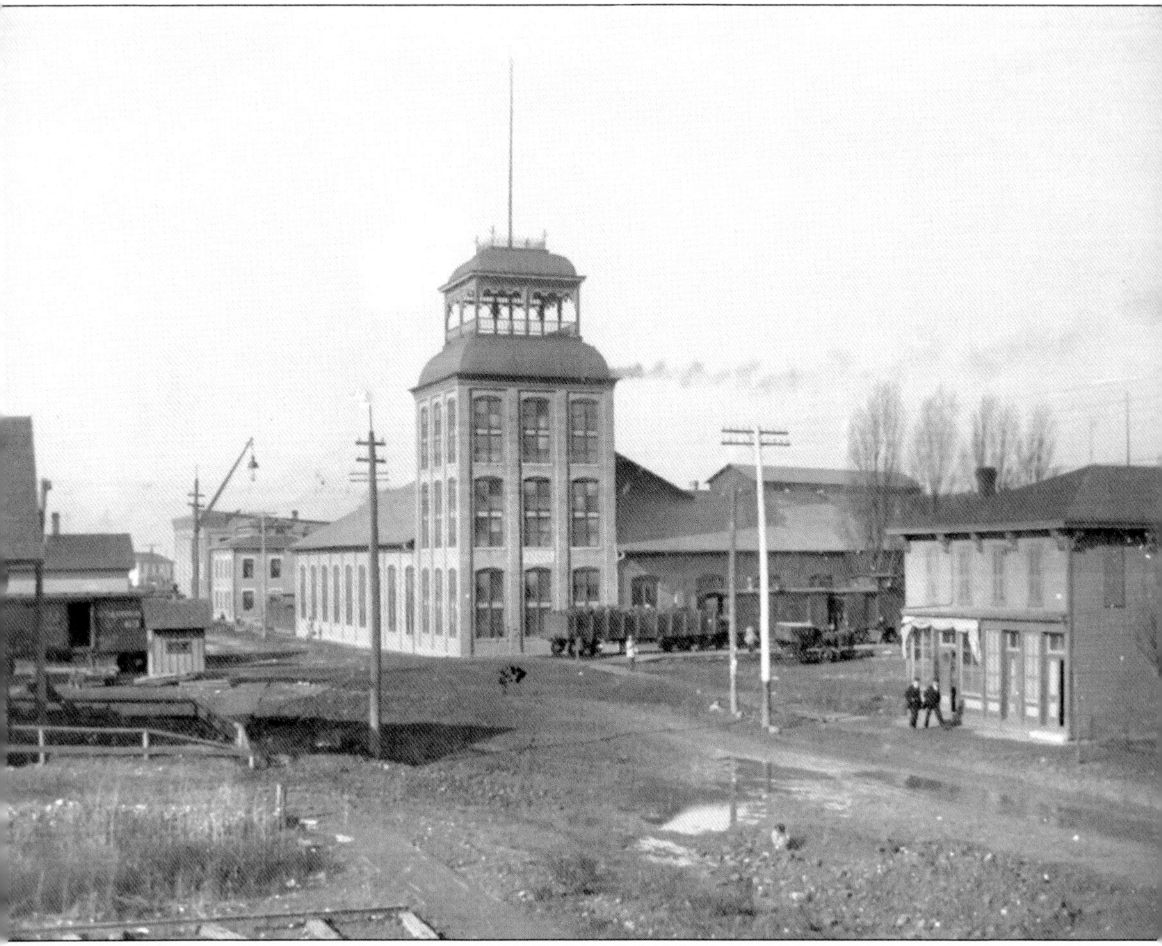

Marion Steam Shovel Company. Henry Barnhart, Edward Huber, and George W. King joined forces in 1884 to form the Marion Steam Shovel Company. Early products included ditching machines, log loaders, and steam shovels. A Marion shovel working on the Panama Canal in 1912 set a world record by moving 5,500 cubic yards of dirt in a day. Other notable projects utilizing Marion shovels were the Hoover Dam and the Hudson River Tunnels in New York City. Renamed Marion Power Shovel in 1946, the company produced dredges, shovels, draglines, and a variety of other products. At its peak in the 1970s, over 3,000 people were employed by the company. Due to a variety of factors, this number shrank to 300 by 1997, with the plant closing soon thereafter. Shown here is the Marion Steam Shovel office building on the north side of West Center Street prior to the street being paved. The frame building to the right was the Nordica Hotel, which is now the site of the Shovel Bar and Lounge. (Courtesy of Bob Turner.)

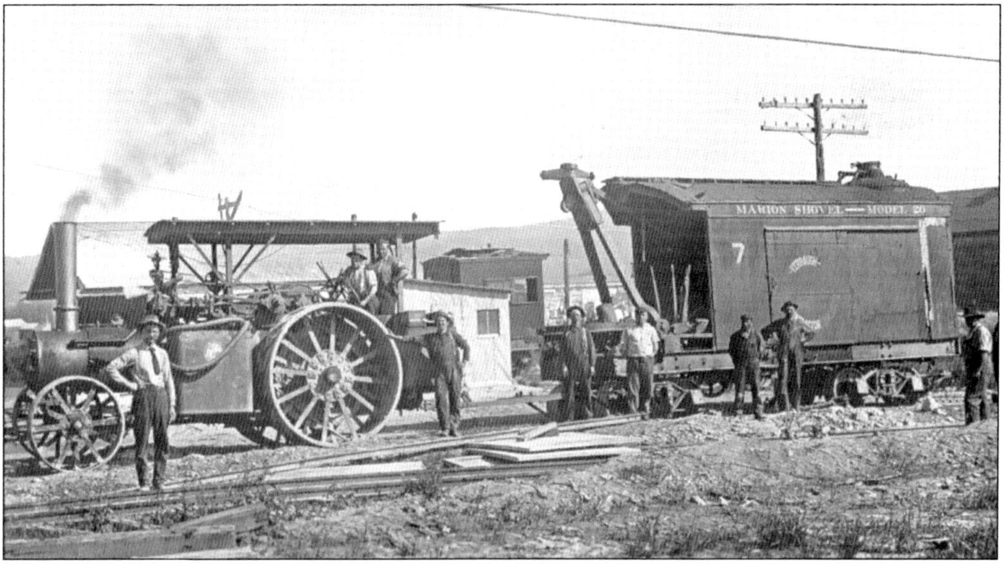

Early Marion Shovel. Early shovels, such as this Model 20 with a 1.25-cubic-yard bucket, were mounted on railcars. In 1916, crawler tracks were added, which significantly increased their mobility. Marion industries such as the Osgood, Fairbanks, and Marion Steam Shovel companies manufactured over 90 percent of the world's steam shovels in the early 1900s and earned Marion the nickname of Shovel City. (Courtesy of Bob Turner.)

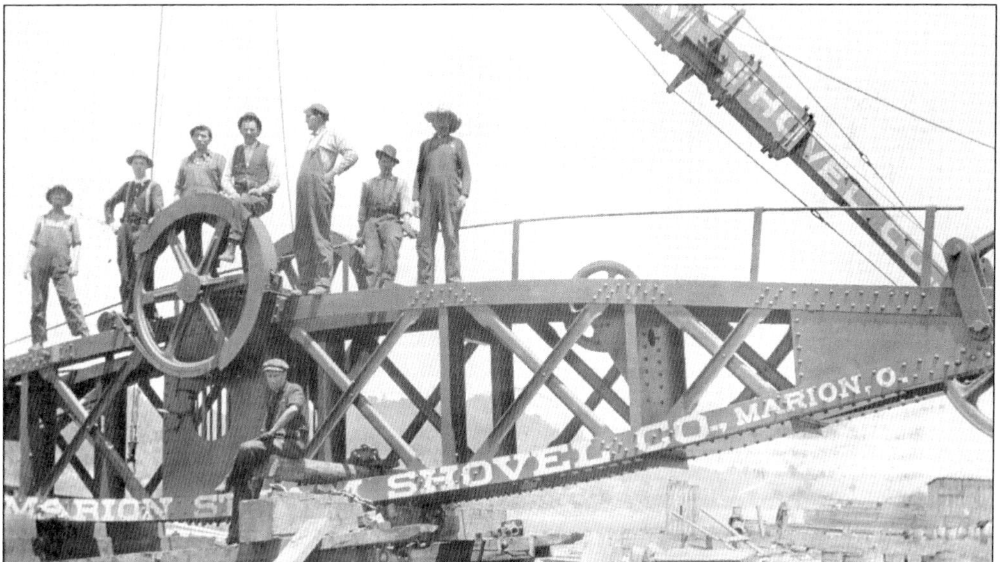

Assembly Crew. Most large shovels and dredges were erected on-site as they were too large to ship fully assembled. The engines and hoist works were assembled and tested in the MSS plant before being disassembled and packed for shipping. Some of the most difficult items to ship were the booms, which varied in length from 32 to 80 feet on the early models. (Courtesy of Richard Carey.)

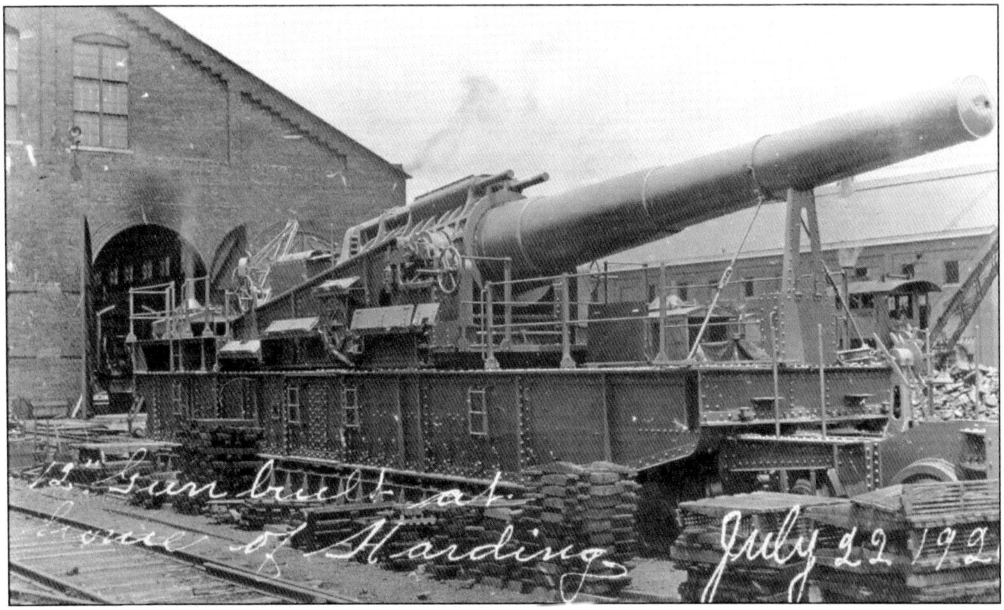

Not Just Steam Shovels. MSS produced 12 long-range cannons beginning in 1919. Each weighed 100 tons, with a specially-designed railcar adding another 160 tons. Manufactured to a tolerance of .001 of an inch, the weapons used a charge of 420 pounds of powder to shoot a projectile weighing 800 pounds a distance of 29 miles. Aeroplane observers reported the accuracy of the shots. (Courtesy of Mike and Linda Perry.)

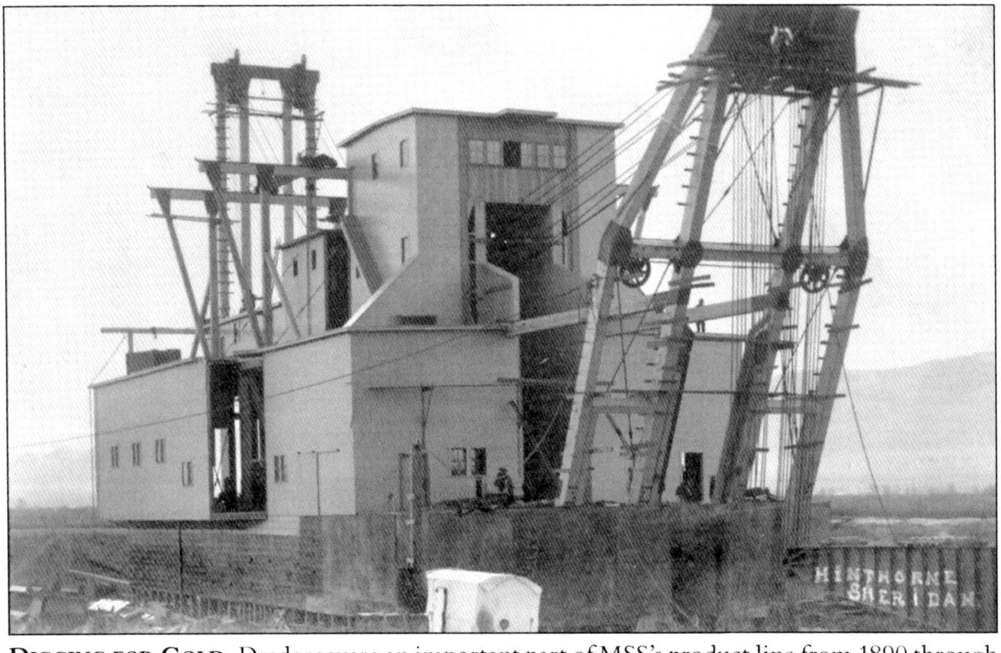

Digging for Gold. Dredges were an important part of MSS's product line from 1890 through the 1920s. Uses included draining swamps, digging canals, dredging harbors, and mining for minerals. This bucket-ladder model was one of 24 manufactured that sold at prices ranging from $48,000 to $178,000. It was used in Montana's Ruby Valley, where over $120 million in gold was dredged in the early 1900s. (Author's collection.)

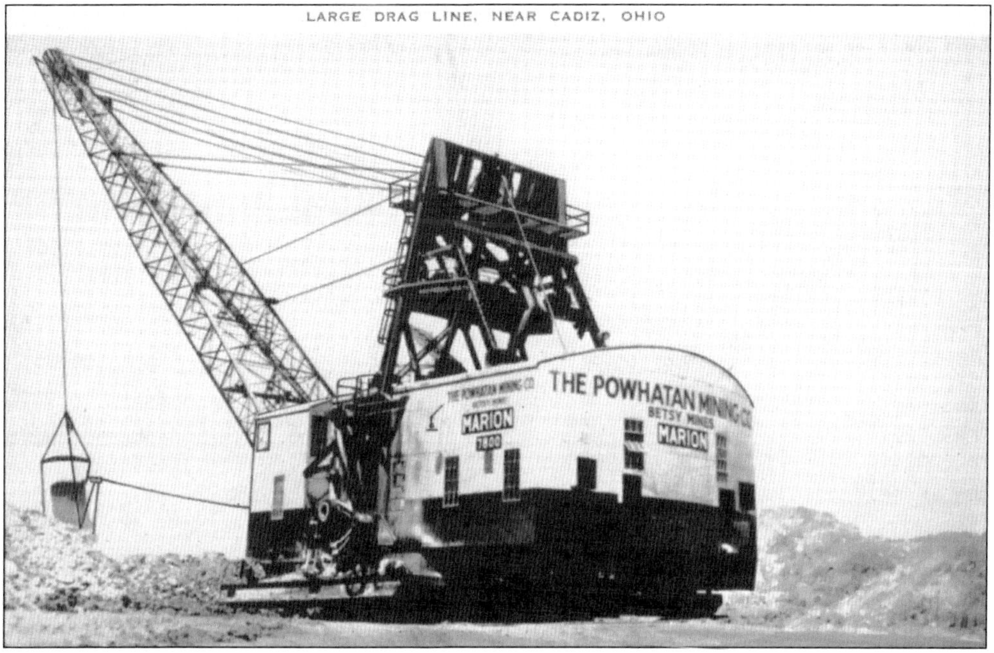

MONSTER SIZE MACHINES. The Model 7800 dragline, with its 35-cubic-yard bucket and 280-foot-long boom, featured an innovative walking system. Hydraulically powered foot pads lifted and slid backwards in a walking motion. The 7800 had an internally mounted 100-ton crane inside the cab that was used for maintenance on the shovel. The largest shovel ever made by Marion had a 180-cubic-yard bucket and weighed more than 15,000 tons. (Author's collection.)

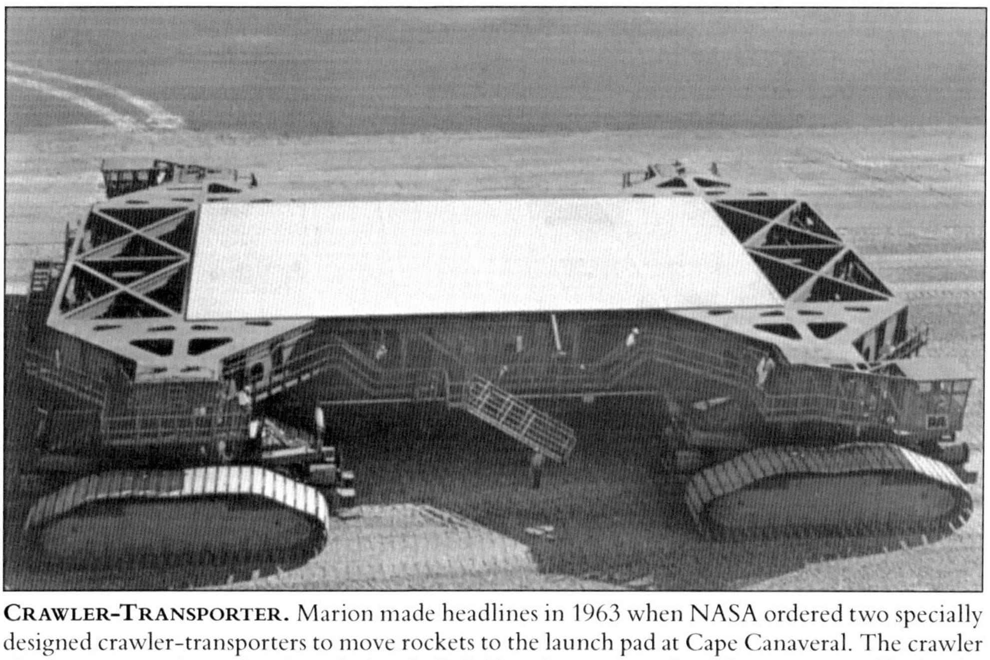

CRAWLER-TRANSPORTER. Marion made headlines in 1963 when NASA ordered two specially designed crawler-transporters to move rockets to the launch pad at Cape Canaveral. The crawler platforms were about the size of a baseball field and were kept level by a system of hydraulic jacks. Each of the four tracks had 57 shoes weighing more than a ton each. Still in use, they have traveled over 2,500 miles. (Author's collection.)

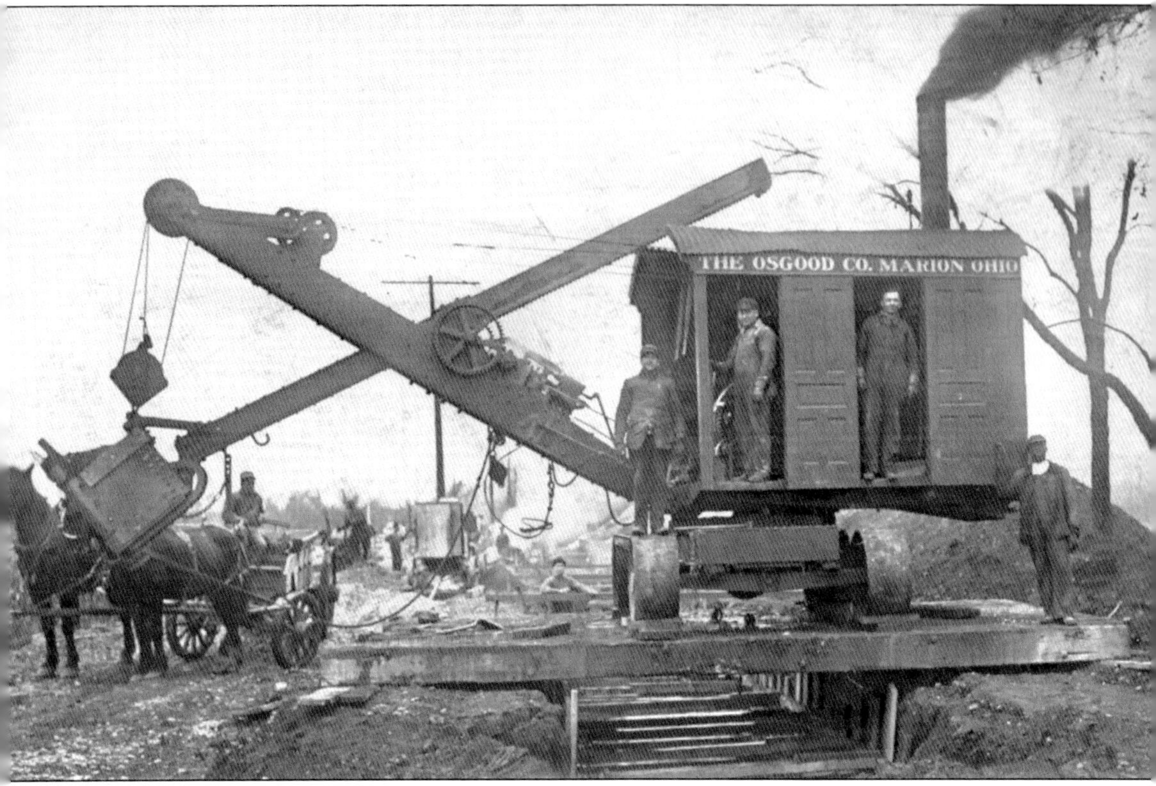

OSGOOD SHOVEL COMPANY. Founded in New York in 1846, the Osgood Company was an innovative competitor to Marion Steam Shovel. Osgood introduced the dragline concept in 1884 and the electrically powered excavator in 1899. In the early 1900s, two disgruntled MSS executives split from the company and formed the Marion Shovel and Dredge Company. In 1910, they purchased the Osgood Company, moved it to Marion, and changed the name to the Marion-Osgood Company before eventually shortening it to Osgood. For the next 45 years, Osgood produced shovels for the construction industry, with a focus on smaller machines. Marion Power Shovel merged with Osgood in 1954 along with the Commercial Steel Casting Company and General Excavator Company. Both of these had been subsidiaries of Osgood. During the 1970s, demand for smaller excavators began to decline, resulting in Marion's engineering and manufacturing efforts becoming more focused on the production of larger machines. The Osgood line was gradually discontinued. (Courtesy of Mike and Linda Perry.)

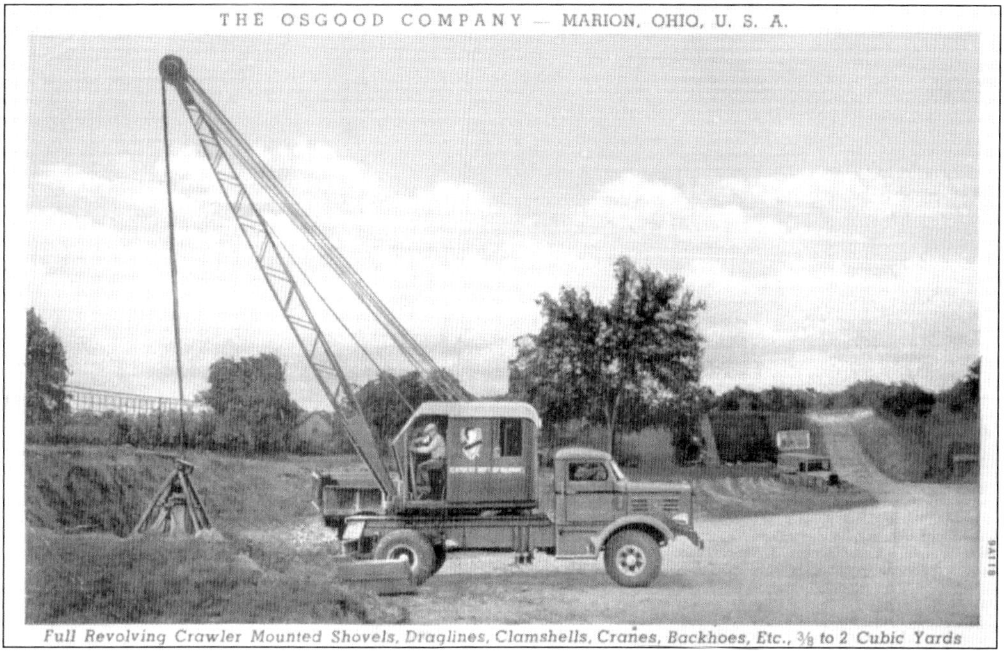

DIFFERENT KIND OF EXCAVATOR. In addition to tracked shovels, the Osgood Company manufactured a line of truck-mounted shovels, including this "clamshell dipper" that is mounted on a Mack chassis. Osgood continued to produce shovels, cranes, and other products into the 1970s. Perhaps its most unique order was 14 truck cranes used in building Atlas missile silos near Lincoln, Nebraska. (Author's collection.)

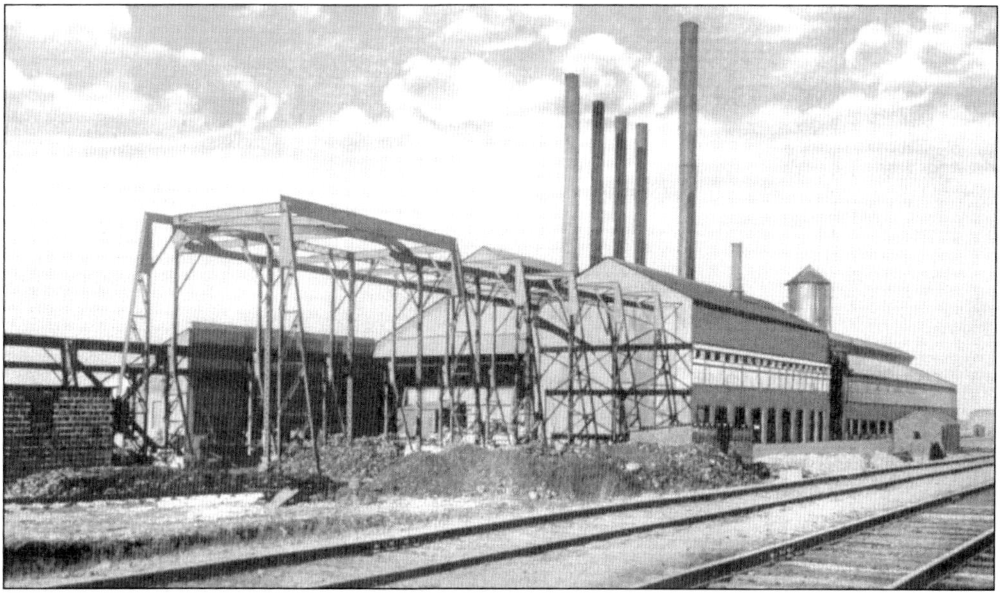

INTERSTATE STEEL COMPANY. Marion's heavy industries required a steady supply of steel for their manufacturing needs. One source was the Interstate Steel Company on Cheney Avenue. Originally located in Cambridge, Ohio, the company was enticed to move to Marion in 1915 with the offer of $60,000 in seed money to build a new production facility. Nucor Steel currently uses the facility to manufacture specialty steel products. (Author's collection.)

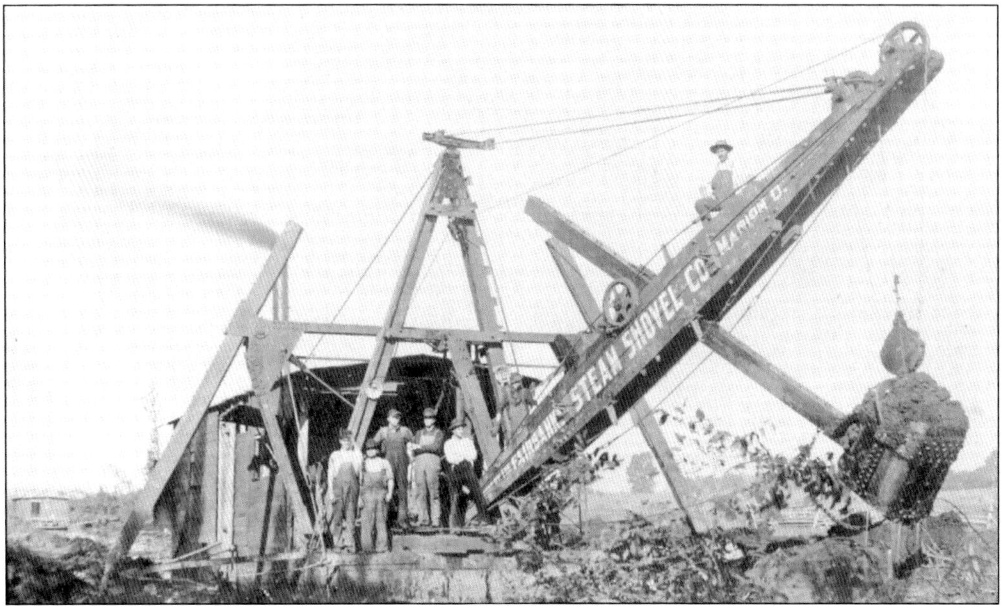

FAIRBANKS SHOVEL COMPANY. James G. Fairbanks established the Fairbanks Steam Shovel Company in 1893 with a plant on East George Street where he also operated a quarry. Products included dipper dredges, steam shovels, locomotive cranes, log loaders, and the Lobo traction engine. (Courtesy of Mike and Linda Perry.)

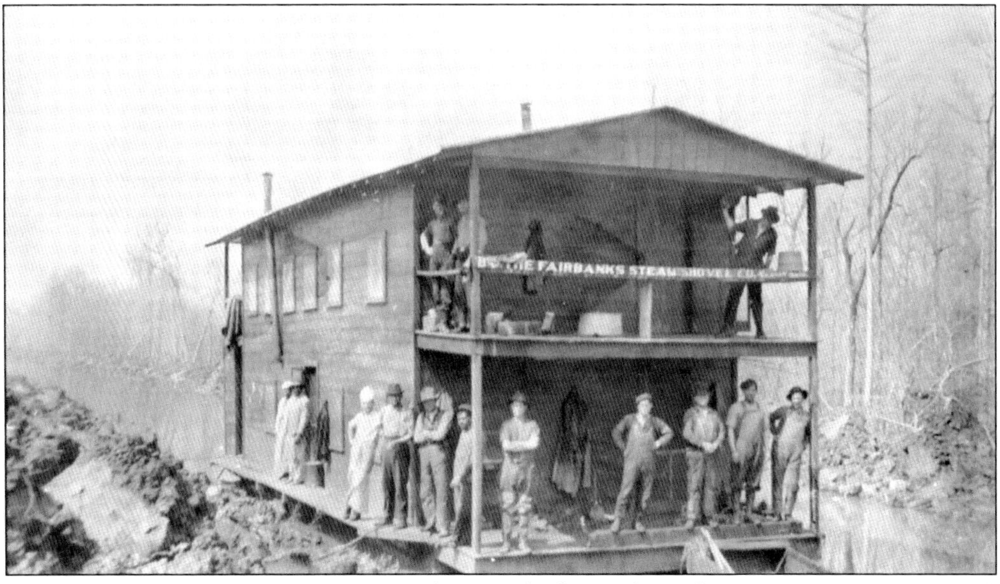

FLOATING BUNKHOUSE. Digging and cleaning ditches and canals was a very important task as new areas were opened for farming and other purposes. Since many of the locations were remote, innovations such as this floating bunkhouse for employees of the Fairbanks Steam Shovel Company made life away from home a little more enjoyable. (Courtesy of Richard Carey.)

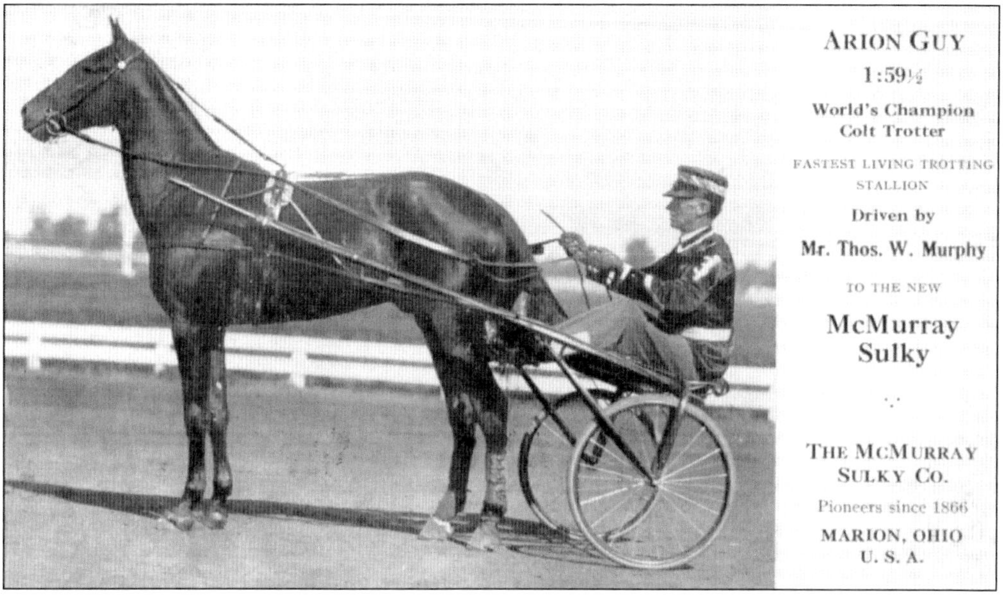

McMurray Sulky Company. Marion could well have been called Sulky City around 1900, as two of the world's predominant racing sulky manufacturers called the city home. McMurray Sulky was formed in 1899 and produced racing sulkies, wagons, buggies, and carts from its factory on North Main Street. It later merged with the Houghton Sulky Company. (Courtesy of Richard Carey.)

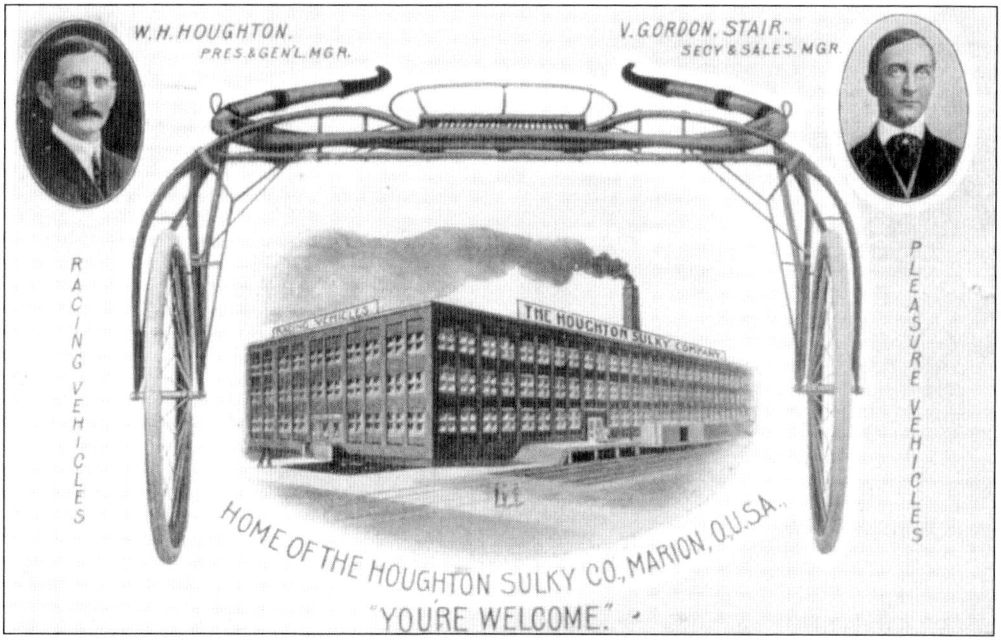

Houghton Sulky Company. William H. Houghton started his sulky company in 1904 in the building shown in this artist's enhanced drawing before moving to the "old stone church" on North State Street. Houghton produced world-class sulkies and wagons for customers such as Czar Nicholas II of Russia, Clark Gable, and Ringling Bros. Circus. After 100 years in Marion, the company was sold to Jerald Sulky Company in 2007. (Author's collection.)

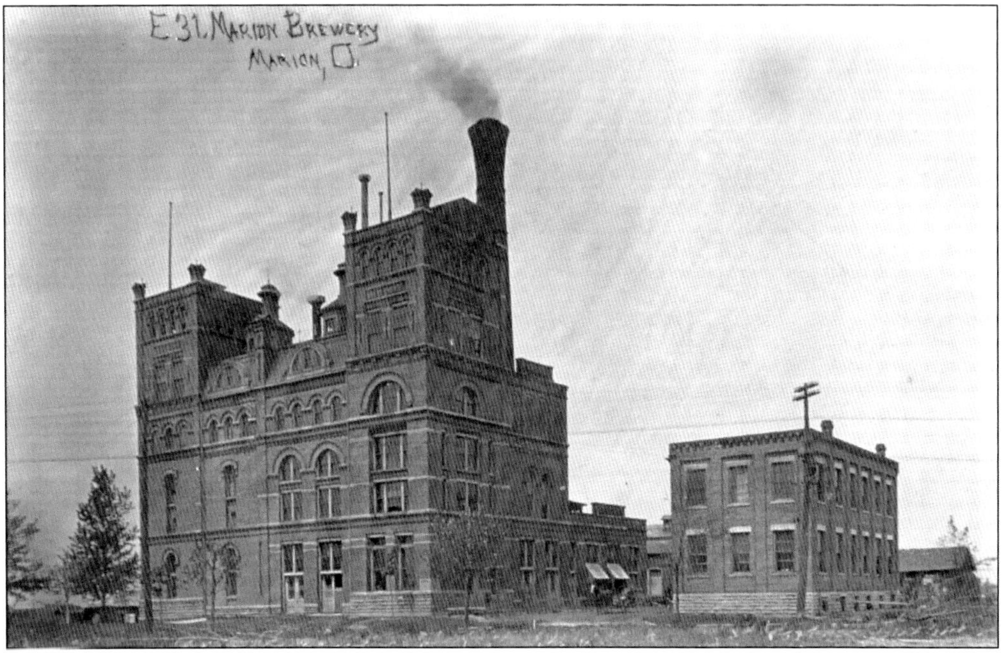

Marion Brewing and Bottling. Started in 1895 on Bellefontaine Avenue near the railroad tracks, the brewer had a first run of 100 kegs of Marion Beer intended mostly for wholesale business. By 1910, Banquet Brew had become a favorite in Marion's taverns. Ohio's 1908 Rose Law and Prohibition combined to eventually force the closure of the company, with the building later being used by the Betty Zane Popcorn Company. (Courtesy of Richard Carey.)

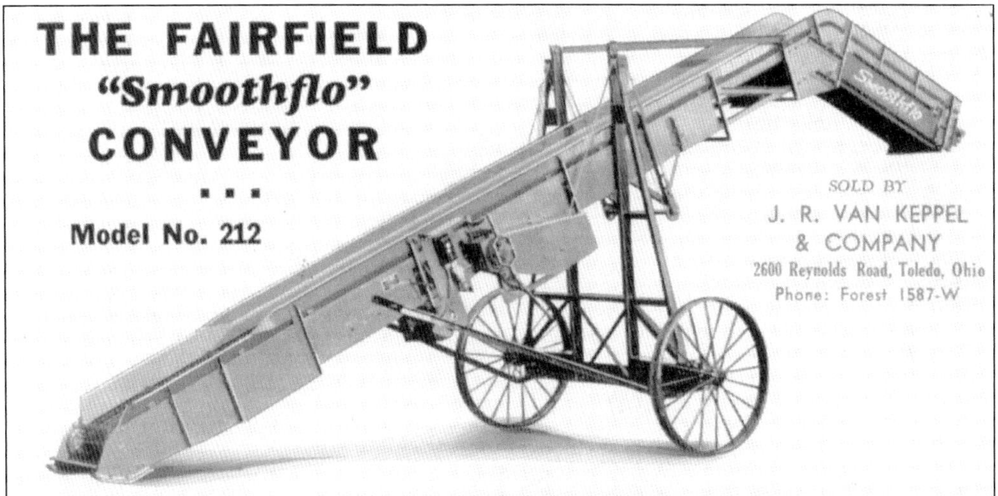

Fairfield Engineering. Properly called a car unloader, conveyors such as this one made by Fairfield Engineering were used primarily to transfer coal from railroad cars. Fairfield, which moved to Marion from Lancaster, Ohio, in 1923, engineered and built a wide variety of conveyance systems in its plant on Barnhart Street. (Courtesy of Richard Carey.)

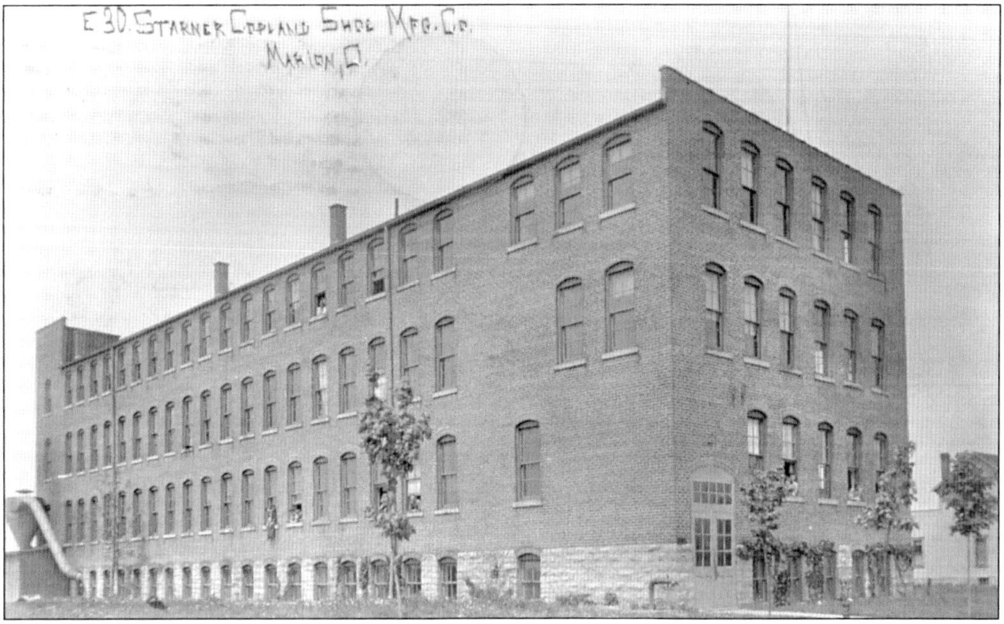

STARNER-COPELAND SHOE COMPANY. Incorporated as the Marion Shoe Manufacturing Company in 1904, the company in this impressive building at the corner of Park Boulevard and Darius Street later had its name changed to the Starner-Copeland Shoe Company. Eventually unable to maintain sufficient sales, the company closed, with the building being razed. It is now the site of a bulk oil facility. (Courtesy of Mike and Linda Perry.)

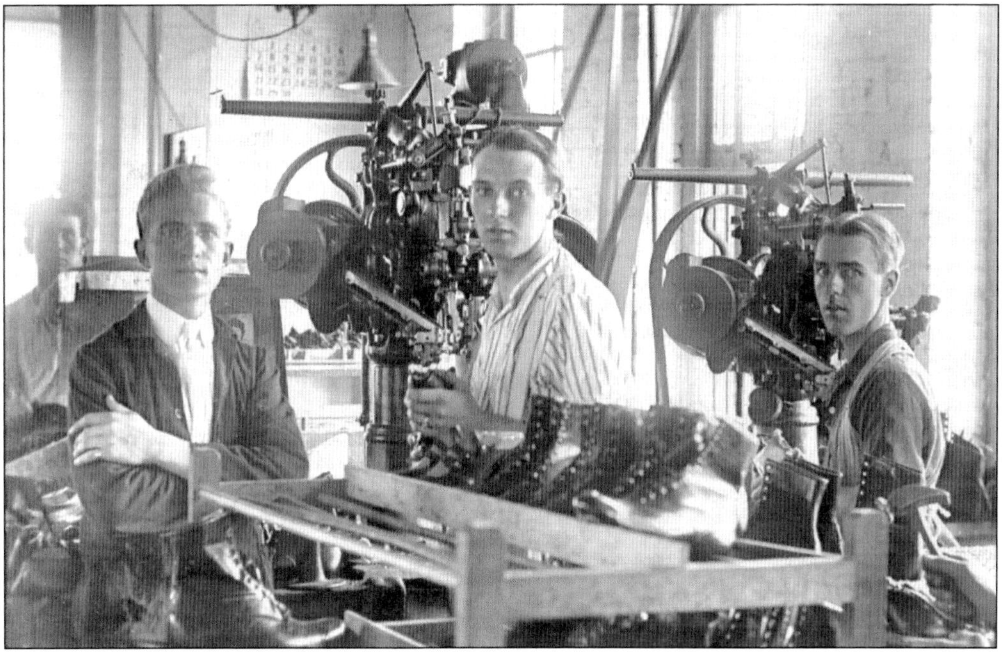

MANUFACTURING SHOES. These workers at the Starner-Copeland Shoe Company crafted fine leather footwear for ladies, misses, and children using machines powered by leather belts that were attached to overhead driveshafts. The 180 employees produced over 25,000 pair of shoes annually, with many of them being exported to European nations. (Courtesy of Richard Carey.)

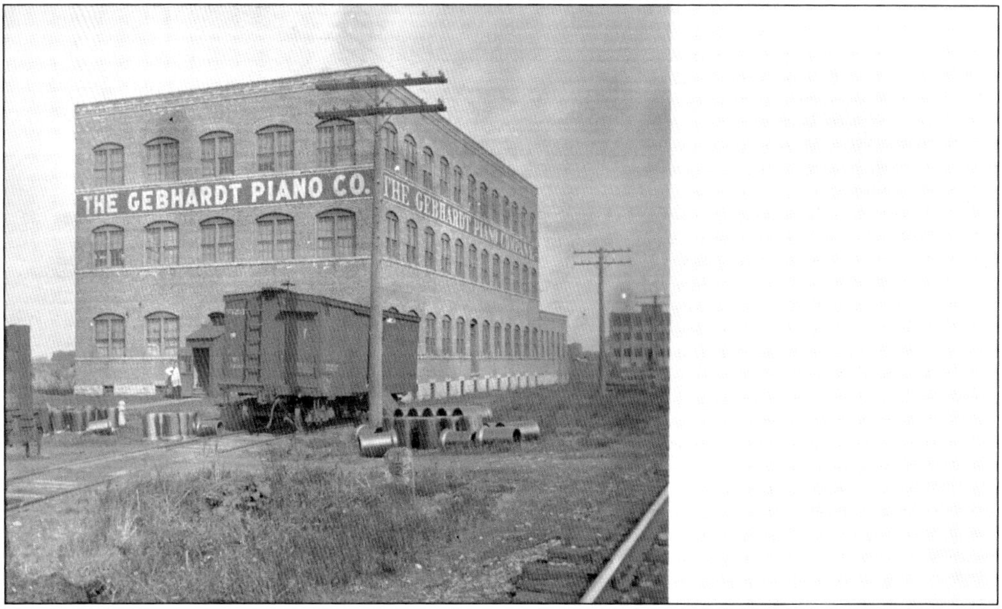

GEBHARDT PIANO COMPANY. Built on Marion's east side in 1902 adjacent to the Pennsylvania and Hocking Valley Railroads as a speculative venture, this building was state-of-the-art, with an electric elevator, sprinkler system, and its own power generator. The Gebhardt Piano Company was the first tenant, followed over the years by Ackerman Piano, Houghton Sulky Company, and Studebaker-Wulff Tires, among others. (Courtesy of Stuart Koblentz Haley.)

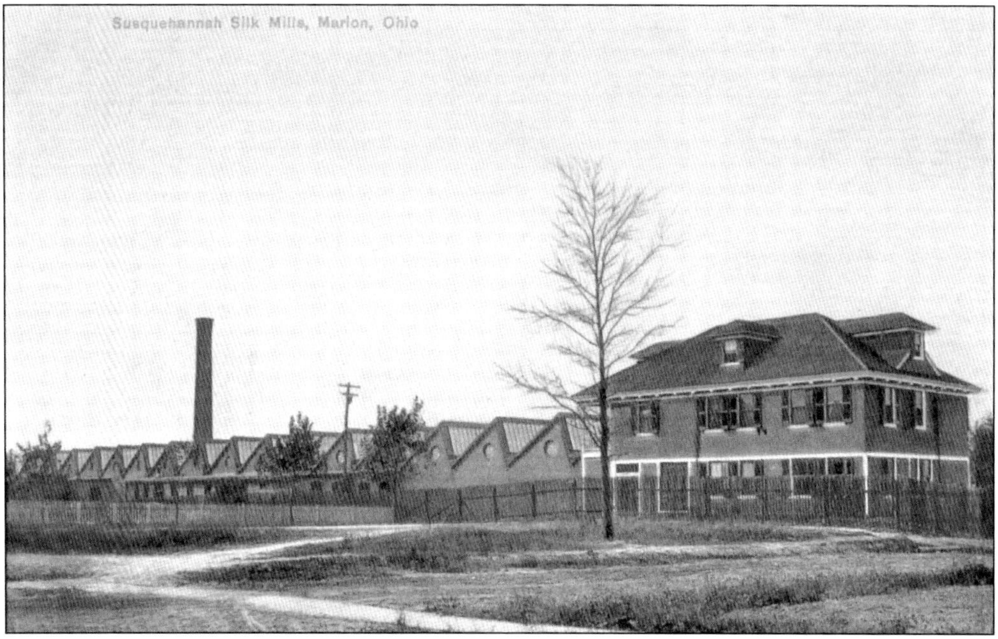

SUSQUEHANNA SILK MILL. Working with thin silk thread as it was woven into silk fabric for a variety of uses was a job best suited for the over 300 female employees of the Susquehanna Silk Mill on Joseph Street. Opened in 1902, the factory provided housing for women employees and plant management on its 54-acre site. Building lots were offered to employees to encourage them to construct houses in the area. (Author's collection.)

Five

Now Leaving the Station

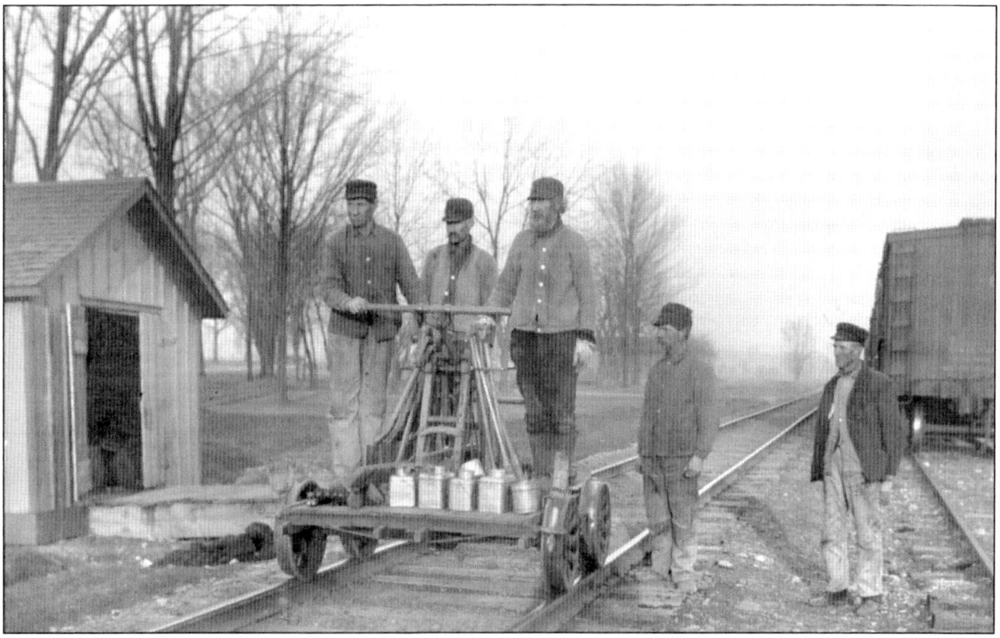

Checking the Track. Railroad workers commonly used hand-powered track cars to inspect and repair the rails. The first railroad through Marion was the Bellefontaine & Indiana Railroad track adjacent to North Street—later Railroad Street, Mill Street, and now Huber Street. The first train arrived from Galion on August 28, 1852, with Howard Copeland as the conductor. (Courtesy of Mike and Linda Perry.)

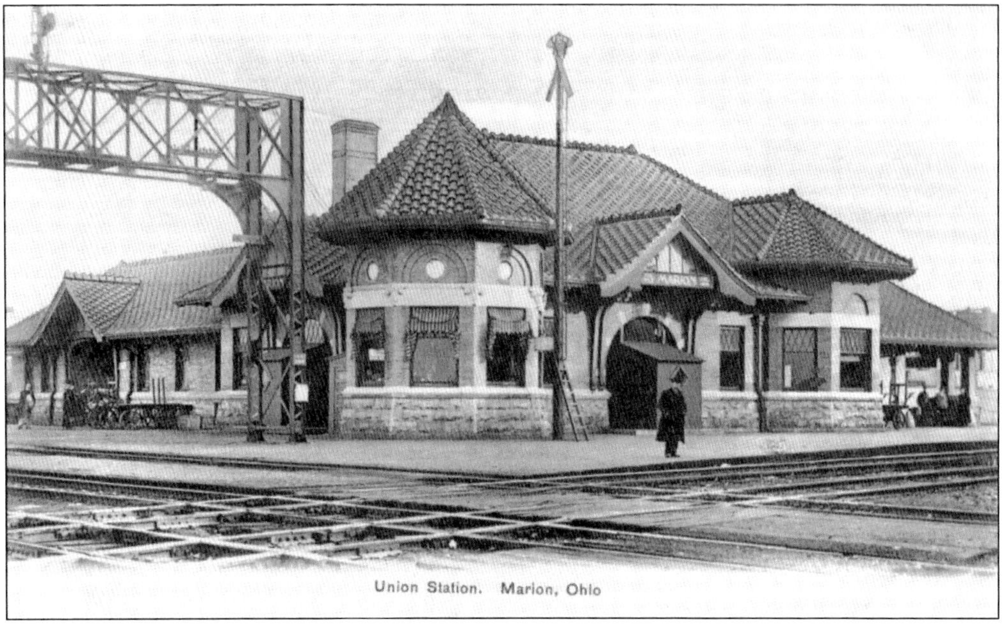

UNION STATION. Marion's rapid industrial growth in the early 1900s underscored the need for a rail depot to replace the antiquated railcar that served the purpose. Several railroads combined to build the Union Station Depot. Opened in 1902, the building featured a stained-glass dome in the waiting area along with golden oak woodwork and a red-glazed ceramic tile roof. (Author's collection.)

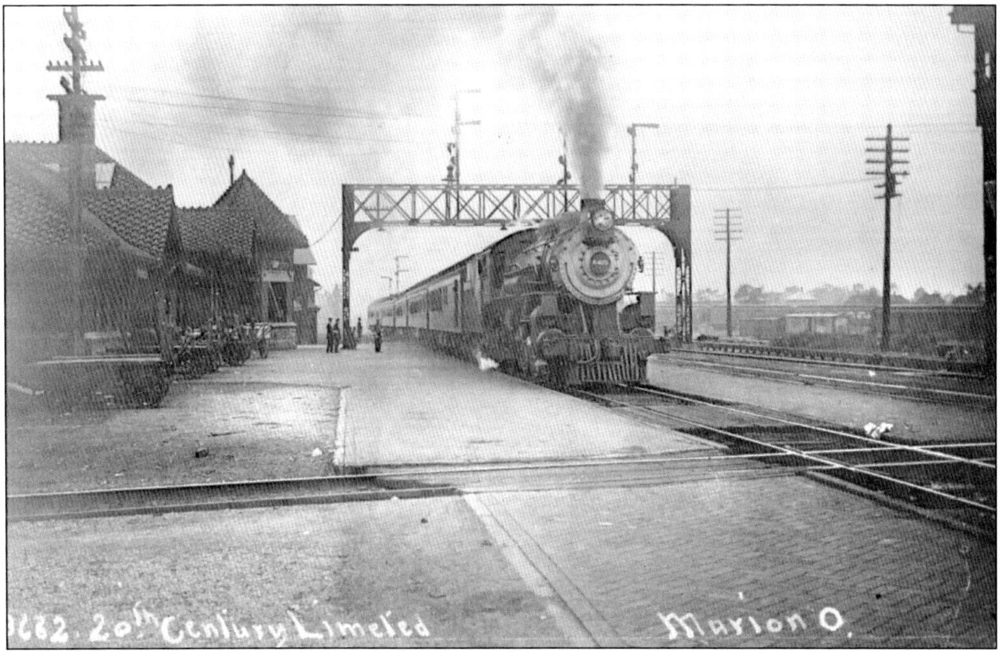

DIFFERENT KIND OF DIAMOND. Marion's rail network grew rapidly in the early 1900s, with more than 38 passenger trains passing through daily. Several rail lines converged near the Union Depot, creating rail "diamonds" where a track crossed another track. Marion was a prosperous town in at least one regard, as it possessed 16 diamonds. (Courtesy of Richard Carey.)

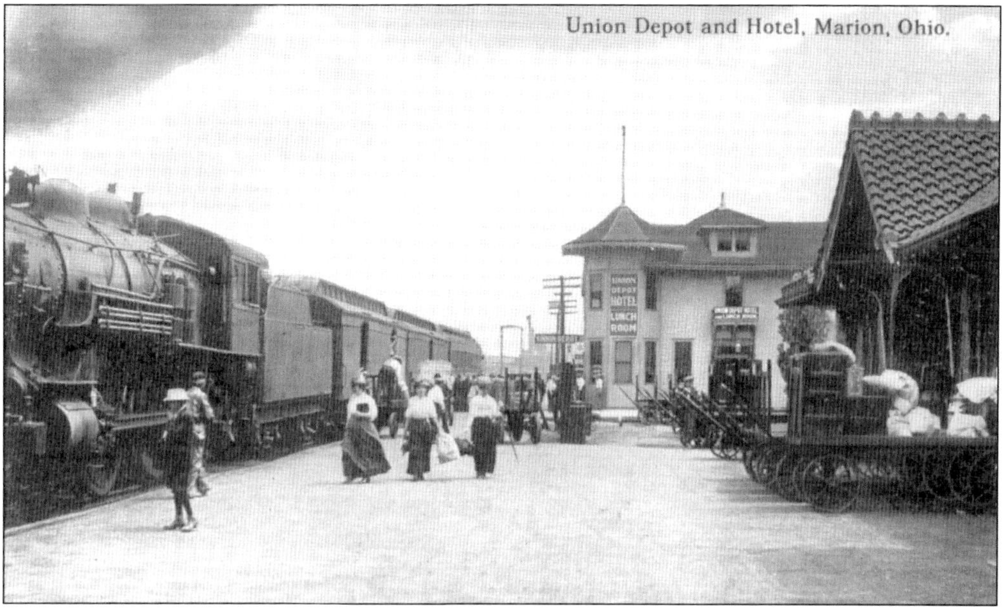

ALL ABOARD! Passengers disperse from their westbound train that is actually sitting on the eastbound tracks to assist in unloading. Some may have stopped in the Union Depot to have a sip of cold water from the special iced-water machine, while others simply wanted their baggage from the waiting carts. On May 10, 1971, the last passenger train left from Marion. (Courtesy of Mike and Linda Perry.)

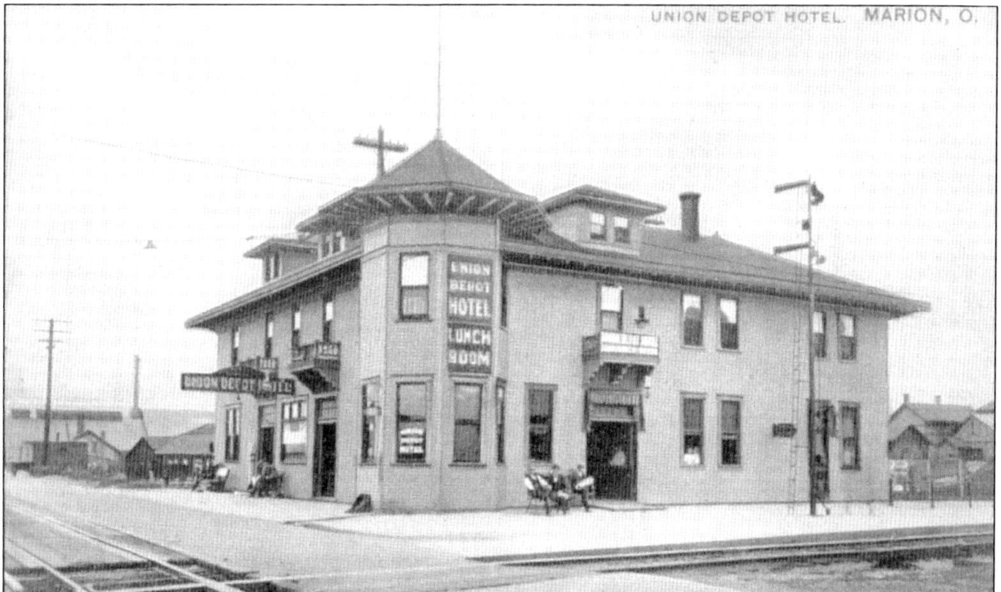

UNION DEPOT HOTEL. In addition to being a very convenient overnight abode for rail travelers, the Union Depot Hotel was also a popular dining establishment for rail workers, Marion Steam Shovel employees, and the local police force. It was known for excellent food—especially its pie. The structure was razed in the 1970s, and the site is now vacant land east of the Union Depot. (Author's collection.)

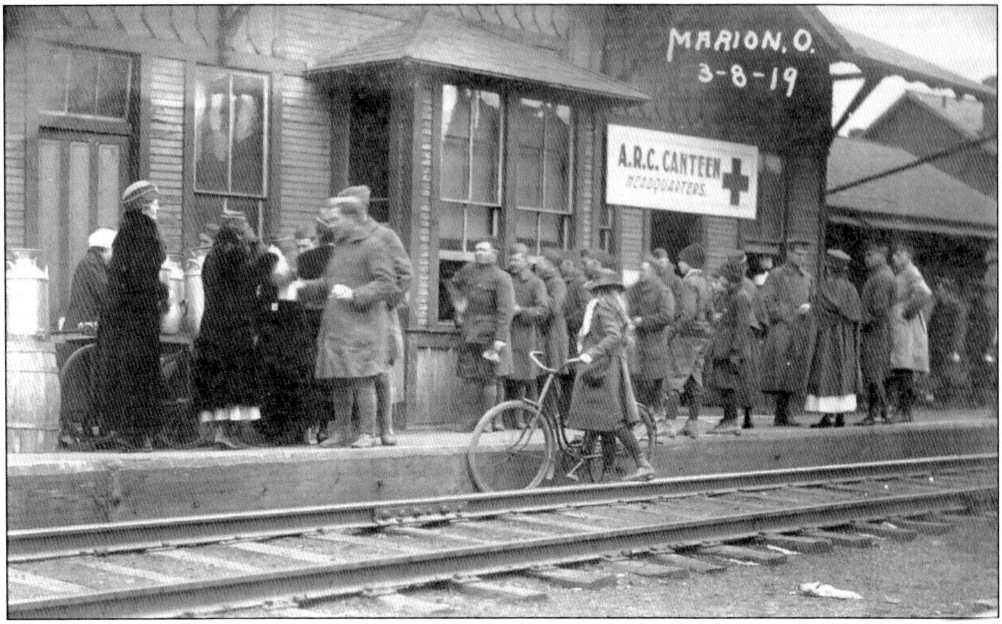

Help for the Soldiers. A friendly smile and a hot cup of coffee provided by the American Red Cross canteen volunteers helped make these World War I soldiers' stop in Marion a little more pleasant. The canteen, one of over 700 nationwide, was housed at the Pennsylvania Railroad station located just south of Union Station. (Courtesy of Richard Carey.)

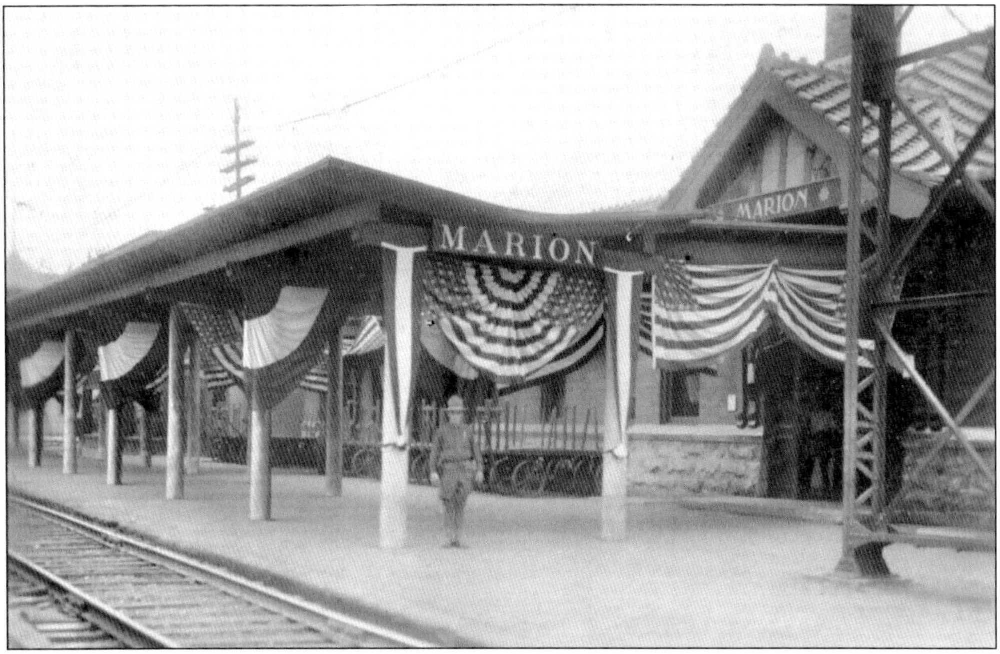

Waiting on a Trophy. In an effort to sell more war bonds, the Liberty Loan Committee sponsored a trophy train's visit to Marion in April 1919. The train featured specially designed railcars that displayed captured German armaments. They included Big Bertha howitzers, guns, helmets, gas masks, and numerous other items captured on the battlefield. A crowd of over 5,000 people toured the train during its stop. (Courtesy of Bob Turner.)

A Moose in Marion. Theodore Roosevelt, seen climbing the side of the railcar, visited Marion in May 1912 during his Bull Moose presidential campaign. Roosevelt's train stopped at West Center Street, where he clambered atop the car to present his campaign pitch to the crowd. The speech may not have been a success, as both Roosevelt and incumbent William Howard Taft were defeated by Woodrow Wilson. (Courtesy of Mike and Linda Perry.)

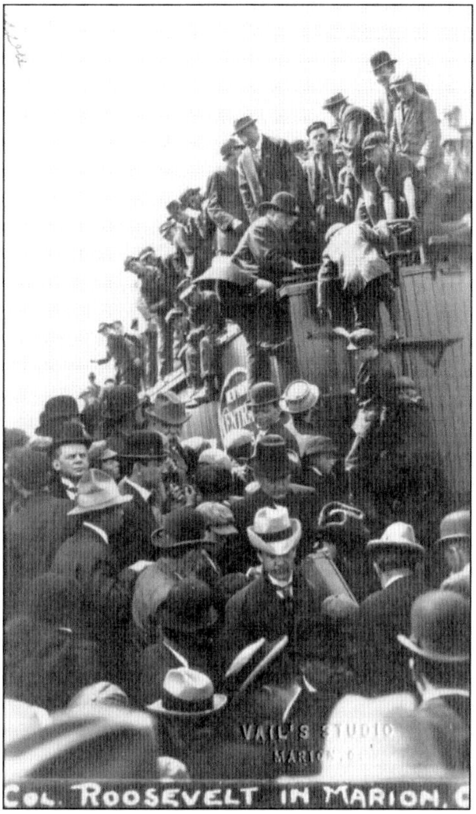

Fishing Excursion. Traveling on the Hocking Valley Railroad in a Pullman-built coach, members of the Marion Fishing Club appear to be enjoying their trip. The Hocking Valley ran from Athens through Columbus to Prospect, Marion, and on to Toledo. It eventually became part of the Chesapeake and Ohio Railway. Some of the line is used today by CSX, while portions south of Columbus host the Hocking Valley Scenic Railway. (Courtesy of Richard Carey.)

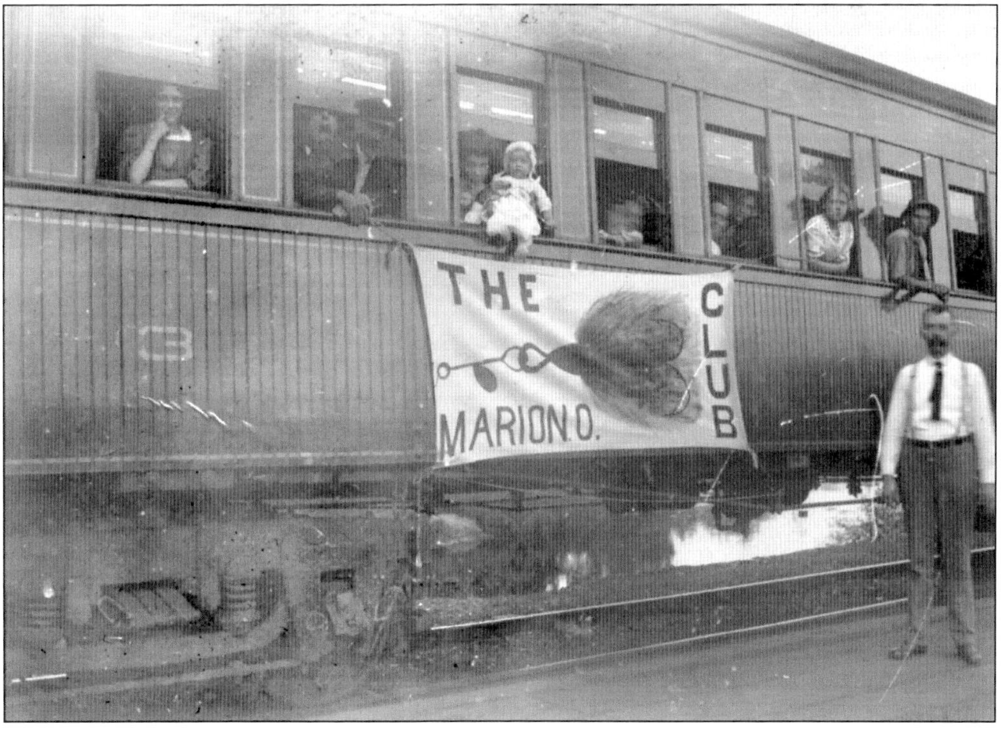

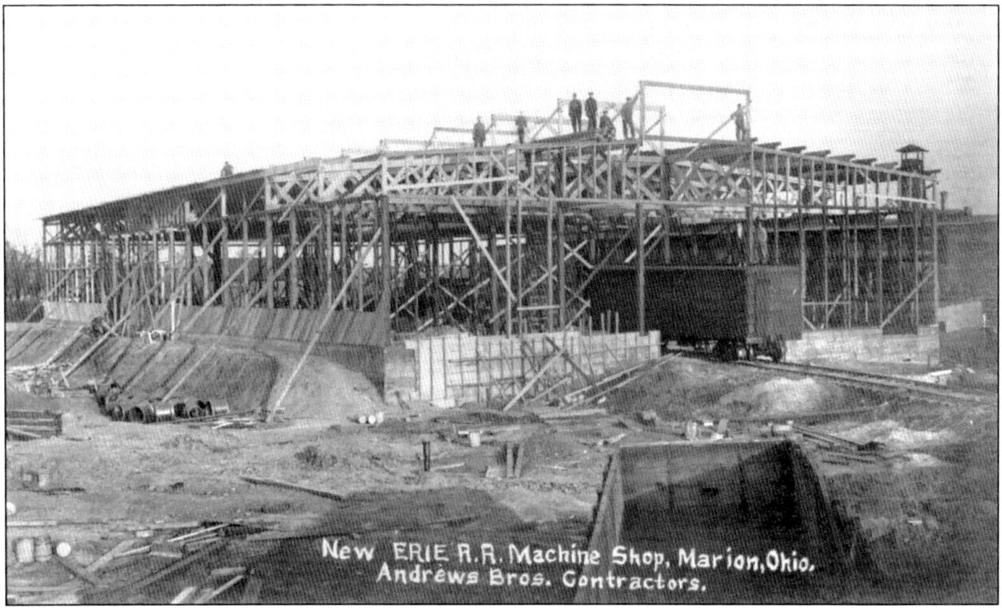

Erie Machine Shop. The Erie rail system built this machine shop on the west side of Marion near the current Union Tank Car facility around 1930. Erie Lackawanna was a major employer in Marion for many years, with over 2,000 employees in the Marion branch in the early 1970s, prior to the company declaring bankruptcy in 1976. Erie then joined six other railroads to form the Consolidated Rail Corporation, or Conrail. (Courtesy of Richard Carey.)

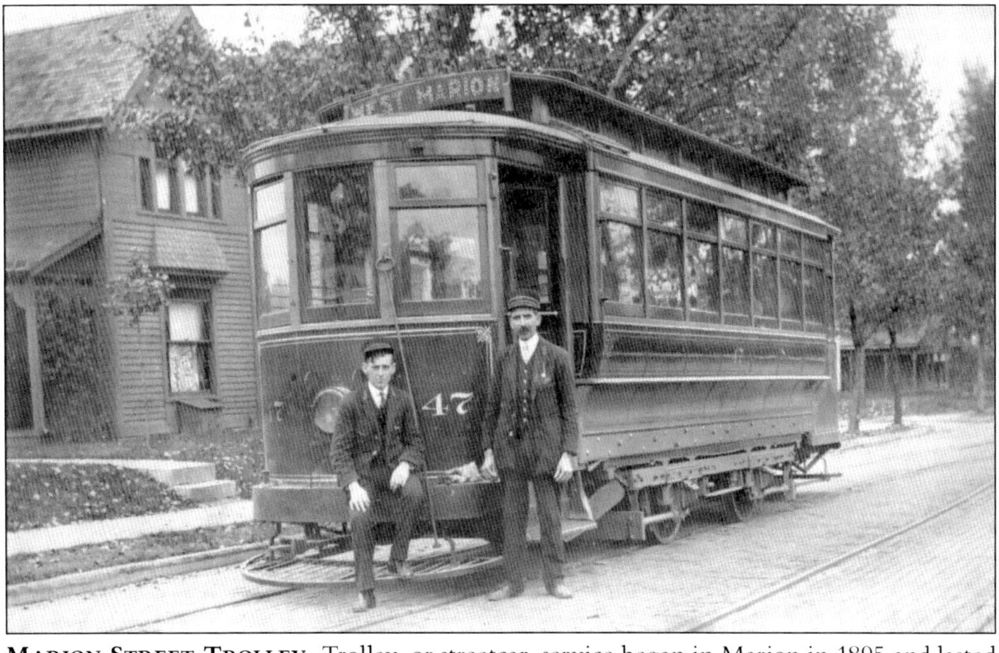

Marion Street Trolley. Trolley, or streetcar, service began in Marion in 1895 and lasted through 1928. The main route covered four miles of track from Bellefontaine Avenue down Davids Street to Center Street, where it headed east to Garfield Park. Passengers had the option of transferring at the courthouse to go to the fairgrounds or the Marion Cemetery. The cost of a ticket was 10¢. (Courtesy of Richard Carey.)

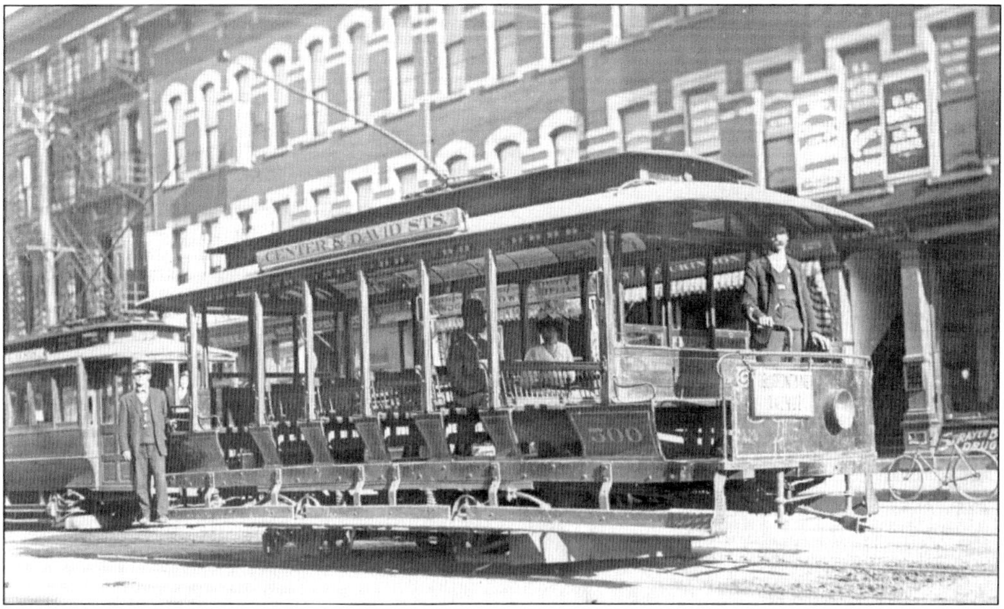

SUMMERTIME TROLLEY. Passengers in this open-air trolley perhaps entertained themselves by reading the advertisements on the trolley's ceiling. Upon reaching the end of the line, the trolley was driven onto a large turntable, spun 180 degrees, and started back in the opposite direction. Special couplings were added to the cars to allow them to pull fire equipment, which had previously been pulled by hand or horse. (Courtesy of Mike and Linda Perry.)

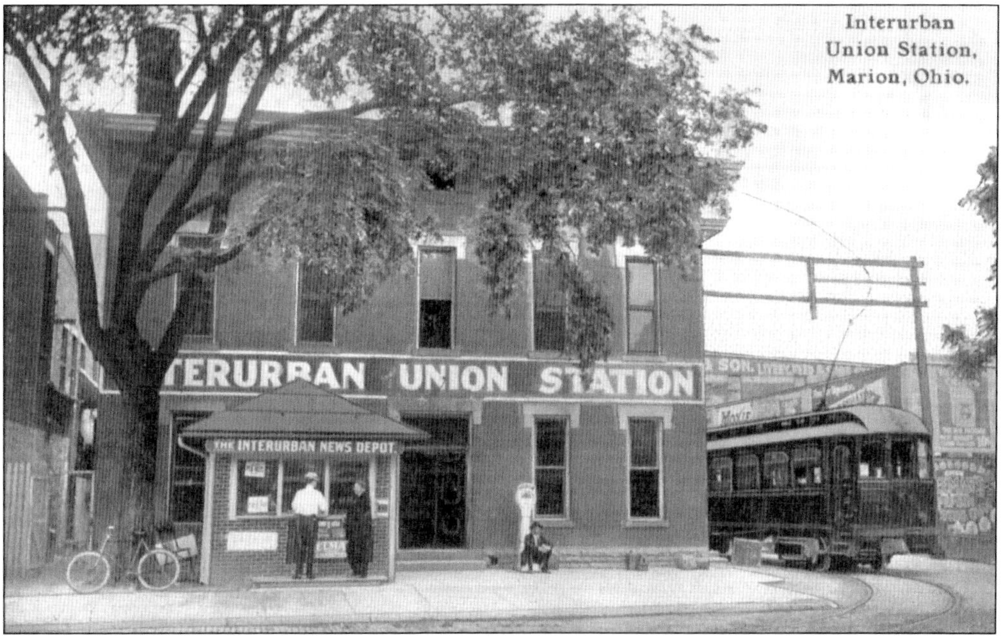

COLUMBUS, DELAWARE, AND MARION INTERURBAN (CDM). Service via the CDM Interurban line began in 1904. Passenger service lasted until 1933, when the growing popularity of the automobile signaled the end of fast rail service. The passenger station was located on North State Street near the railroad, while the freight house was on West Center Street in the building now housing the Warehouse Restaurant. (Author's collection.)

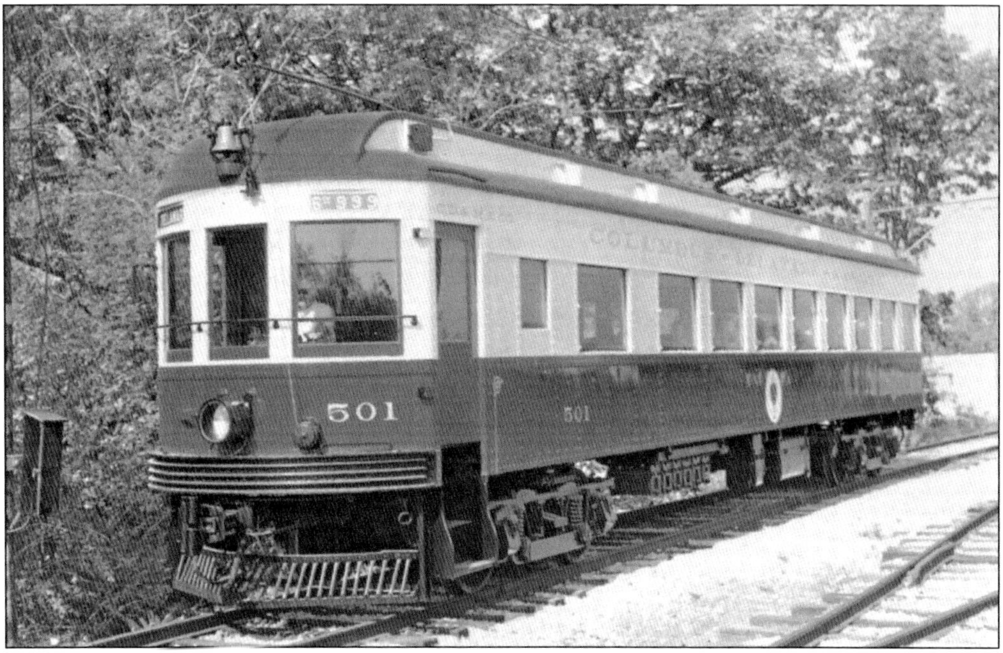

PRIDE OF THE PACK. Two elaborate parlor cars known as Redbirds, due to their vivid red color scheme, were purchased by the CDM in 1925 at a cost of $36,000 each. The front of the car was a smoker, with the remainder a parlor car with swivel seats. They made the 1.5-hour round-trip from Columbus to Marion six times each day. (Courtesy of Marion County Historical Society.)

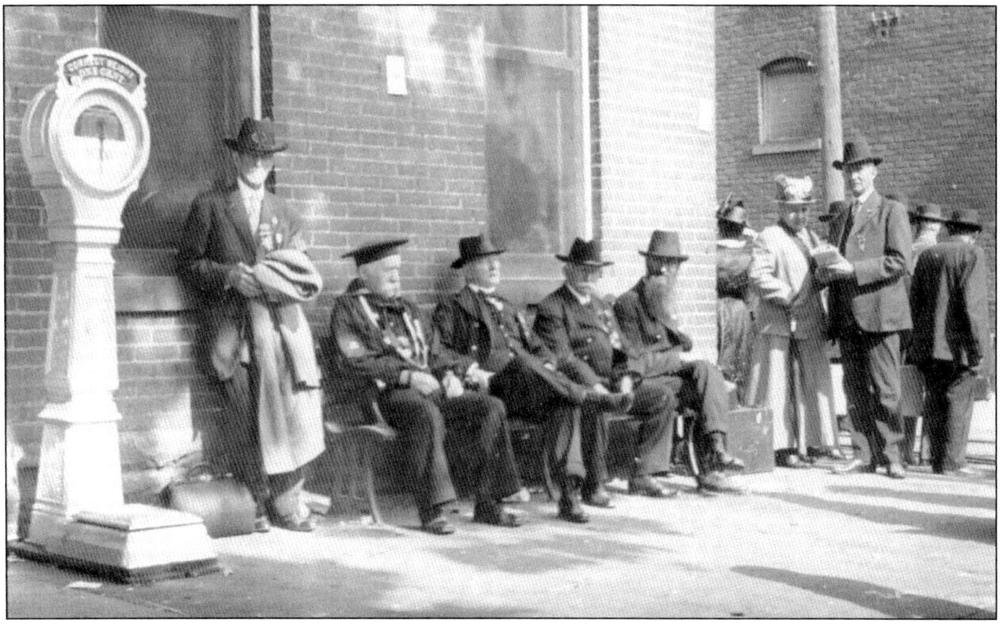

WAITING ON THEIR RIDE. These Civil War veterans wait outside the Marion CDM station to travel to Columbus for the 1919 National Grand Army of the Republic Convention. The GAR, composed of veterans of the American Civil War, was a fraternal organization and was one of the first advocacy groups in American politics. After reaching a peak of 490,000 members in 1890, it was dissolved in 1956 when the last member died. (Courtesy of Mike and Linda Perry.)

Six

Houses of Worship and Places of Rest

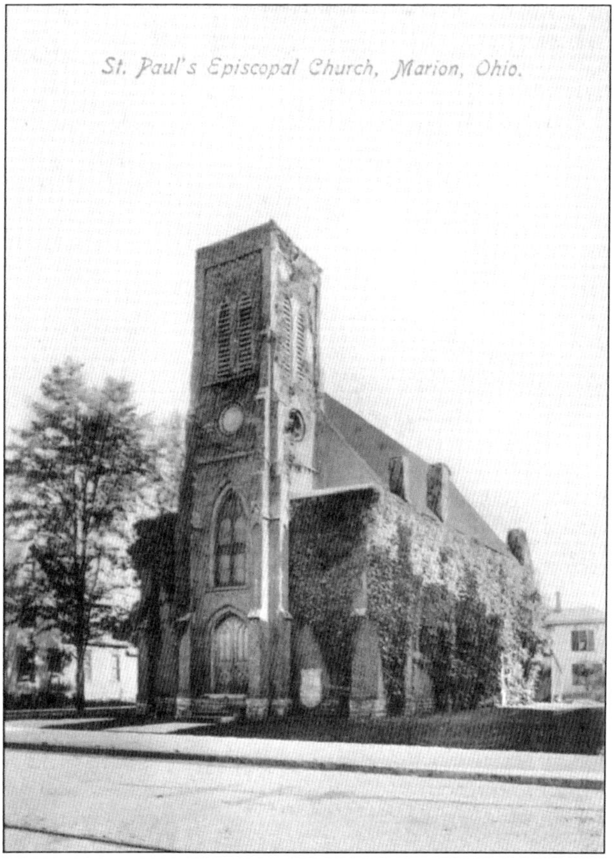

St. Paul's Episcopal. Marion town father Eber Baker donated a lot at the southwest corner of Center and High Streets as well as $1,000 toward construction costs for the English Abbey–style building with its Gothic-style stained-glass windows. St. Paul's is believed to be the oldest congregation still meeting in its original building in Marion, completed in 1858. (Courtesy of Mike and Linda Perry.)

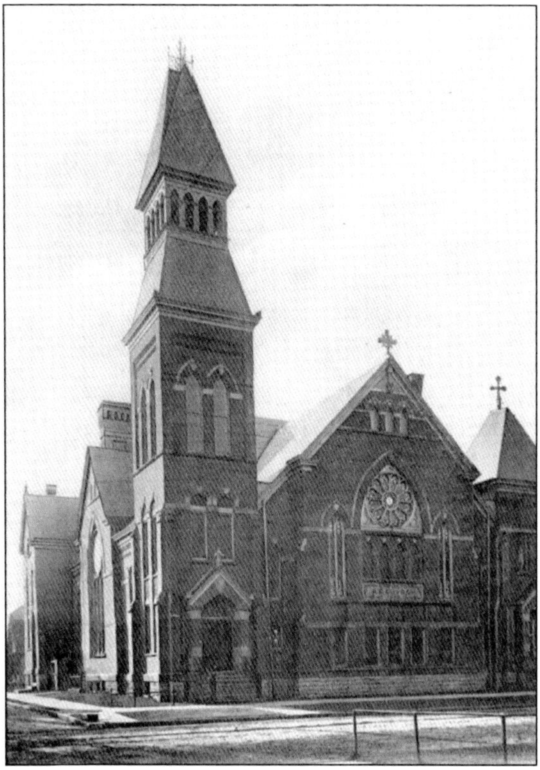

Epworth Methodist Episcopal. The founding members of Epworth first met in 1820 before Marion officially became a village. The congregation held services in a number of locations before moving into this High Victorian Gothic building at the southwest corner of Center and Vine Streets in 1891. By 1931, its 2,800 members made it the largest Methodist church in the state of Ohio. (Courtesy of Mike and Linda Perry.)

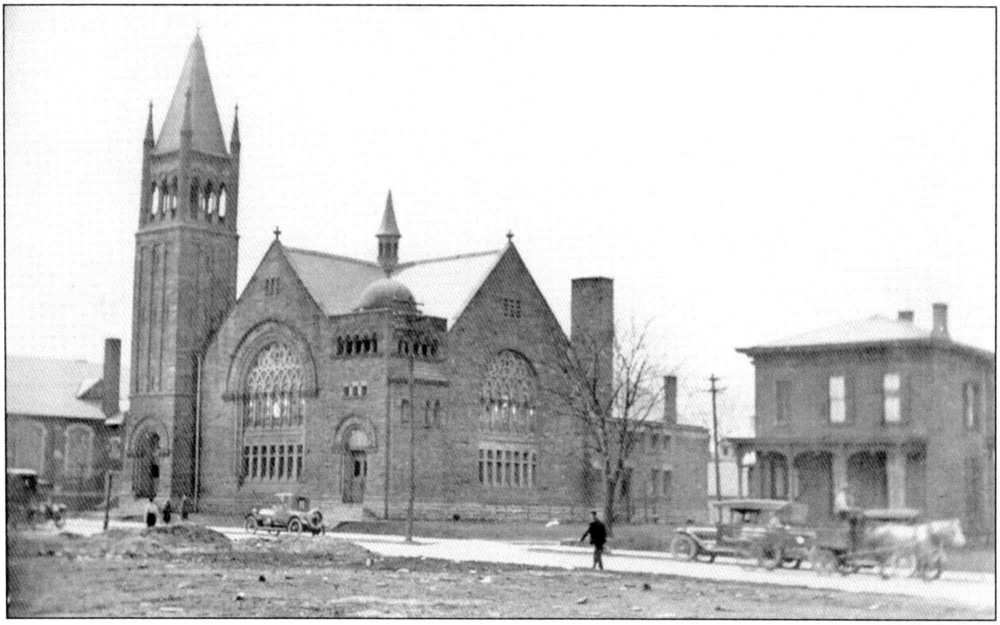

First Presbyterian. Marion's Presbyterians first met in 1828. Services were held in several locations preceding the1893 building of "The Great Stone Church" at the northwest corner of Prospect and Church Streets. This view was taken prior to the 1925 building addition, which was made necessary by the donation of an organ. The sanctuary features beautiful stained-glass windows, including one from Tiffany Studios. (Courtesy of Mike and Linda Perry.)

TRINITY BAPTIST. Trinity traces its roots to the Free Will Baptist Church organized in Marion in 1824. This Old English–style building located on South Main Street was completed in 1908 at a cost of $67,500, which included the furnishings and organ. In 1912, members of the First Baptist congregation merged with the Free Baptists to create Trinity Baptist. (Courtesy of Mike and Linda Perry.)

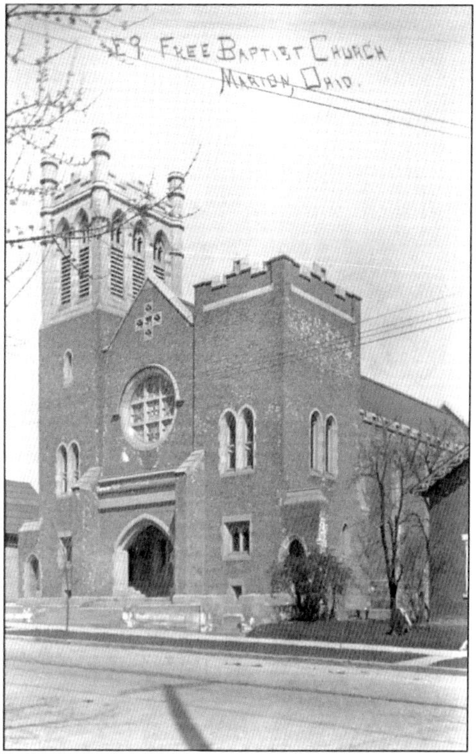

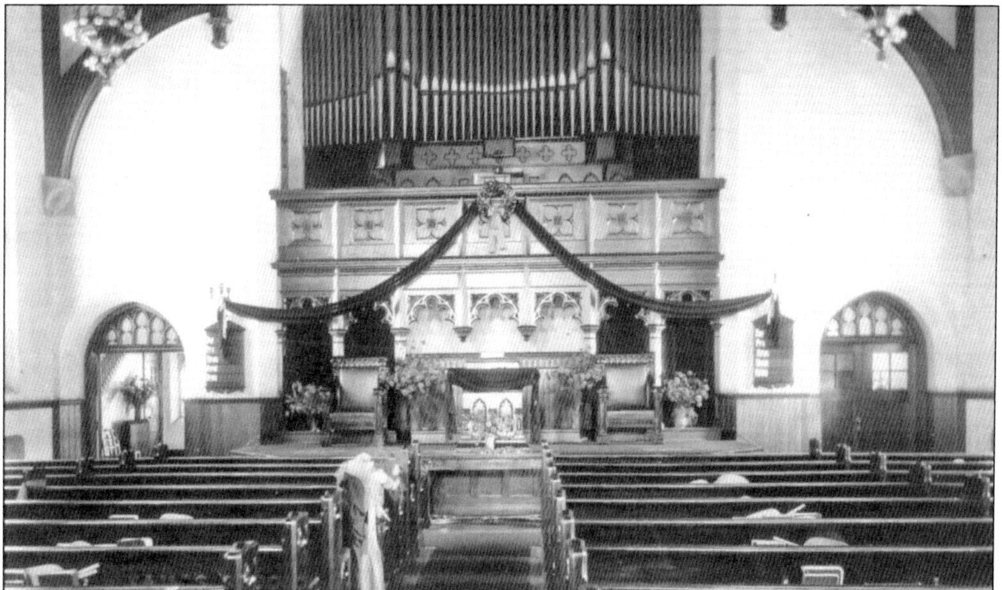

MOURNING A NATION'S LOSS. Warren G. Harding was a member of Trinity Baptist for 40 years and served as a trustee for 35 years. Upon his death, the pew where he normally sat was draped in mourning cloth for 30 days. During that time, the church doors were left open and over 11,000 people visited. A bronze plaque was placed on the pew. (Courtesy of Marion County Historical Society.)

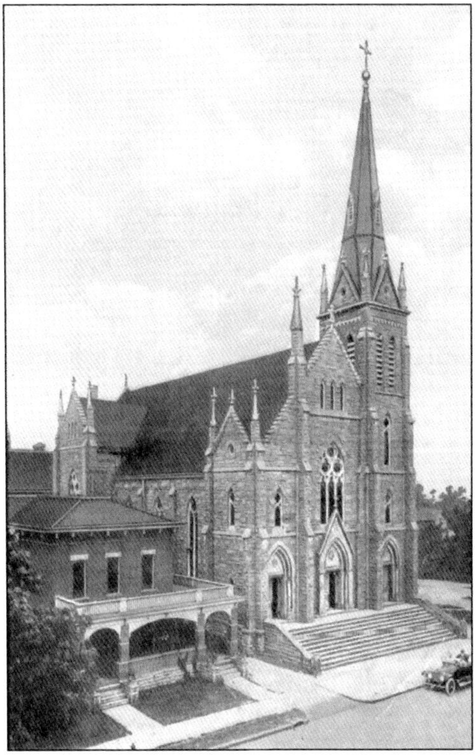

St. Mary Catholic. The first Catholic church services in Marion were conducted in 1849 by Father Burgess. Local banker Timothy Fahey donated land in 1861 for a church at the site of what is now St. Mary School. This High Victorian Gothic building was constructed on North Main Street at a cost of $75,000. More than 2,000 people attended its dedication in October of 1895. (Courtesy of Mike and Linda Perry.)

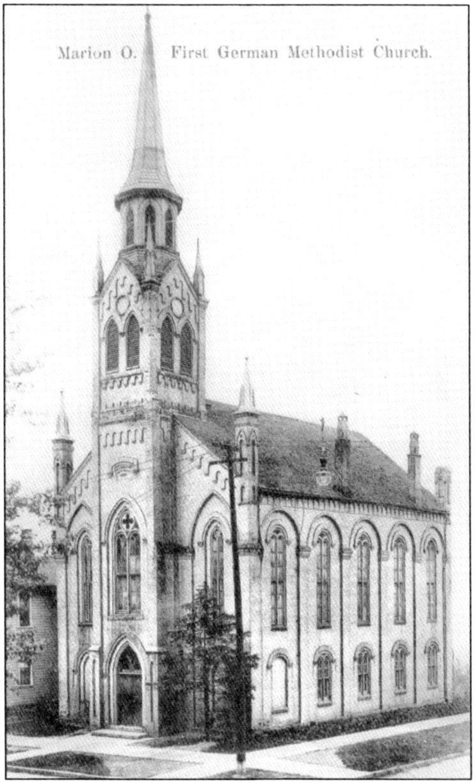

First German Methodist. The opening year of 1869 is set in the date-stone over the front entrance of this hall-style church with a second-floor sanctuary. It was built on the site of the former Duncan's Brewery at the southwest corner of Church and Prospect Streets. The church was used until 1914, when it was replaced with the "Red Brick Methodist," current home of Prospect Street United Methodist Church. (Author's collection.)

EMANUEL LUTHERAN, COLUMBIA STREET. Founded in 1874 as St. Matthew's English Mission Evangelical Lutheran, services were conducted in both English and German for many years. Renamed Salem Evangelical Lutheran in 1879, the congregation built this church in the swale at the corner of Prospect and Columbia Street in 1886 and changed names again to Emanuel Evangelical Lutheran. The congregation moved to a new building in 1918. (Courtesy of Mike and Linda Perry.)

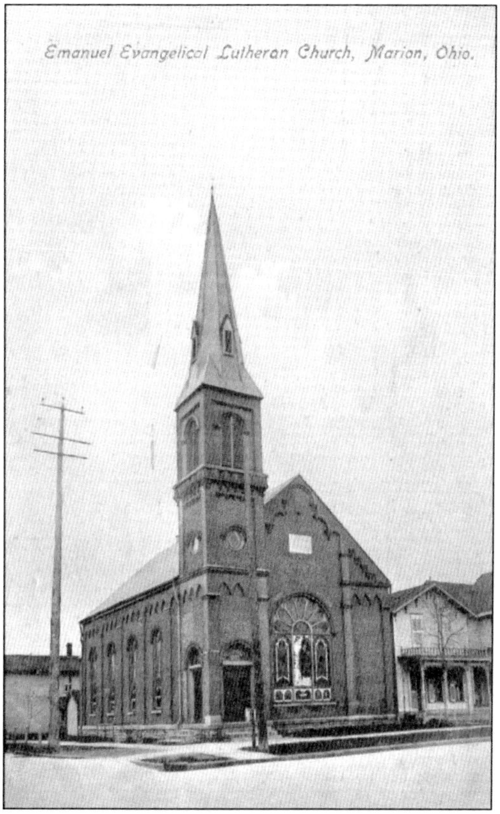

EMANUEL LUTHERAN, SOUTH PROSPECT STREET. Architect J.W.C. Carbsuier used a design that featured a Latin cross with a nave (body of the cross) supported by huge wooden beams. The chancel (head of the cross) had an elaborate altar made of oak, which was backed by three large stained-glass windows. The church opened in 1918 with the final German-language worship service held in 1924. (Author's collection.)

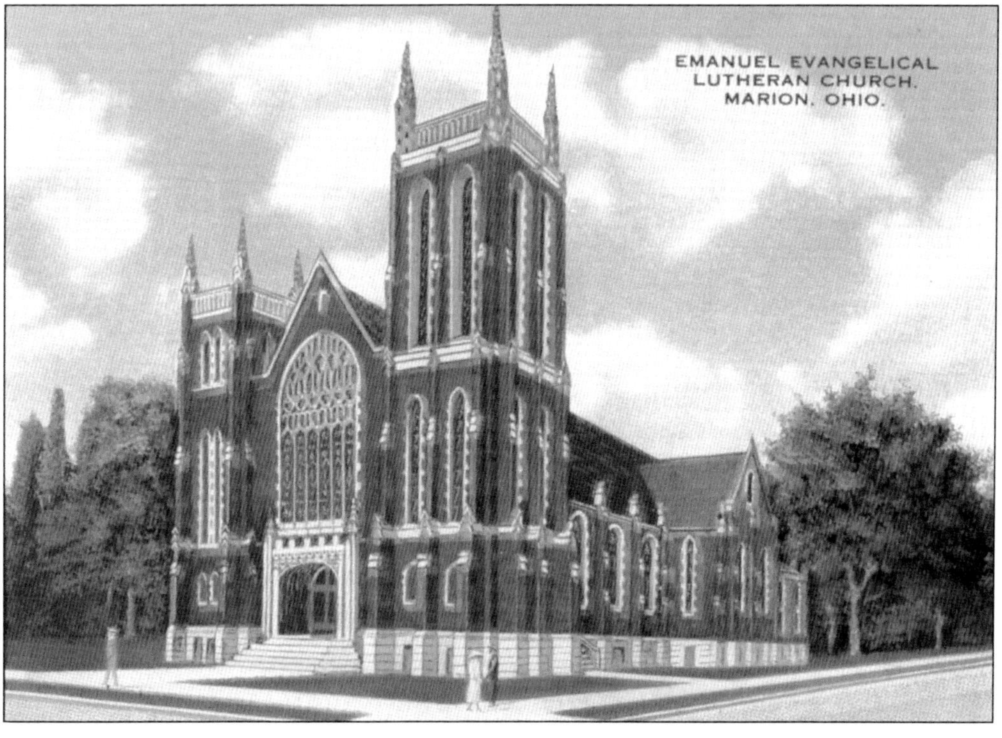

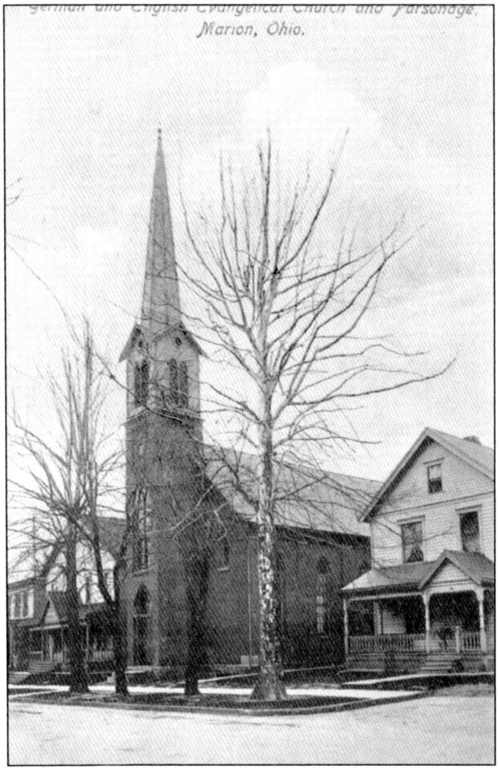

German and English Evangelical. Built in 1883 on East Church Street, the imposing tower had no bell until one from Marion's 1833 courthouse became available. An extensive remodeling in 1928 changed the building's profile. It also included the removal of a large copper rooster on the steeple that was a favorite target of local sharpshooters. Known by many as the "Rooster Church," it is the home of Salem Evangelical Church. (Courtesy of Mike and Linda Perry.)

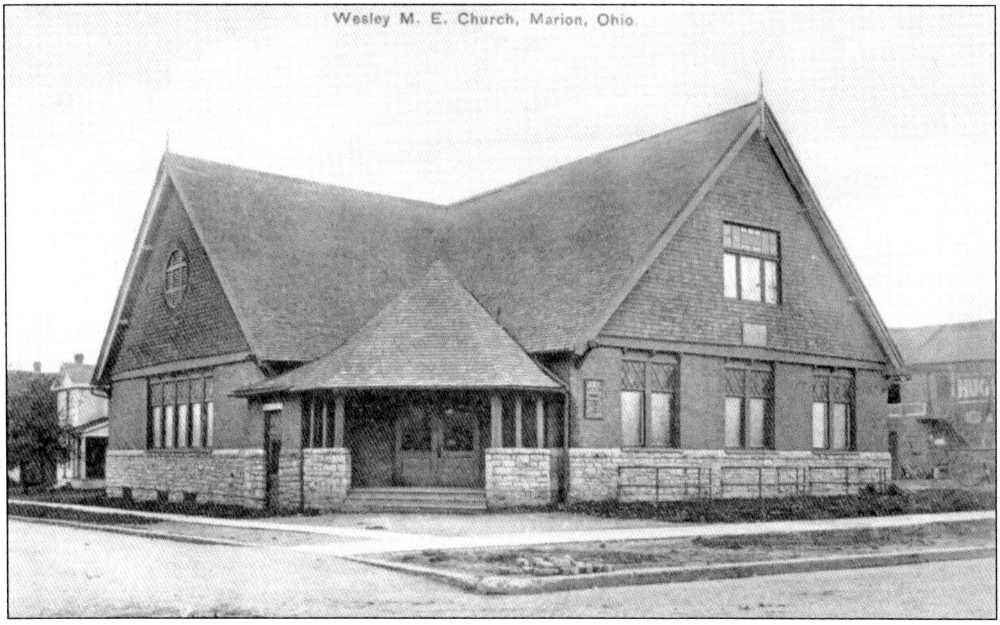

Wesley Methodist Episcopal. This Arts and Crafts–style church opened in 1901 at the corner of Center Street and Olney Avenue on land donated by Edward Huber. It served its congregation until 1923, when a new building was erected farther south on Olney Avenue. This building became the site of an L-K Restaurant. In 2004, Wesley Methodist merged with Prospect Street United Methodist (Author's collection.)

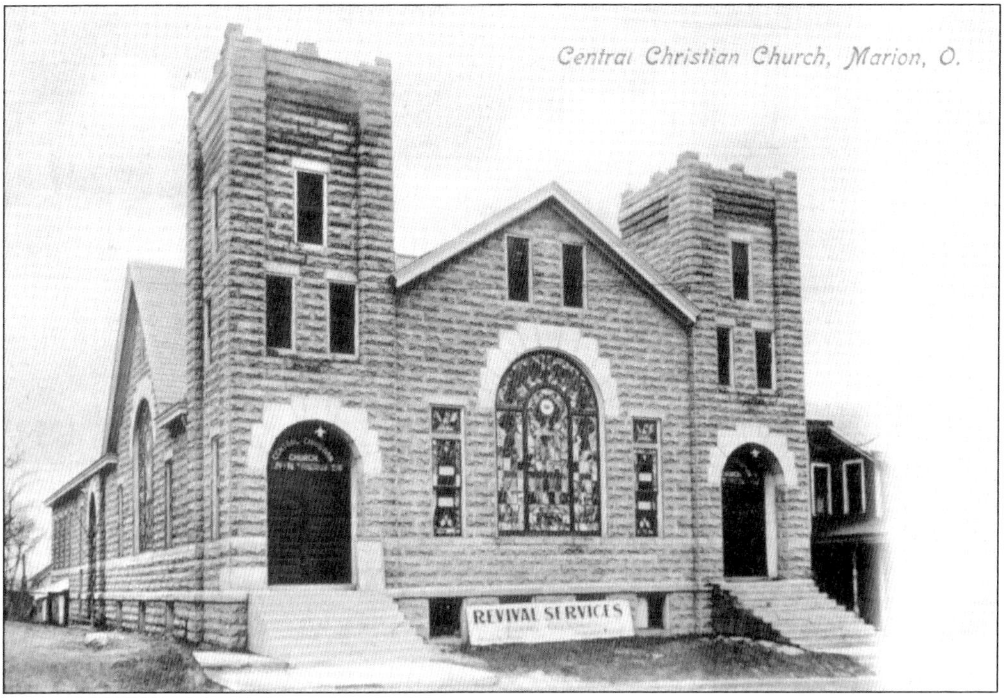

CENTRAL CHRISTIAN. Central Christian Church's first services were held in 1902 when 37 members from the First Christian Church met in the Masonic Temple. In 1906, this church was built on West Church Street across from Marion High School using concrete blocks designed to look like stone. The building was sold to the Nazarene Church in 1947, and the congregation moved to the former King Mansion on Mount Vernon Avenue. (Author's collection.)

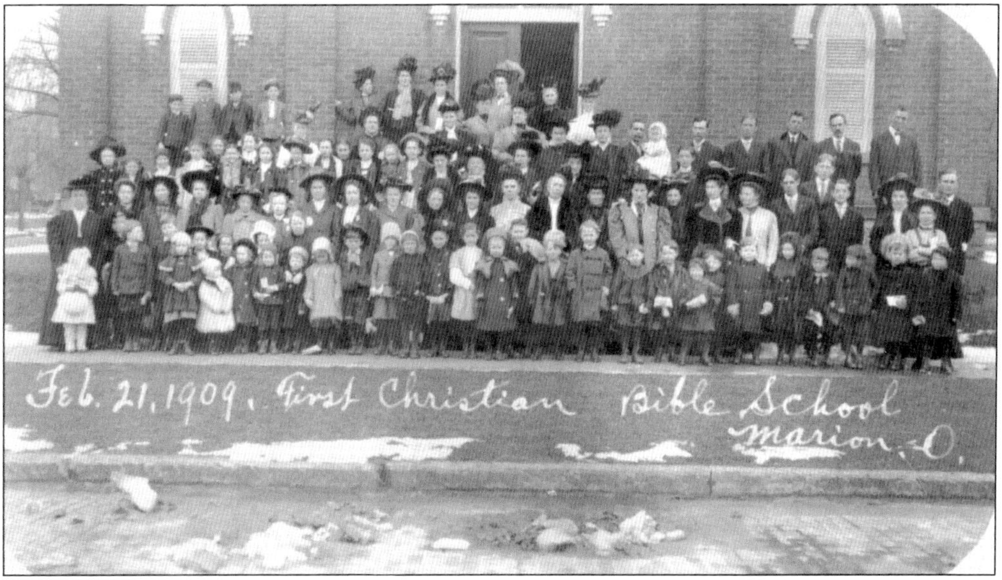

FIRST CHRISTIAN BIBLE SCHOOL. The First Christian congregation was very supportive of its Bible school, as evidenced by the turnout in this 1909 view. The church eventually closed when a new building was opened on Richland Road and the name changed to Richland Road Church of Christ. (Courtesy of Stuart Koblentz Haley.)

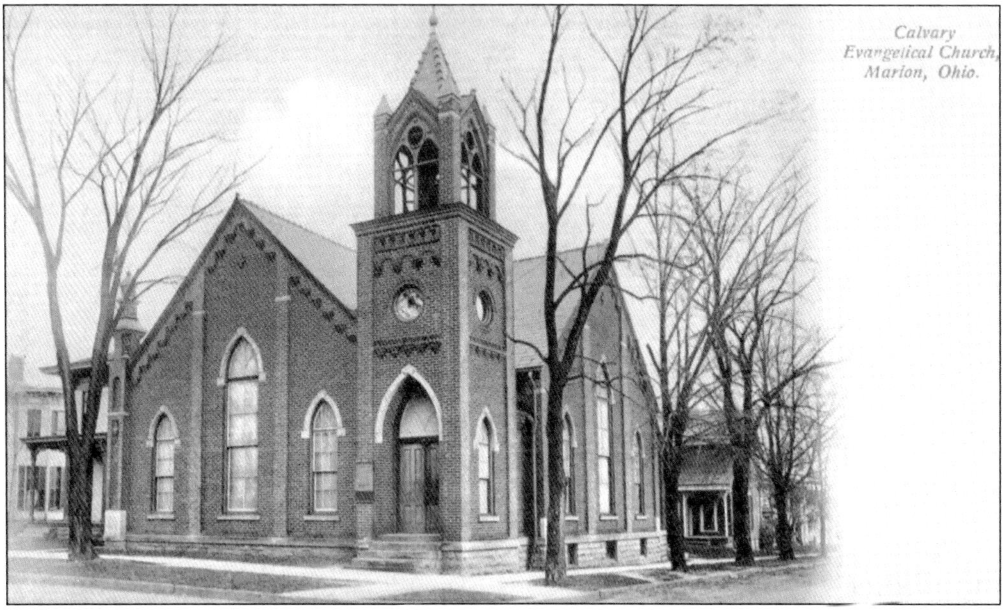

CALVARY EVANGELICAL. Located at the southeast corner of Church and High Streets, Calvary Evangelical utilized the design of many Marion buildings, with a limestone base supporting a brick structure. It served from 1855 until 1918, when a new building featuring a large copper dome was erected. In 1946, Calvary merged with the United Methodist Church. This is now the worship center for Gethsemane Evangelical Lutheran Church. (Author's collection.)

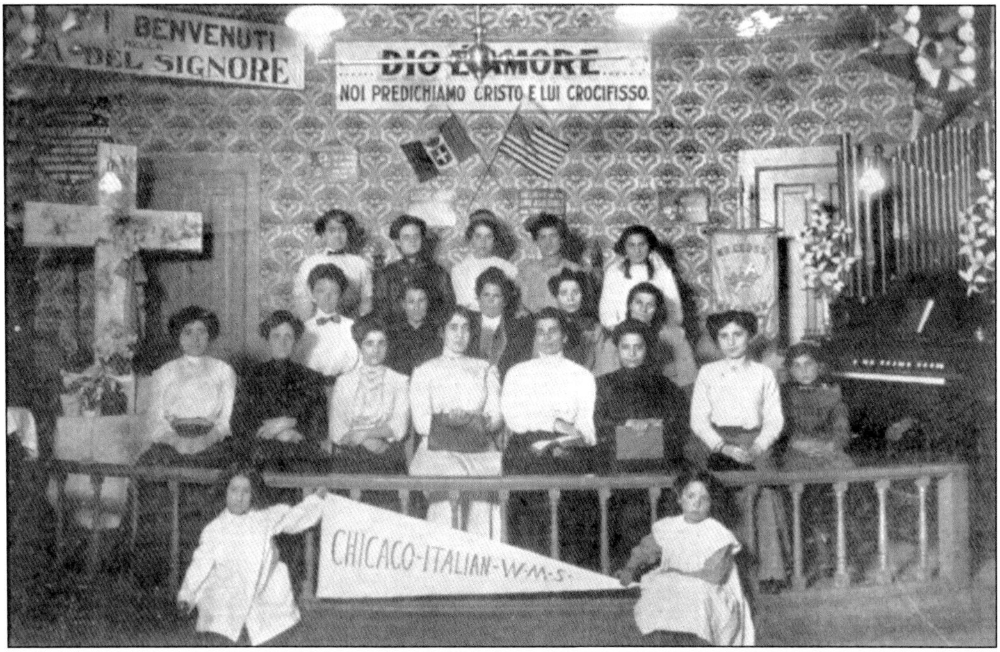

MISSIONARY RALLY. Postmarked in Marion in 1914, this card invites the recipient to attend a missionary rally at Calvary Church. The banner in the middle reads "God is Love, We Preach Christ and His Cross." Also shown are Italian flags and a banner for the Chicago Italian Women's Missionary Society. (Courtesy of Mike and Linda Perry.)

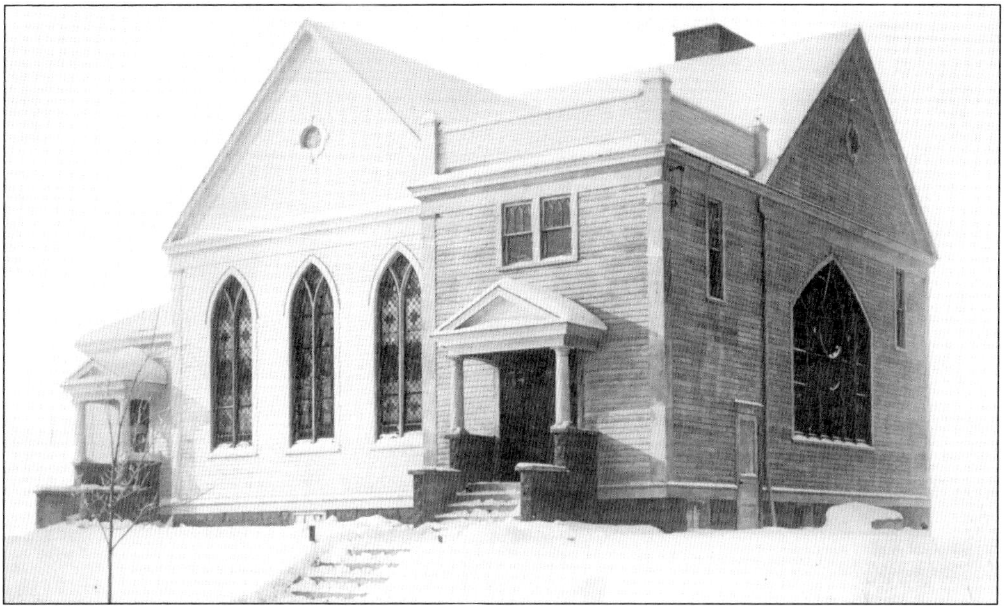

English Lutheran. Located on the northeast corner of Windsor Street and Bellefontaine Avenue, the former English Lutheran Church with its gothic windows and clapboard siding became the home of the Seventh-day Adventist Church congregation in 1965. The Lutheran congregation was first established in 1888 with Phoebe Harding, mother of Warren G. Harding, as one of the founding members. (Courtesy of Stuart Koblentz Haley.)

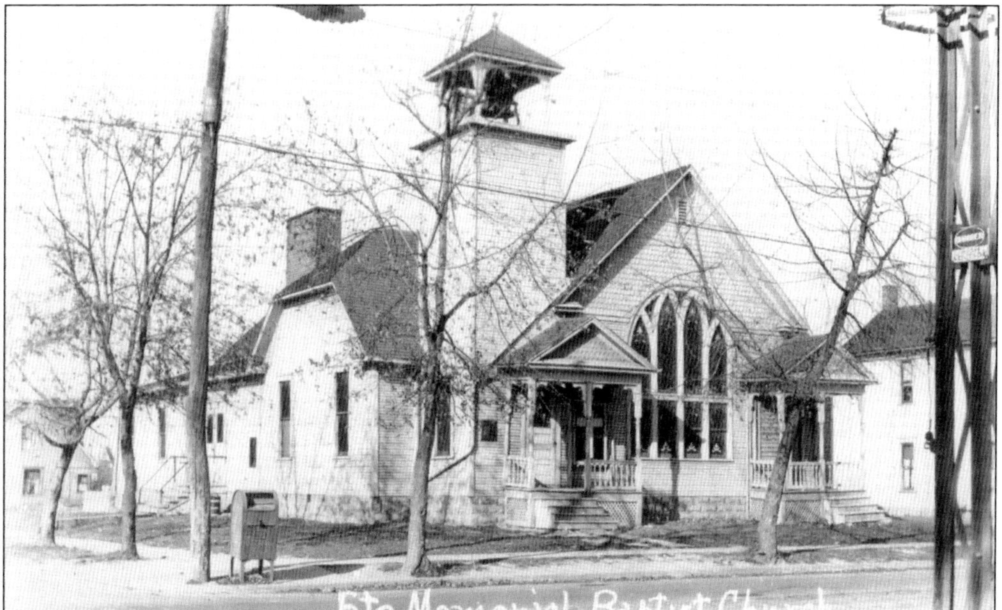

Fite Memorial Baptist. The west side of Marion was growing rapidly in the early 1900s, but there were few churches. Trinity Baptist's Anna Fite organized services in a small cottage, which eventually led to the building of this church at the corner of Davids and Darius Streets. Named Fite Memorial Church in Anna's honor in 1913, it was replaced in 1966 with the current building. (Courtesy of Stuart Koblentz Haley.)

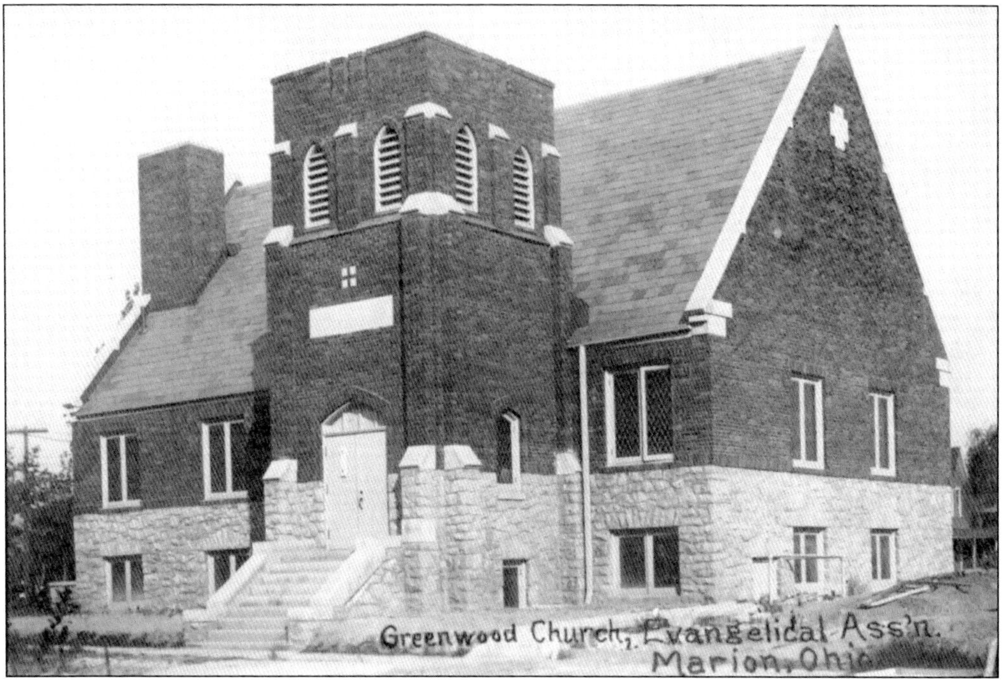

Greenwood Evangelical. The founders of Greenwood Evangelical started meeting in 1914 for Sunday school classes in a rented building. With the support of Calvary Evangelical, attendance grew and the cornerstone for this building at the northeast corner of Greenwood and Mark Streets was laid in 1915. Numerous mergers and affiliation changes have occurred over the years, with the building now being used by Greenwood United Methodist. (Author's collection.)

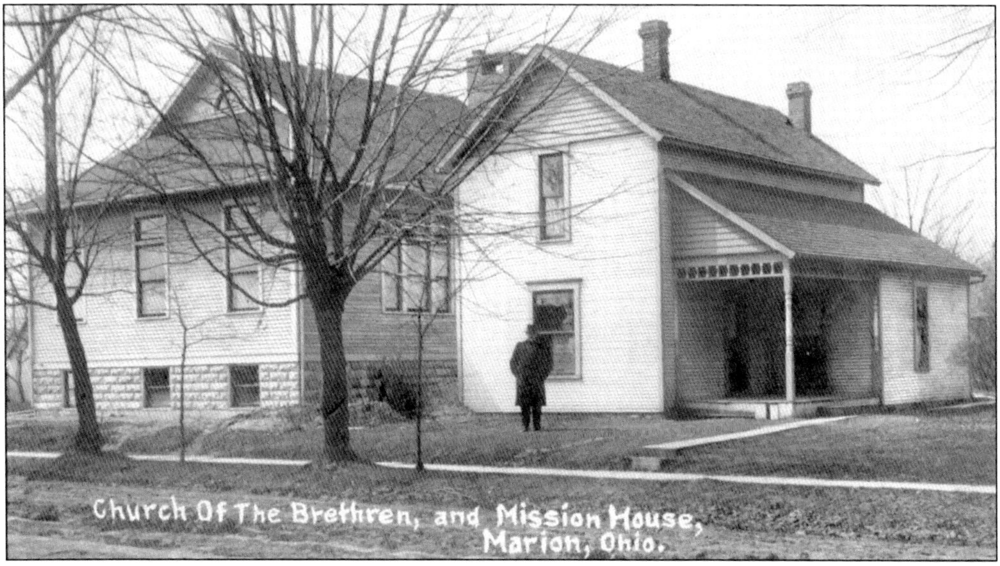

Church of the Brethren. The First Church of the Brethren in Marion began services in 1912. Property at the northwest corner of Church Street and Reed Avenue was purchased, with a church built that was later converted to a parsonage. In 1918, a new church was completed and then underwent numerous additions and remodeling projects until the present building was completed in 1958. (Author's collection.)

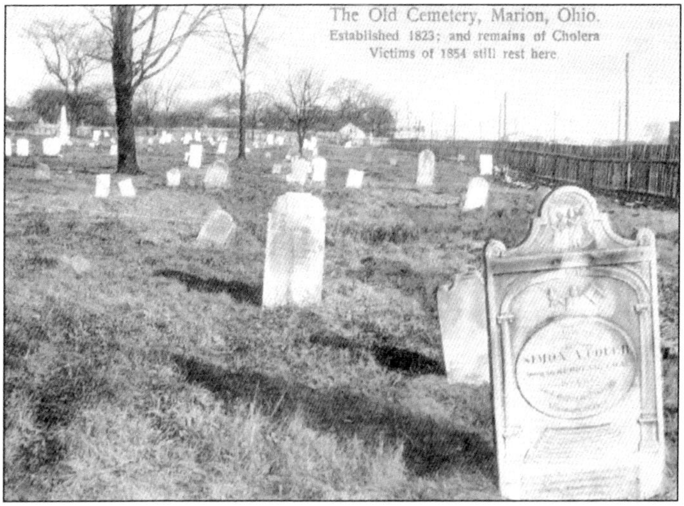

PIONEER CEMETERY. Eber Baker donated land on Quarry Street for a public cemetery soon after Marion was founded. Shallow soil over a limestone base that held water as well as a location next to the railroad tracks made it a less than desirable site for a cemetery. In 1854, many victims of a cholera epidemic were buried here. A new cemetery was later opened on the south side of Marion. (Courtesy of Mike and Linda Perry.)

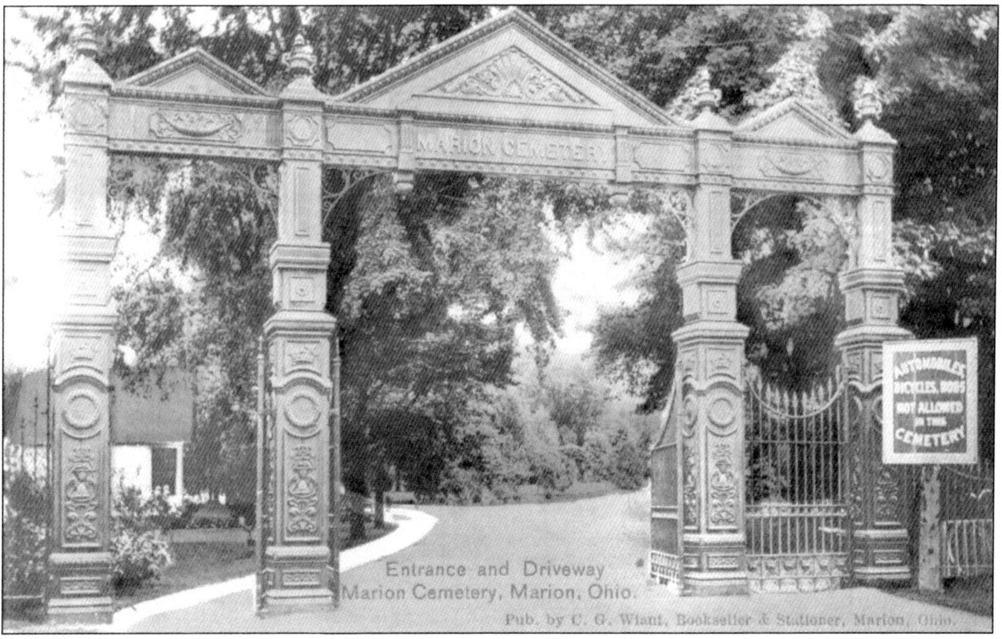

MARION CEMETERY. Beautiful cast-iron gates once welcomed visitors and "soon-to-be-residents" alike to the scenic grounds of Marion Cemetery on Delaware Avenue. Started in 1858 on 47 acres purchased for $4,347, the cemetery grounds were laid out by Dr. H.A. True, a well-known Marion physician. Prominent Marion businessman Peter Sharpless selected and planted the trees and shrubs. Lot prices were 15¢ per square foot. (Author's collection.)

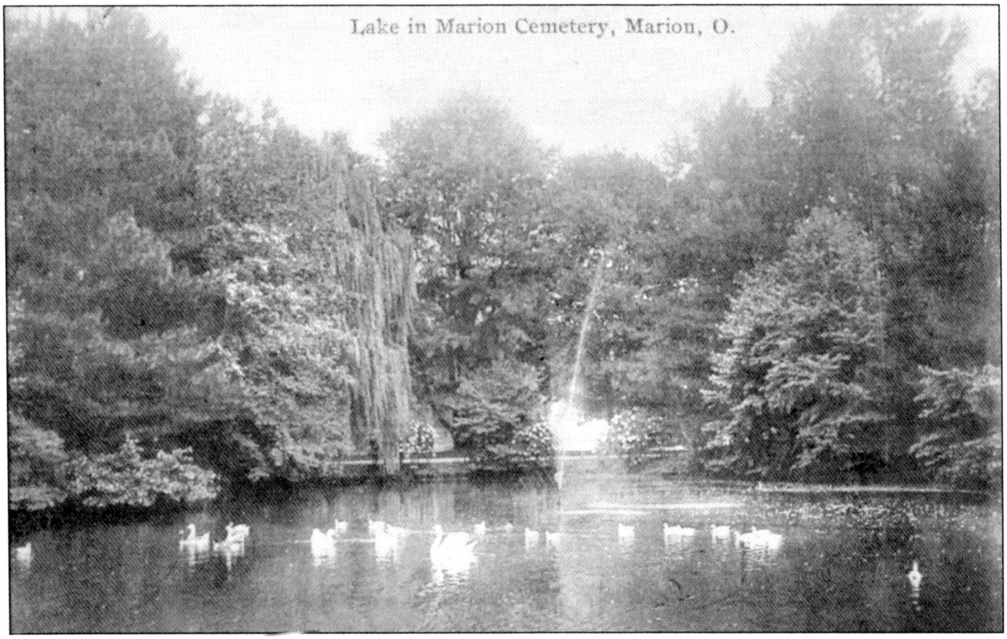

CEMETERY LAKES. Helping to complement the natural beauty of the cemetery were four artificial lakes scattered throughout the grounds. The lake pictured here was known as Swan Lake, due to the swans that were sometimes less than gracious to visitors who came too close to their home. The lakes were eventually drained and filled in for use as burial grounds. (Courtesy of Bob Turner.)

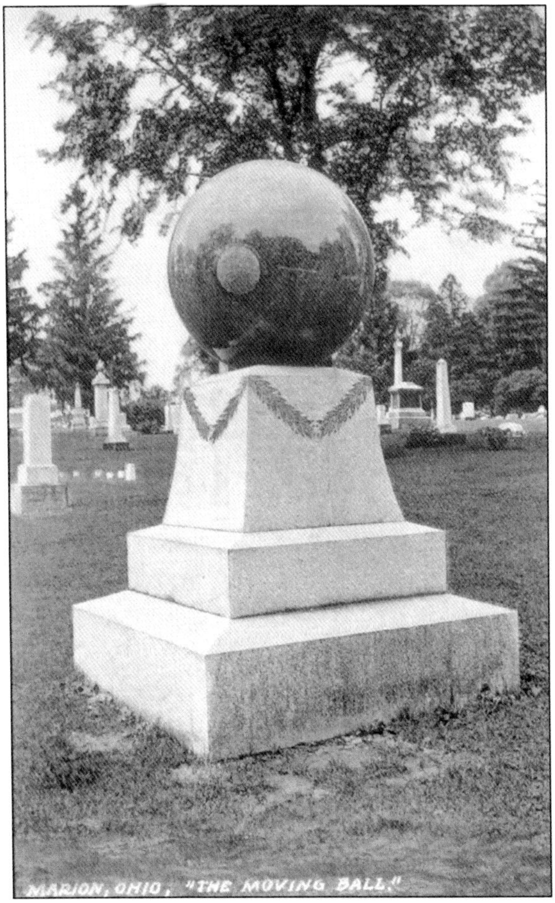

MERCHANT BALL. Charles Merchant's centralized marker for his family's grave plot consisted of a 5,200-pound polished granite ball resting in a socket atop a granite pedestal. Soon after being installed, the ball began a barely perceptible rotation which exposed an unpolished spot. The ball was reset in a bed of tar in 1898 but soon began its rotation again. The movement inexplicably continues to this day. (Author's collection.)

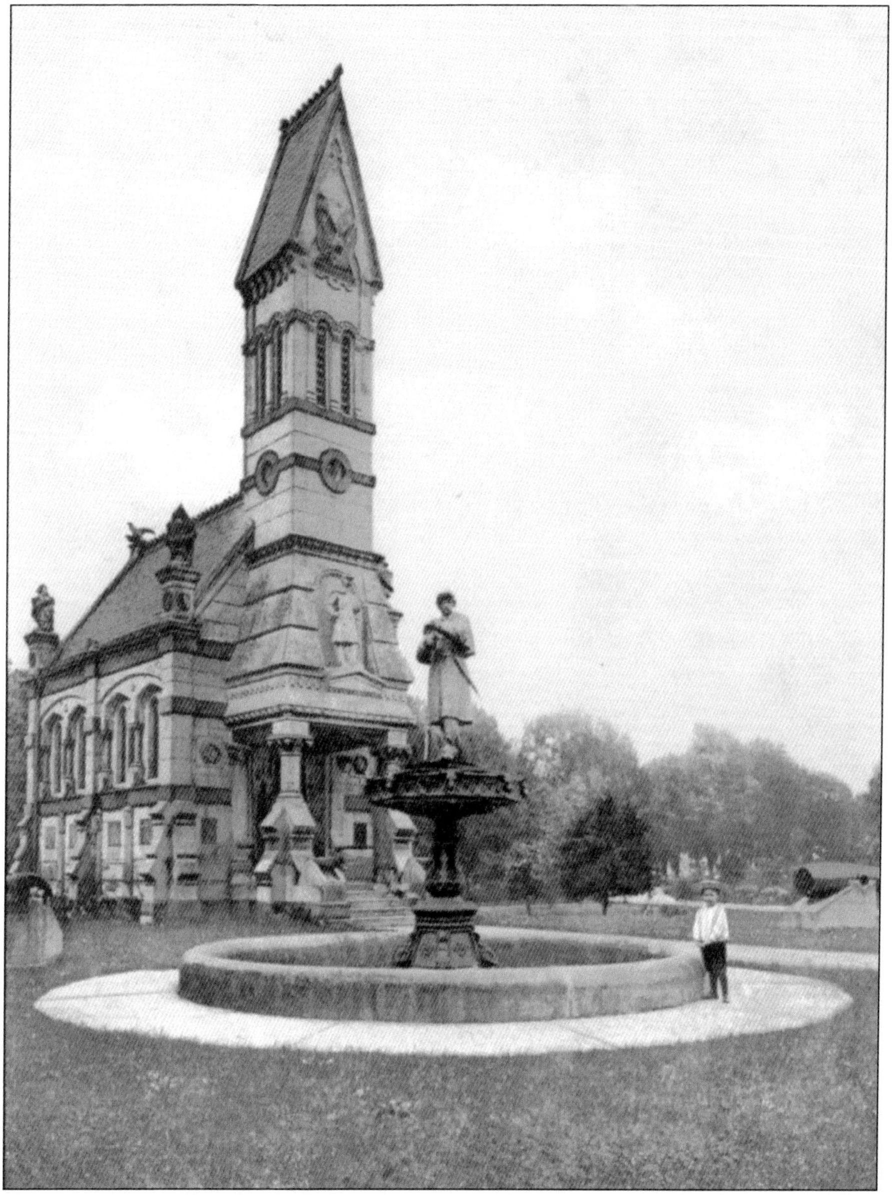

SOLDIERS AND SAILORS MEMORIAL CHAPEL. Built at a cost of almost $15,000 using funds raised by a tax levy, the memorial was dedicated in August 1888 in front of a huge gathering. The exterior features statues of soldiers in uniform guarding the entrances. The interior has Italian marble tablets with the names of more than 2,800 men from Marion County who served for the Union as well as those who were residents of the county when the levy was passed. Also included are names of soldiers from the Revolutionary War and War of 1812 who had been residents of the county. Added to the National Register of Historic Places in 1995, the chapel has 16 cathedral-glass windows and several carved portraits. The fountain featured goat heads that spouted water from their mouths and a statue representing all Civil War soldiers. The statue was believed to be modeled after Pvt. Sturgess Herbert Cooper, the first Marion County soldier killed in the conflict. The statue remained after the fountain was removed but was later destroyed in a 1979 windstorm. (Courtesy of Mike and Linda Perry.)

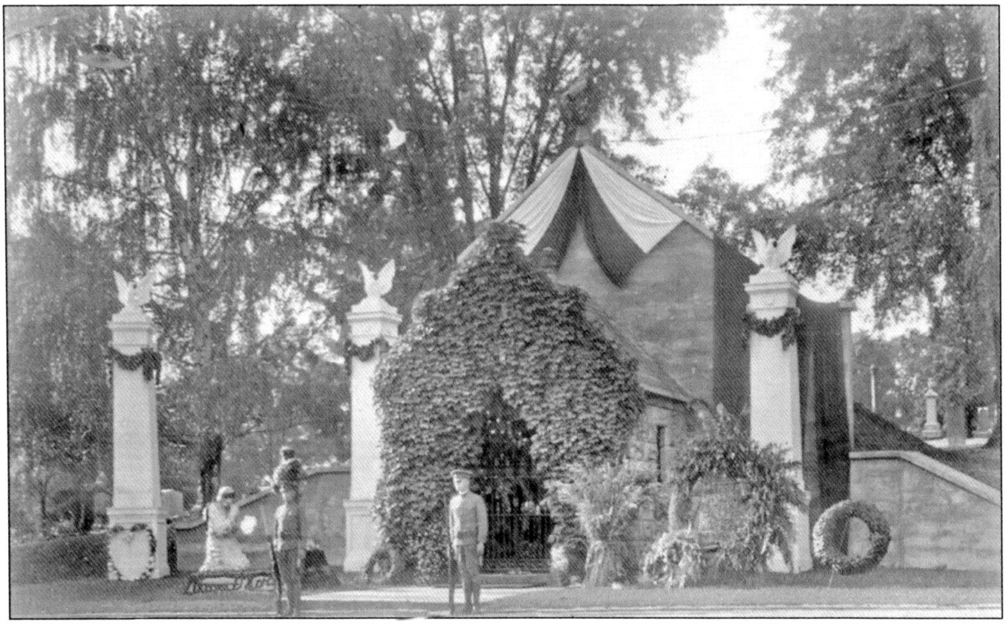

Holding Vault. Vaults such as these were common in the late 1800s as a means of preventing bodies from being stolen for medical dissection purposes. Built in 1879 at a cost of $2,900, this vault was later used for the bodies of former president Warren G. and Florence Kling Harding. Honor guards stood watch from the time of Harding's interment until he and Mrs. Harding were moved to the Harding Memorial in 1927. (Courtesy of Marion County Historical Society.)

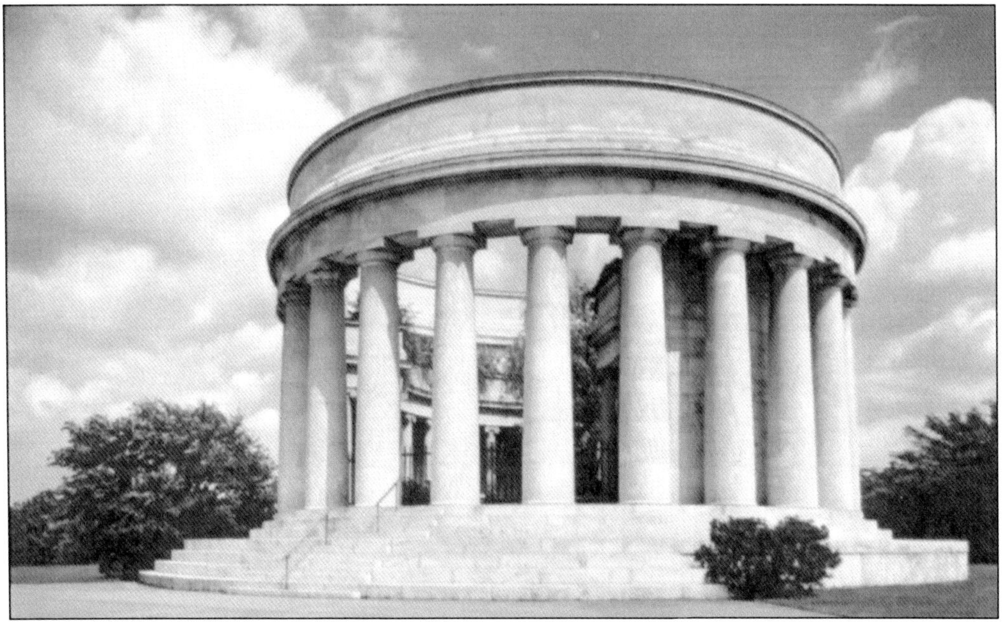

Harding Memorial. Shortly after President Harding's unexpected death in 1923, efforts began to build a memorial to him. Fundraising efforts quickly generated over $977,000. The memorial was completed in 1927 on land adjacent to the Marion Cemetery. Due to concerns surrounding some of Harding's political appointees, the official dedication was not held until 1931, more than five years after construction had begun. (Author's collection.)

Seven

Bells, Books, and Blackboards

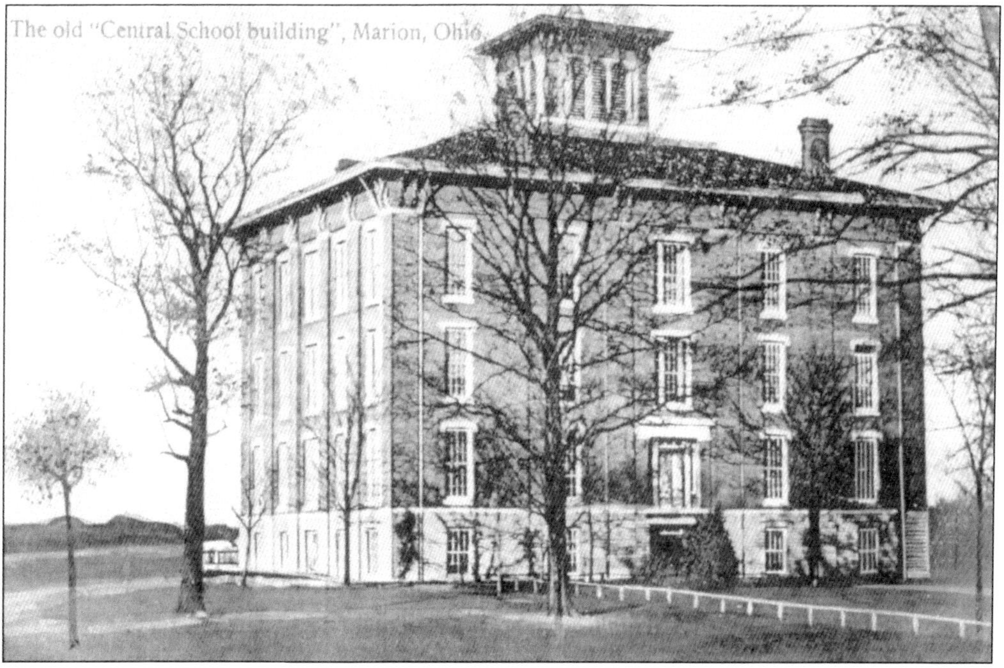

Union School. Classes began in 1858 in the Union School located at the northwest corner of Center and Oak Streets. The building stood four stories tall with a belfry and dry moat. E.B. Olmstead was superintendent at a salary of $800 per year. He did not stay for long; along with most of the male students of suitable age, he enlisted for service in the Civil War. (Author's collection.)

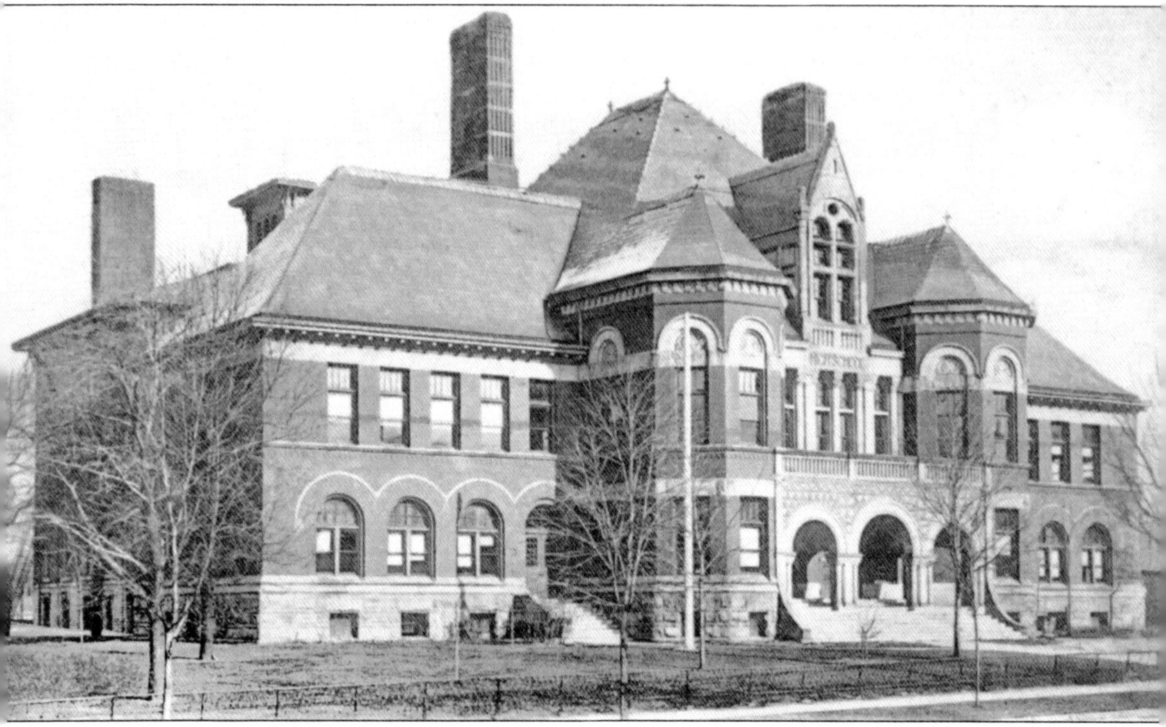

MARION HIGH SCHOOL NO. 1. Marion's new Romanesque Revival–style high school was located on West Center Street directly in front of the Union School whose cupola is visible behind the left portion of the roof of the new building. Opened in 1894 at a cost of $39,995, the high school was modeled after a school in Hamilton, Ohio. A library with over 200 books, science classrooms, and running water were among the notable features. Numerous changes were made over the years, including adding a gymnasium in 1899. A passageway was built that connected the new school to the Union School, which was eventually altered by the removal of its top floor and cupola due to deterioration. In 1915, the high school was changed to Central Junior High as a result of the opening of a new Marion High School on Church Street. Closed in 1951 when State Street Junior High opened, the property was sold for $261,000. Marion's first shopping center was later built on the site. Today, it is the location of the Marion County Office Building. (Courtesy of Mike and Linda Perry.)

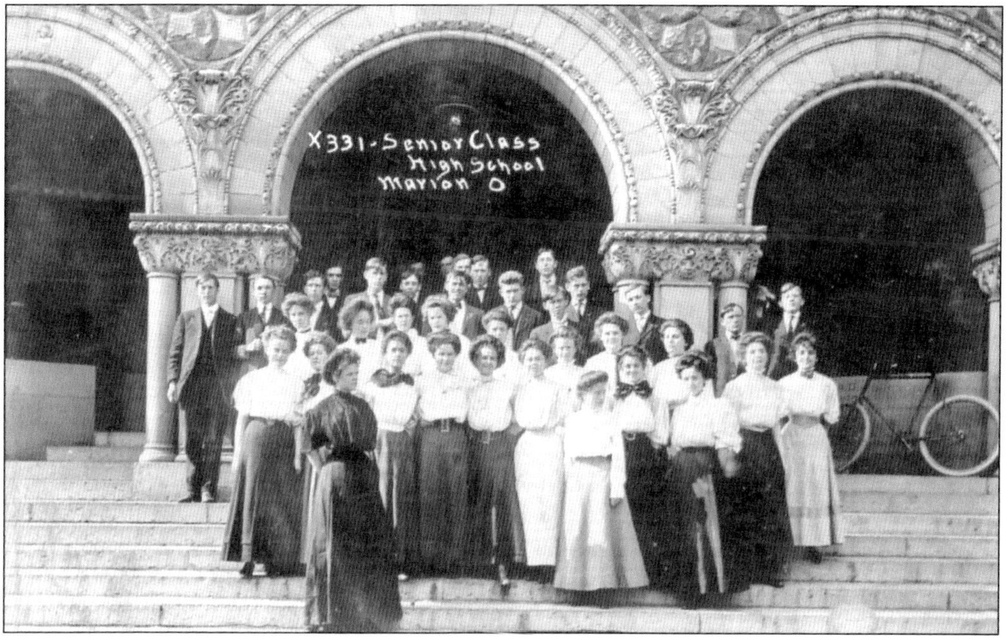

Senior Class Picture. Standing in front of the elaborate stonework and arches of the Marion High School, the senior class poses for one last group picture in this c. 1900 view. This class was significantly larger than the first one to have graduated from the Union School in 1872, which had only two members. (Courtesy of Michael Crane.)

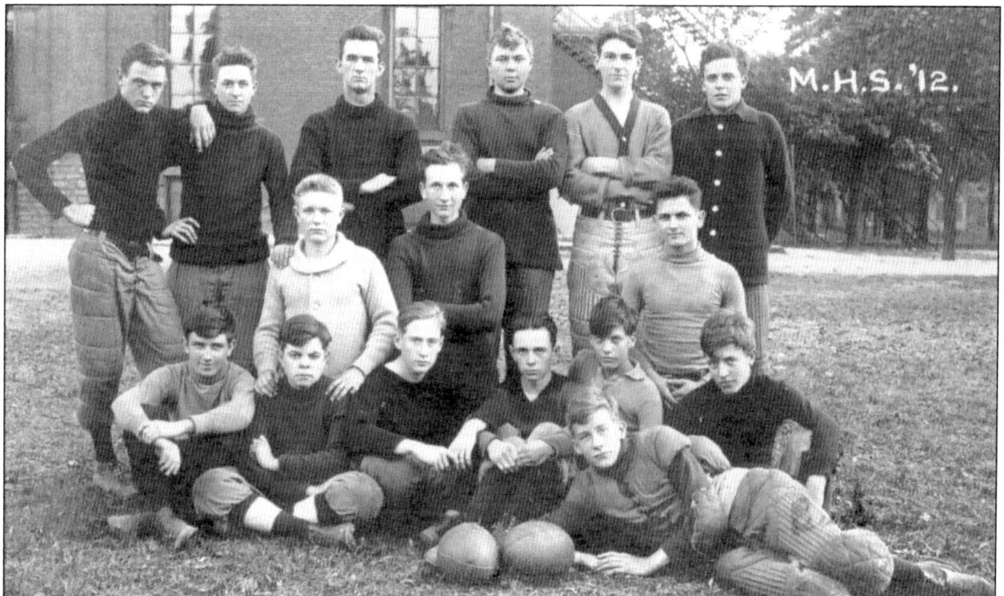

1912 Football Team. The first interscholastic sport for Marion schools was track and field in 1898. Football began in 1901, with games held at the Marion County Fairgrounds until the completion of Harding Stadium in 1935. Noticeable differences in the uniforms of the time were the lack of helmets and shoulder pads as well as heavy padding sewn directly into the pants. (Courtesy of Richard Carey.)

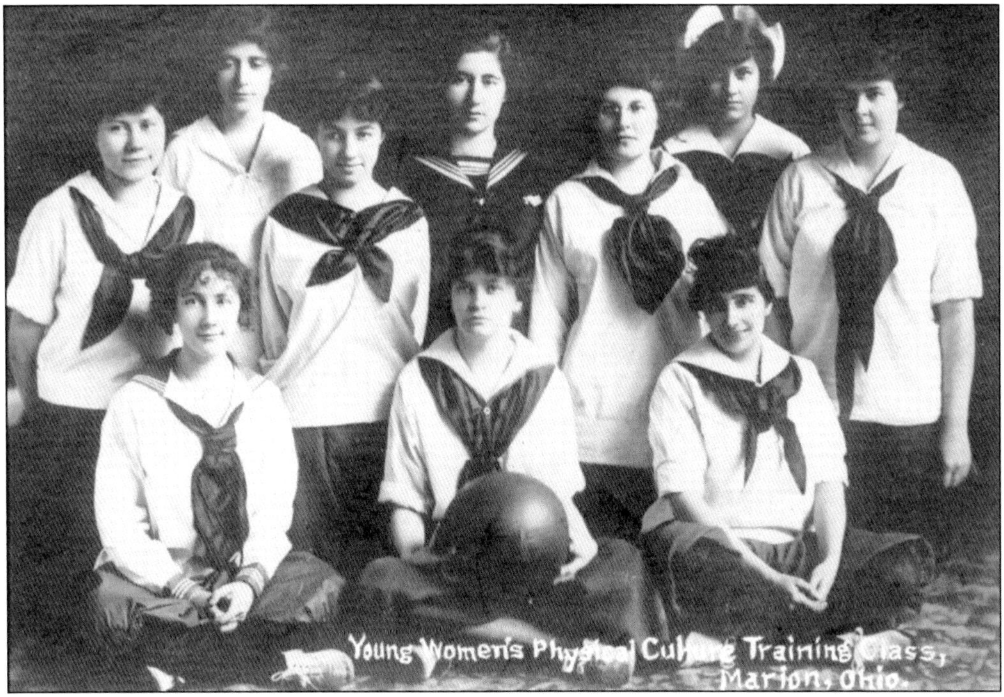

PHYSICAL CULTURE TRAINING CLASS. As a result of industrial growth of the late 19th century, a theory was formulated that "diseases of affluence" were becoming prevalent in American cities. The result was the development of physical culture programs, which were promoted throughout the education system. These young ladies are ready for some exercise with their medicine ball. Other equipment might have included Indian clubs or dumbbells. (Courtesy of Richard Carey.)

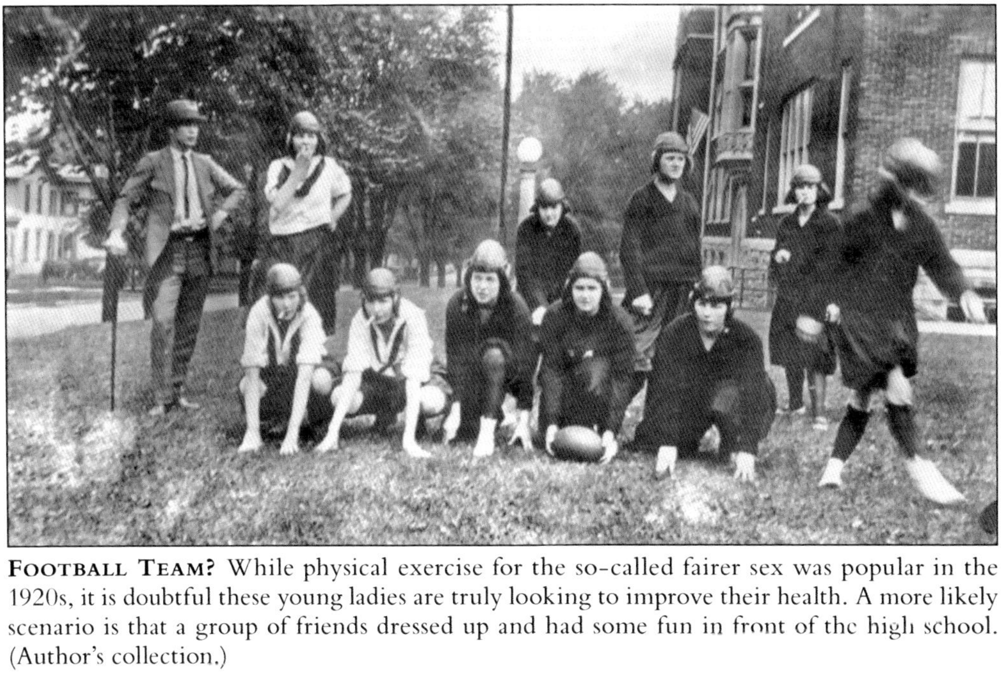

FOOTBALL TEAM? While physical exercise for the so-called fairer sex was popular in the 1920s, it is doubtful these young ladies are truly looking to improve their health. A more likely scenario is that a group of friends dressed up and had some fun in front of the high school. (Author's collection.)

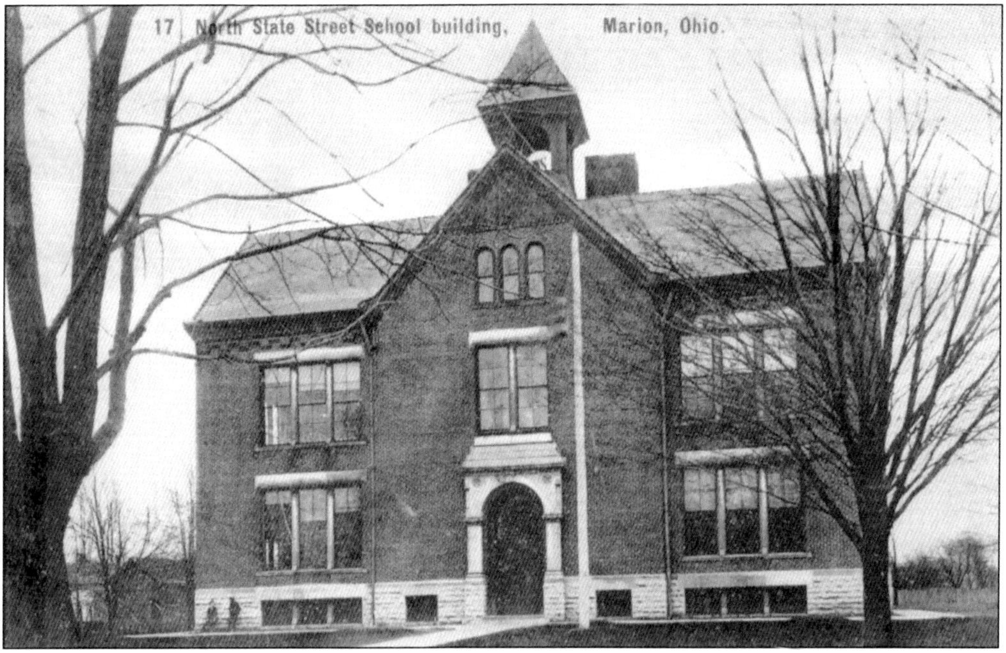

NORTH STATE STREET SCHOOL. The eclectic Victorian style of North State Street School was a popular option for builders in 1877 when the building opened. It had a total of eight rooms, each designed to accommodate 50 students. In 1900, Marion's first kindergarten classes were held here. Closed in 1934, the site was later used for the new North State Street Junior High, which was renamed Robert A. Taft Junior High. (Author's collection.)

DAVIDS STREET SCHOOL. Marion Schools experienced a building boom around 1900 as the town's swelling population required more classrooms. Davids Street School, located at Davids and Bennett Streets, was one of 14 schools built between 1877 and 1917. Closed in 1931, the site was sold to the Marion Steam Shovel Company for use as a company parking lot. (Author's collection.)

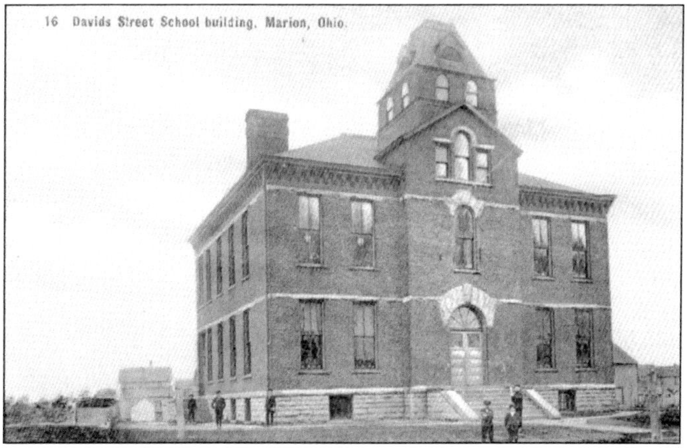

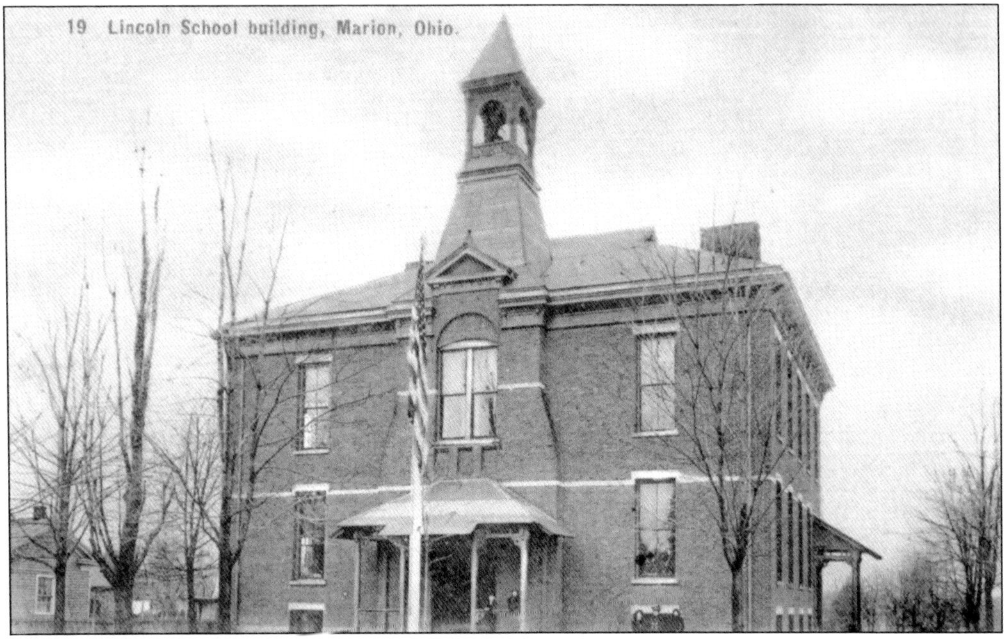

LINCOLN SCHOOL. Also known as South Prospect Street or South School, the building opened in 1884 on South Prospect Street south of Hill Street. It served as an elementary school until 1930, when Pearl Street School was enlarged. The building was given new life with a 1936 Works Progress Administration remodel and served as the Marion City Schools Administration Center until 1971. (Author's collection.)

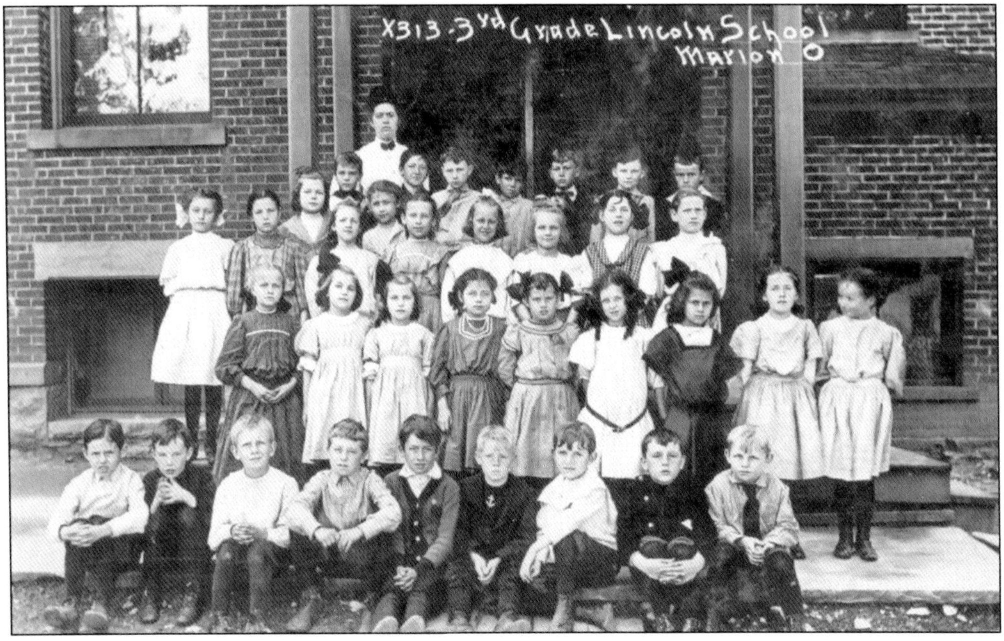

ON THEIR BEST BEHAVIOR. Students in this third-grade class are certainly on their best behavior as they pose for their class picture. Perhaps part of their motivation was a result of the presence of their teacher standing in the back row. Hair bows were apparently the style of the day for the young ladies. (Courtesy of Mike and Linda Perry.)

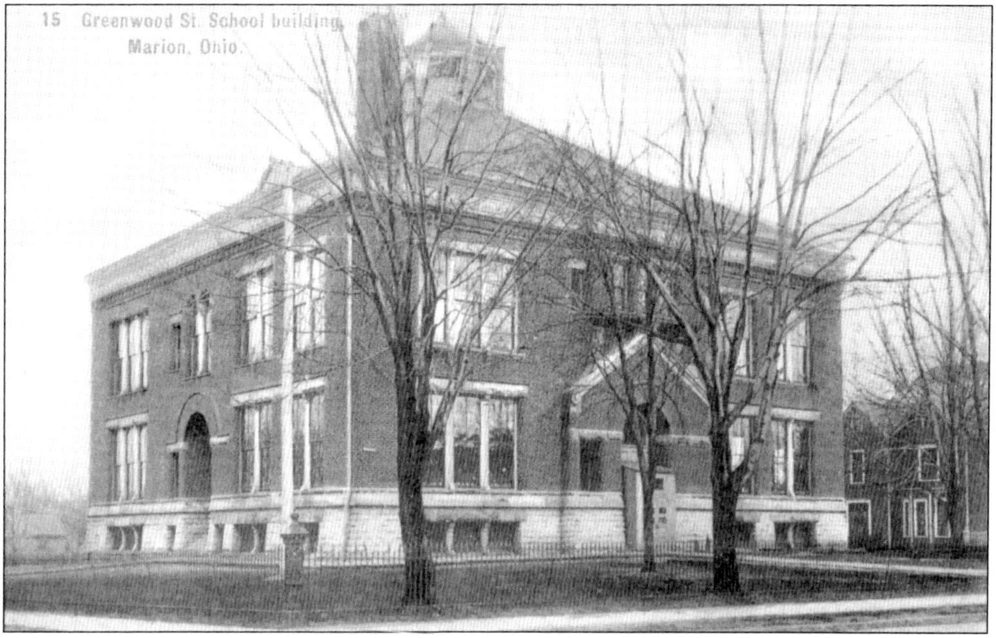

GREENWOOD STREET SCHOOL. Many of Marion's schools were built with a construction style similar to the 1888 Greenwood Street building. A half-basement of limestone block topped by brick and an open cupola helped promote a flow-through ventilation system as cooler air was drawn in through the basement windows and exited the cupola. This building was razed in 1964, and the site is now home to the Marion Public Library. (Author's collection.)

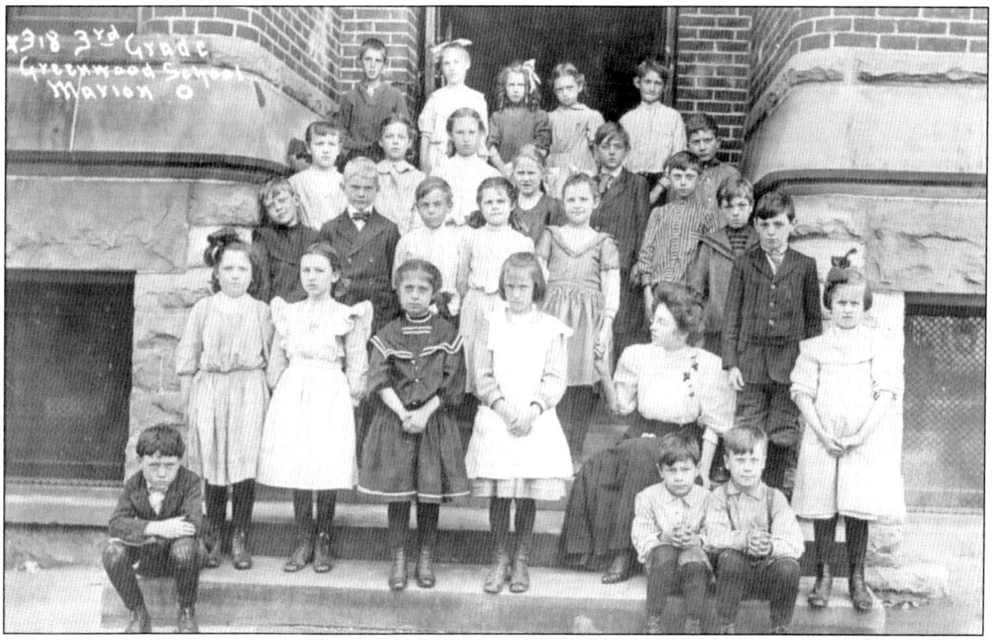

WHERE ARE THE SMILES? These third-grade students at the Greenwood Street School may not be having a good day, if judged by the young man sitting in the front left corner. The teacher appears to have more concerns about keeping an eye on her students than looking at the camera. (Courtesy of Marion County Historical Society.)

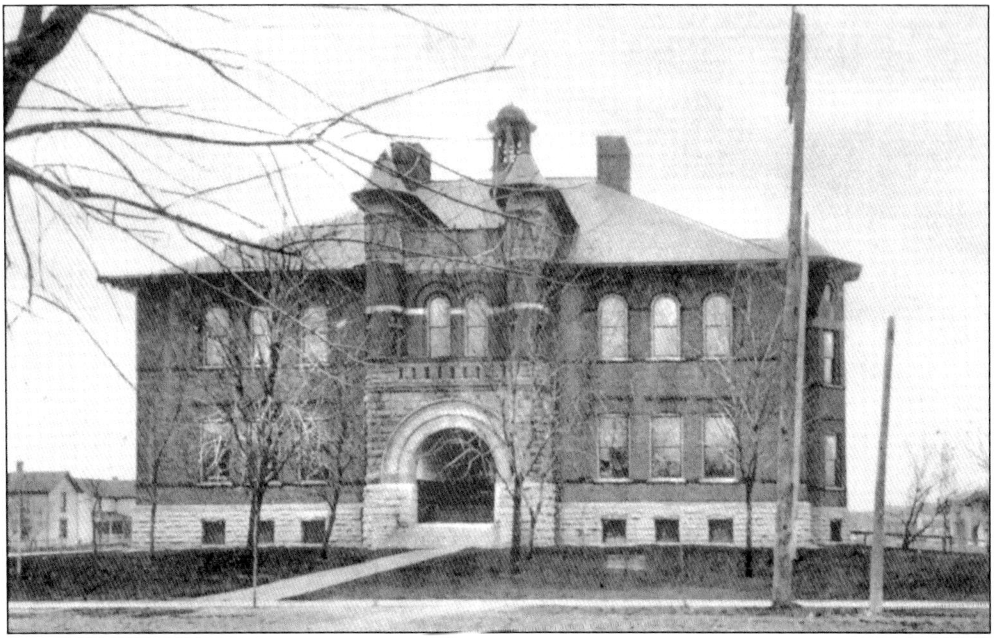

SILVER STREET SCHOOL. Looking very similar to a castle minus its moat and drawbridge, Silver Street School was opened in 1895 at a cost of $39,995. Numerous changes and additions were made to the building located at 750 Silver Street prior to its being razed in 1963. A new school was built on the same site. (Author's collection.)

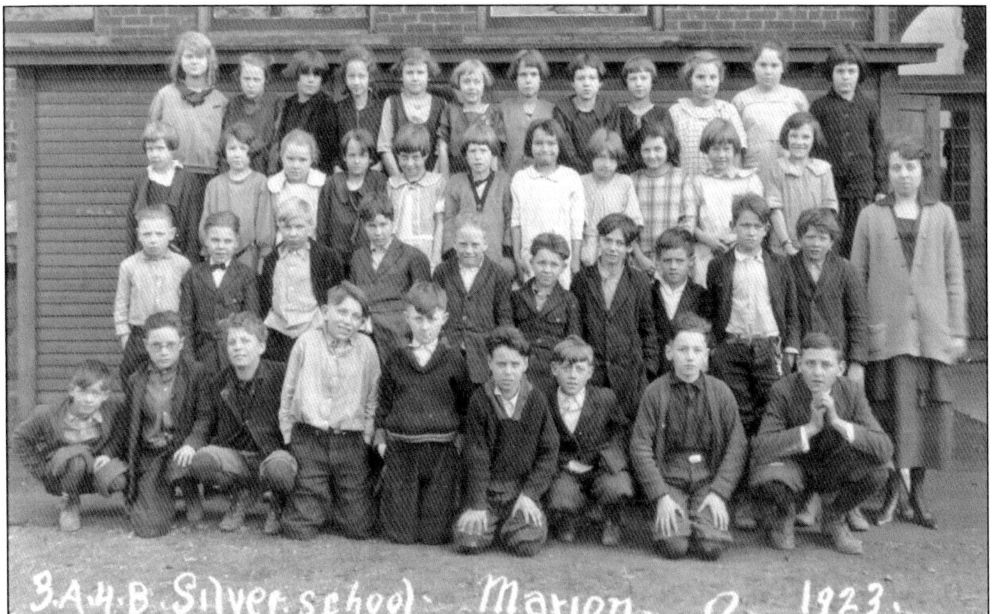

A FULL CLASSROOM. While it is unknown if all 42 students from "3A-4B" were taught as a group by this young teacher, large class sizes were not uncommon in Marion's schools in the early 1900s. Rapid industrial growth spurred by companies such as Huber Manufacturing and Marion Steam Shovel led to a population increase of 150 percent from 1900 to 1920. (Courtesy of Maureen Cole, from the Ed McKinney collection.)

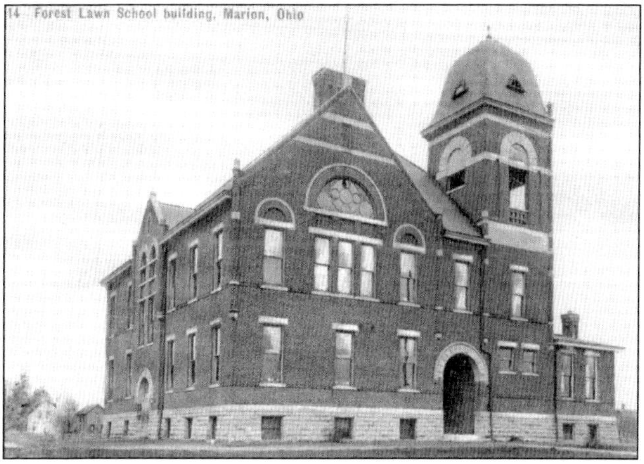

FOREST LAWN SCHOOL. A casual observer could easily have mistaken Forest Lawn School for a house of worship, with its bell tower and stained-glass windows. Jacob Apt, who also built St. Mary School, was the contractor for the 1899 building at the corner of Reed Avenue and Church Street. After the school closed in 1953, the building was razed, with the Marion City Schools Administration Center built on part of the lot. (Author's collection.)

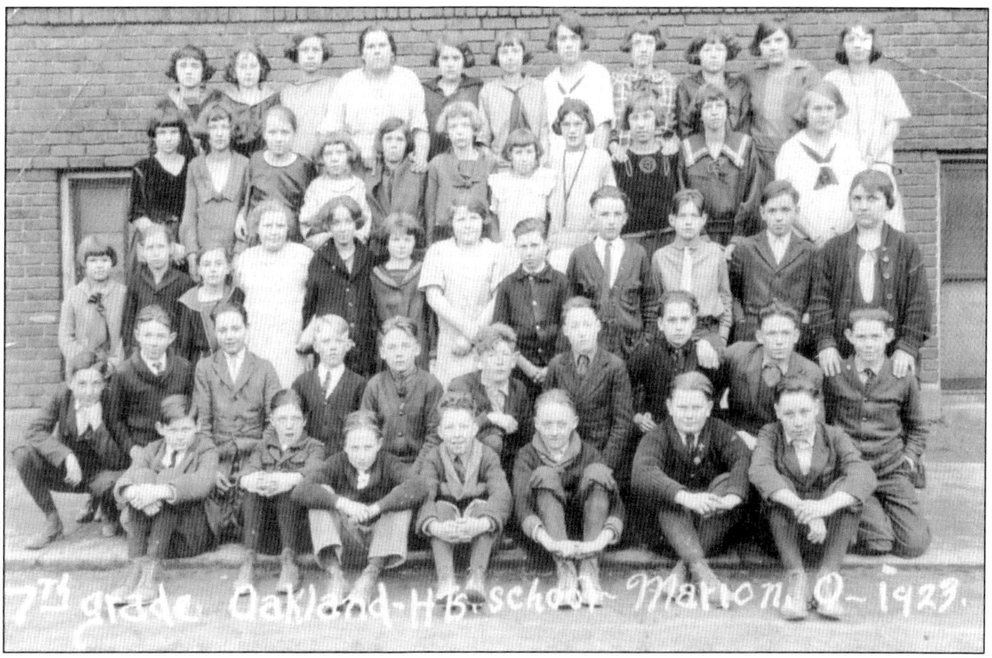

OAKLAND HEIGHTS SCHOOL STUDENTS. Marion's west end underwent very rapid growth in 1913, when the Erie Railroad transferred several hundred families from Galion to Marion. Many of them bought homes in the Oakland Heights area, which had the flavor of a community of its own within the city of Marion. The school was located at the corner of Uncapher and Woodrow Avenues. (Courtesy of Mike and Linda Perry.)

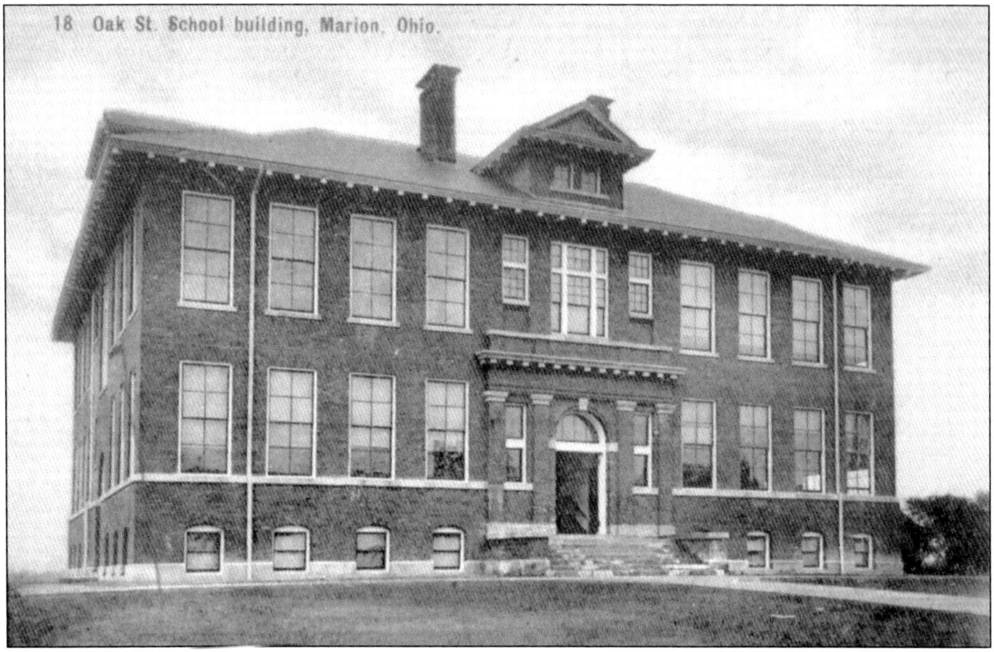

OAK STREET SCHOOL. While most of the buildings in Marion's rapid school expansion of the late 1800s and early 1900s were unique in their designs, there was a set of twin schools. Oak Street and Olney Avenue Schools were virtually identical inside and out. Oak Street, located at the corner of Oak Street and Klerx Avenue, opened in 1907. It closed in 1965 when a new building was opened. (Author's collection.)

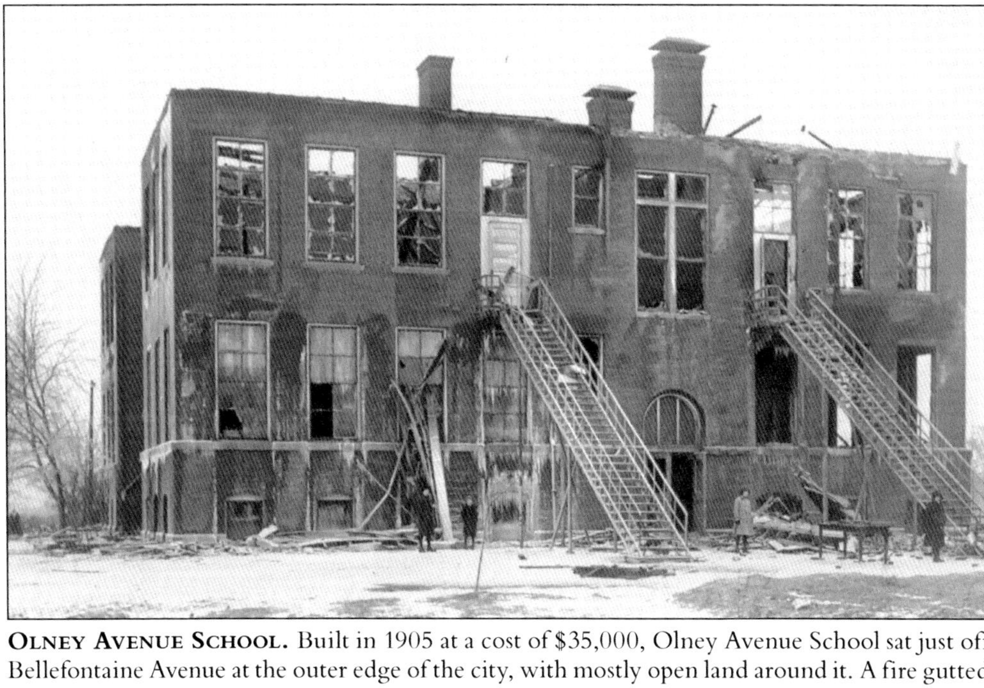

OLNEY AVENUE SCHOOL. Built in 1905 at a cost of $35,000, Olney Avenue School sat just off Bellefontaine Avenue at the outer edge of the city, with mostly open land around it. A fire gutted the building in 1915. The school was rebuilt using the original shell, which was not heavily damaged by the fire. A large addition was made in 1957. (Author's collection.)

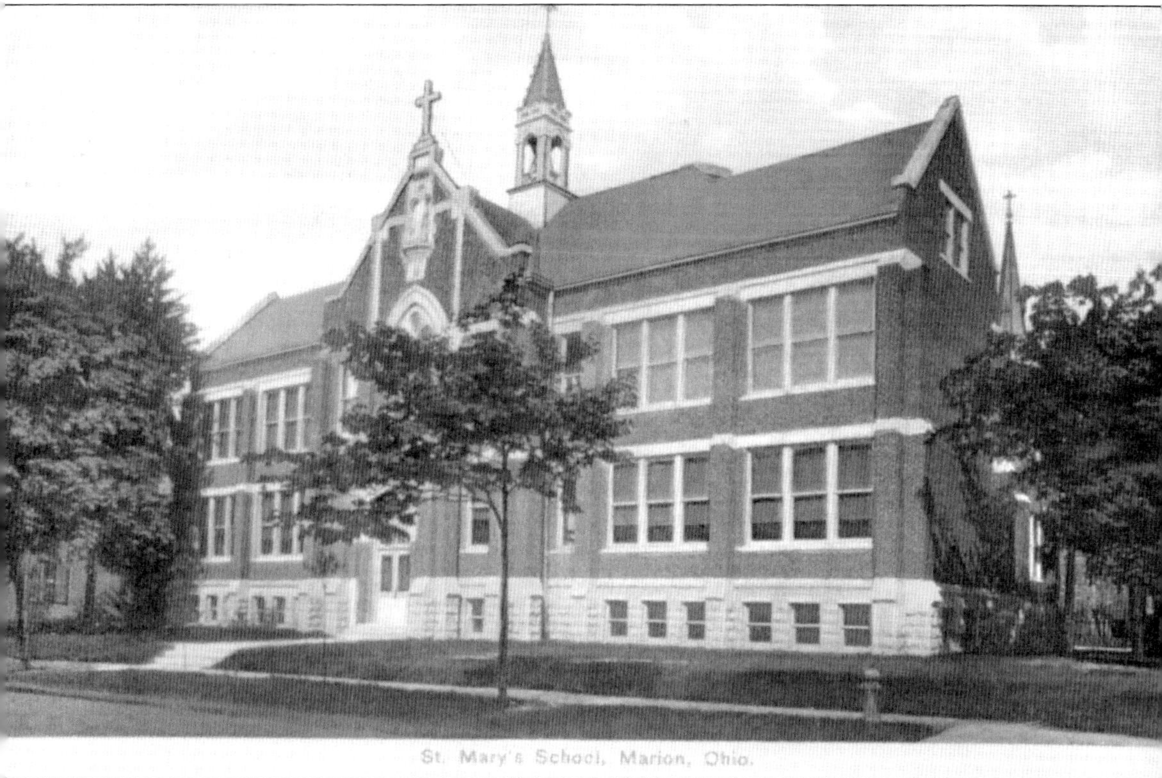

ST. MARY SCHOOL. The first parish school for Marion's Catholics opened in 1875 under the leadership of Father Quattman. The building was also the home of three Sisters of Charity from Mount St. Joseph who served as the teachers. By 1905, a larger school was needed, which resulted in St. Mary School being built on North Prospect Street at a cost of $35,710. A new convent was built next to the school in 1906. Attendance at the school continued to grow, necessitating an addition in 1927. St. Mary School originally served both elementary and high school students until the opening of Marion Catholic High School on Mount Vernon Avenue in 1957, when grades 7 through 12 moved to the new building. With the closing of Marion Catholic at the end of the 2013 school year, grades seven and eight returned to St. Mary School. (Author's collection.)

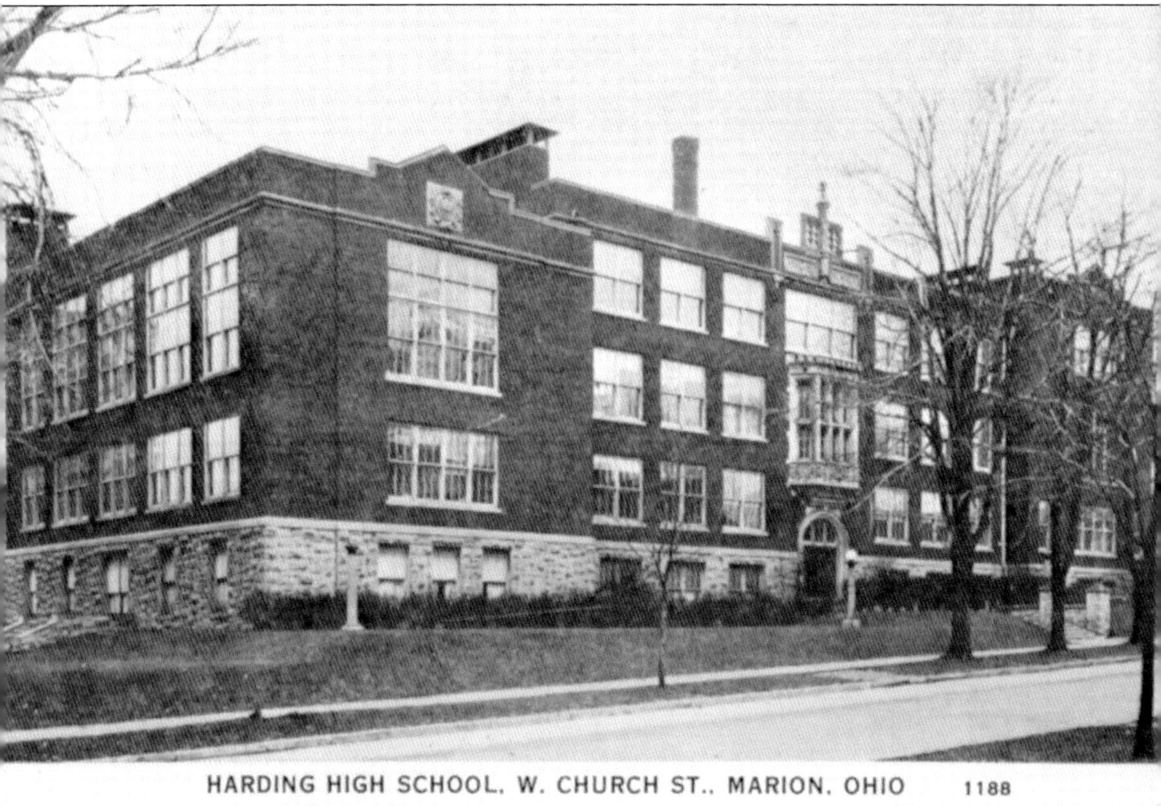

MARION HIGH SCHOOL NO. 2. The need to relieve overcrowding at the high school on Center Street resulted in a new Marion High School being built at West Church and Orchard Streets in 1915. The Jacobean-style building with its innovative stairstep design on a sloped lot filled most of a city block. In 1920, the name was changed to Harding High School in honor of Warren G. Harding's election as president of the United States. For the next 76 years, it would serve a wide variety of grade levels under a variety of names: Harding High School, 1920–1953; Eber Baker Junior High, 1953–1969; and Harding Freshman Building, 1969–1983. Closed at the end of the 1983 school year as a result of the combining of grades 9 through 12 at Harding High School, the building was eventually sold to the City of Marion. It was demolished in 1996, with only the gymnasium left standing. It is now the home of the Marion City Recreation Department. (Author's collection.)

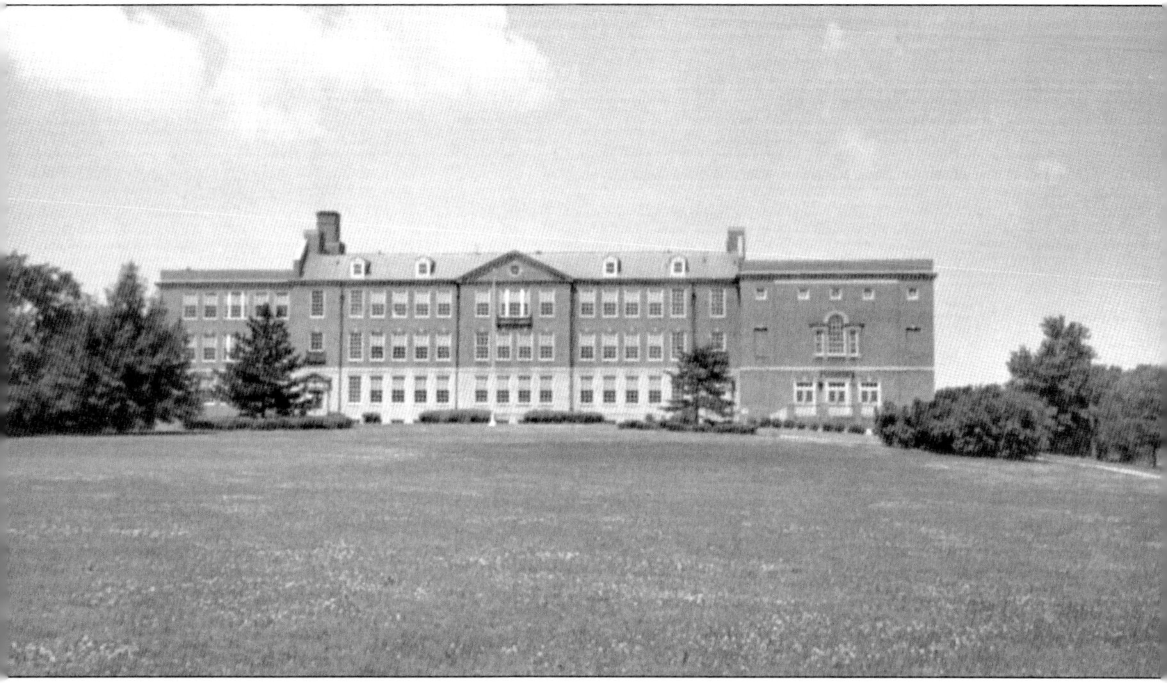

THOMAS EDISON SCHOOL. Situated at the rear of its nine-acre site on Chatfield Road, the New England Colonial–style building provided a spectacular view looking over its expansive front lawn. Opened in 1931, it had a 700-seat auditorium with a separate gymnasium. B.Q. Skinner, state director of education for Ohio, stated it was "one of the finest junior high buildings in the state of Ohio." Filling a need for additional room for students in higher grades, Edison originally housed grades 7 through 11. The students completed their senior year at Harding High School. Edison changed to a more conventional junior high format of grades six through eight in 1953, when a new high school opened that could accommodate all the district's high school students. In 1969, the building was converted to a middle school format and housed students in grades six through eight. It was closed in 2004 as part of a comprehensive school construction and remodeling effort of the Marion City Schools. The building was razed, with McKinley Elementary School built behind the original building site. (Author's collection.)

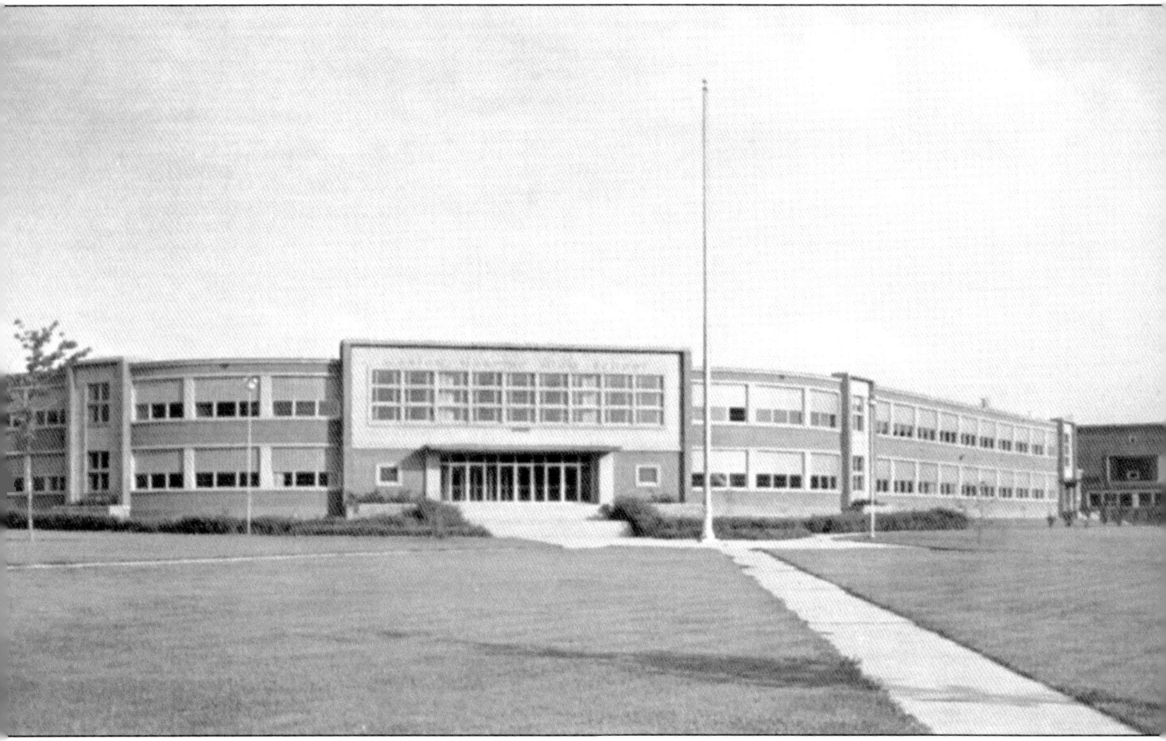

MARION HIGH SCHOOL NO. 3. The need for more space for high school students was answered in 1953 when a new Marion Harding High School opened on a 40-acre site at the corner of Mandana and Seminole Avenues. A notable feature of the $2.9-million building was its central courtyard, which allowed natural light into the interior classrooms. Classes began on September 8, with 1,078 students in attendance under the leadership of principal Cecil Gabler. As part of the festivities, a new Harding High School alma mater was written by Lucille Forman and Richard Meyers. Myers also wrote a new fight song, entitled "The Red and Black." A second gymnasium was added in 1970 to provide additional room for the growing enrollment. In 1976, Tri-Rivers Joint Vocational School opened, allowing numerous curriculum and facility changes as several hundred students chose to attend the vocational school. The building was converted to Grant Middle School after a major remodeling and enlargement in 2003, when a new Marion Harding High School was built on State Route 309 east of Marion. (Author's collection.)

Eight

For a Good Time

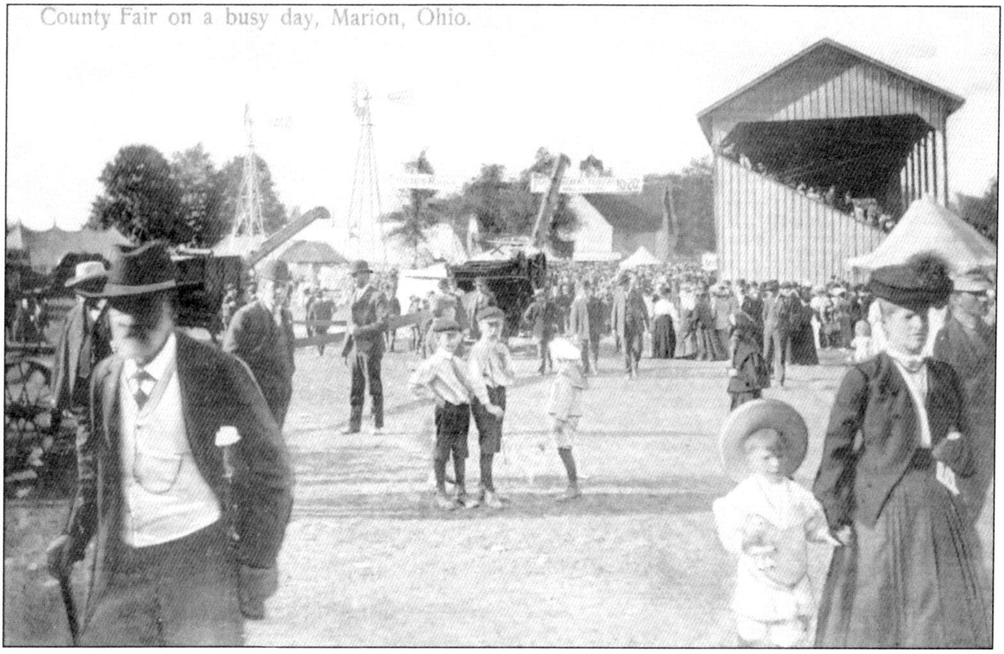

Marion County Fair. First held in 1851 on the county courthouse lawn, the Marion County Fair is the oldest entertainment event in the county. Over the years, fairs were held in a variety of locations, including Copeland's Woods on Ballentine Avenue and also on Kenton Avenue. The fair moved to its present location in 1868 when 26 acres were purchased on Garden City Pike, which was late renamed Fairgrounds Street. (Author's collection.)

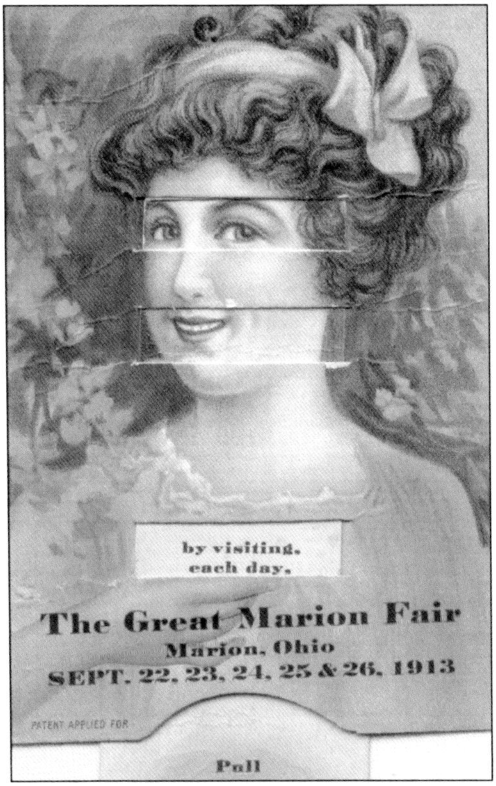

REASON TO SMILE. The lady on this mechanical novelty card changed from a grouchy mood to all smiles when she decided to attend the 1913 Marion County Fair. If she visited the fairgrounds several years later in 1943, she could have watched the filming of the horse racing movie, Home in Indiana (originally titled The Phantom Filly), staring Walter Brennan, Lon McCallister, and Jeanne Craine. (Author's collection.)

SALES OPPORTUNITY. Vendors have been a part of the county fair since its inception. A spot under the grandstand was ideal for this Ford Motor Car dealer to set up his display advertising Visco Auto Oil along with stacks of sales literature and a chance to closely examine a Ford motor as seen in this c. 1910 view. (Courtesy of Mike and Linda Perry.)

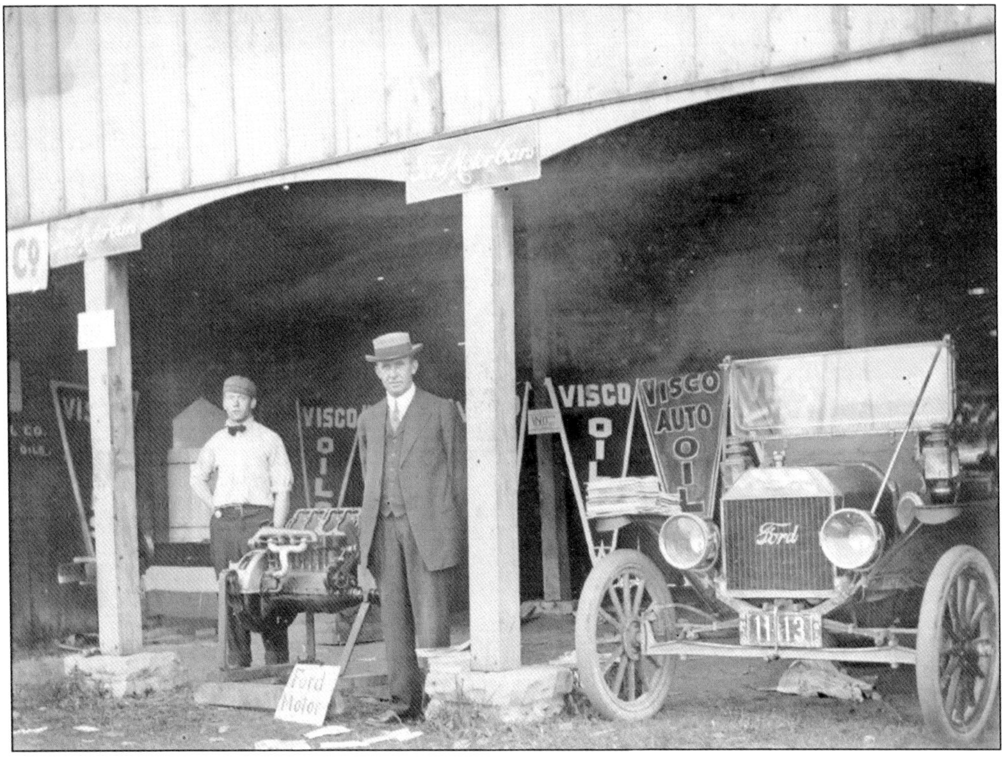

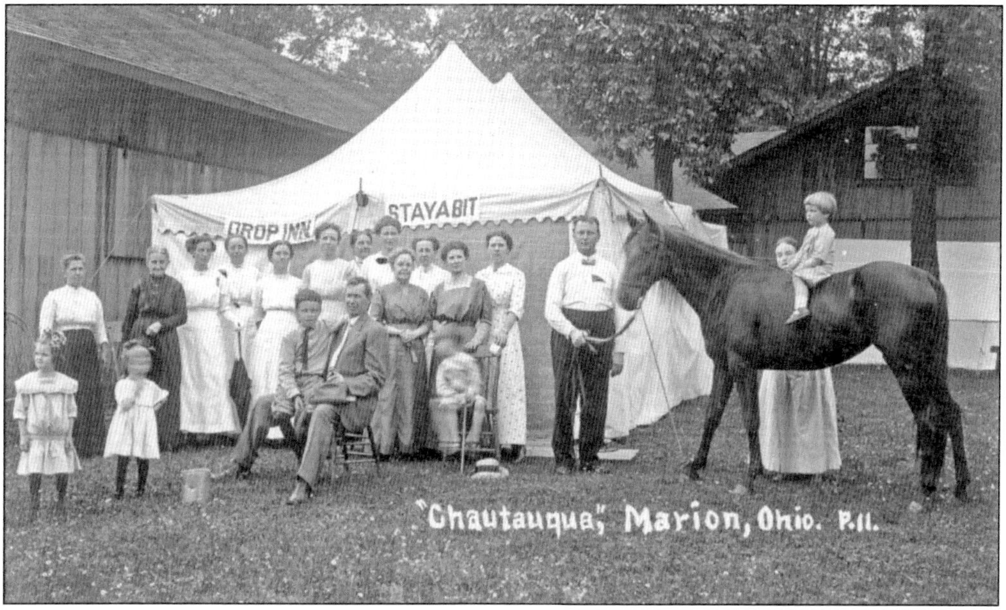

Drop Inn at the Chautauqua. The first Chautauqua was held in 1874 in New York State on the shores of Lake Chautauqua. Designed as an educational summer camp for families, the concept became known as the Chautauqua Institution and was very popular at the turn of the 20th century. Marion County's Chautauqua Association was organized in 1910, with its first event held at the Marion County Fairgrounds. (Courtesy of Shelby Needham)

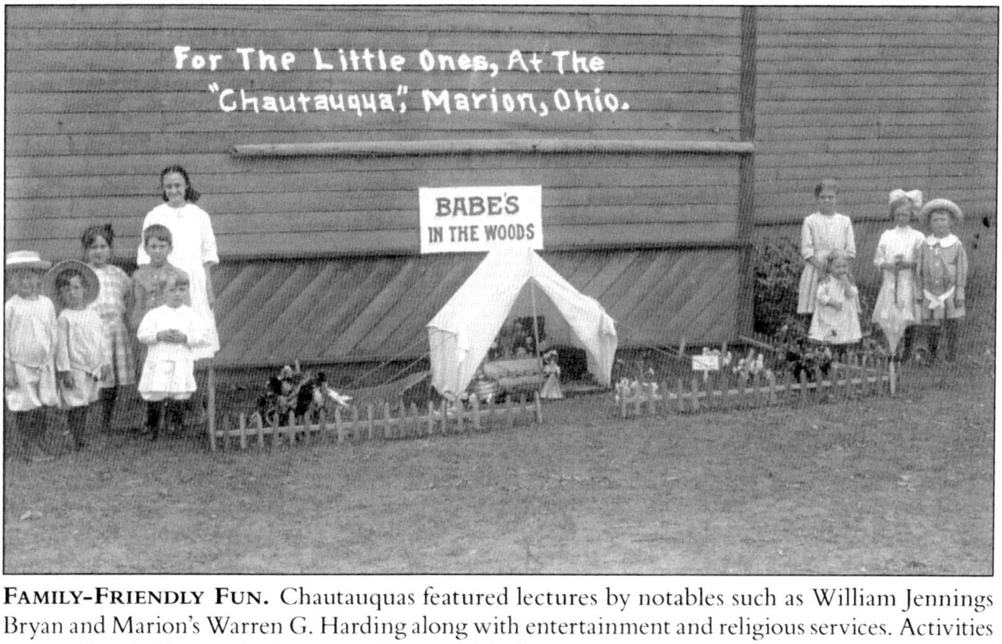

Family-Friendly Fun. Chautauquas featured lectures by notables such as William Jennings Bryan and Marion's Warren G. Harding along with entertainment and religious services. Activities such as this dollhouse display were also available for children. The price to attend was normally quite reasonable. The 1911 Marion event featured 25 assemblies and more than 40 concerts at a cost of $1.50 for the entire nine days. (Courtesy of Richard Carey.)

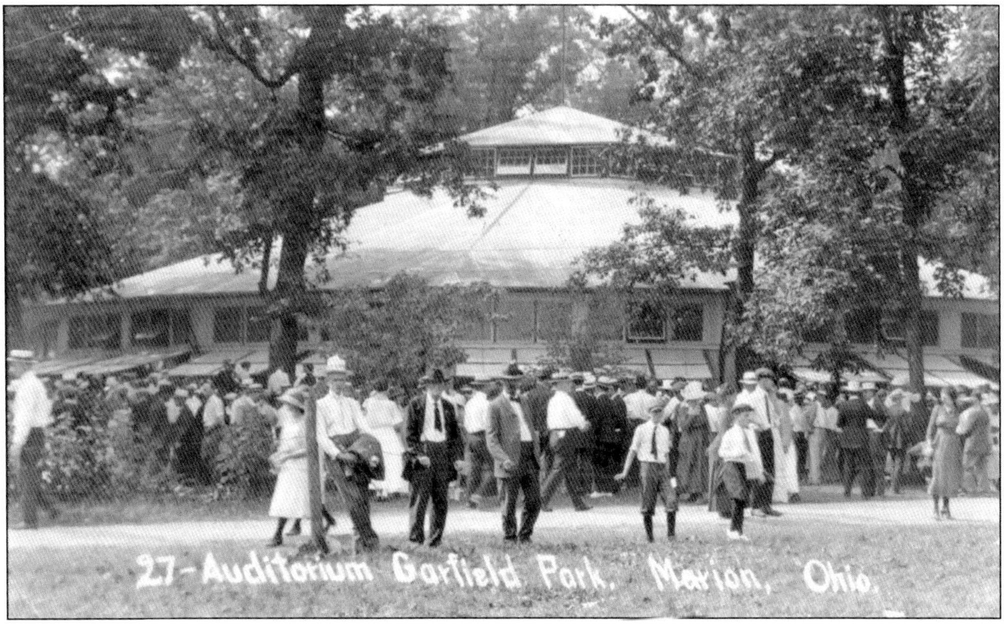

Chautauqua Pavilion. The City of Marion purchased 11 acres at Merchant's Grove on East Center Street in 1905 for $6,000 and renamed it Garfield Park. The Chautauqua pavilion was erected in 1913 at a cost of $12,000, with seating for 2,300 people and a stage that could hold 100 performers. One unforeseen problem was the lack of sufficient parking for hundreds of automobiles. A modern-day revival of the Chautauqua returned to Marion in 2004. (Courtesy of Mike and Linda Perry.)

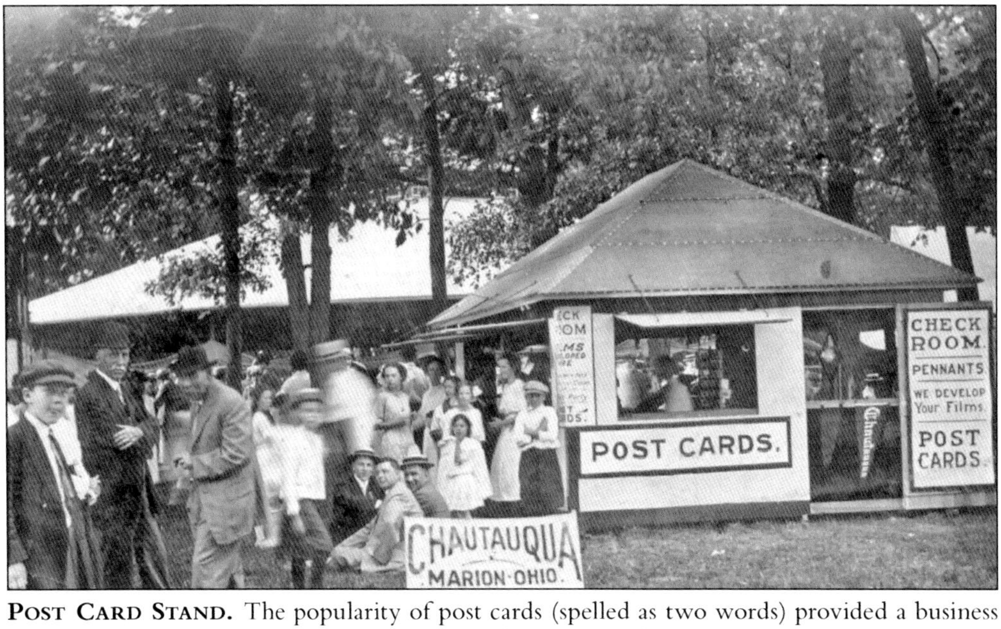

Post Card Stand. The popularity of post cards (spelled as two words) provided a business opportunity for this entrepreneur at the Marion Chautauqua. The Chautauqua movement began to fade in popularity by the late 1920s, as radios brought entertainment into the home. Ohio has one Chautauqua still providing entertainment and enlightenment. Lakeside, near the town of Marblehead on Lake Erie, has been in continuous operation since 1873. (Courtesy of Carol Robinson.)

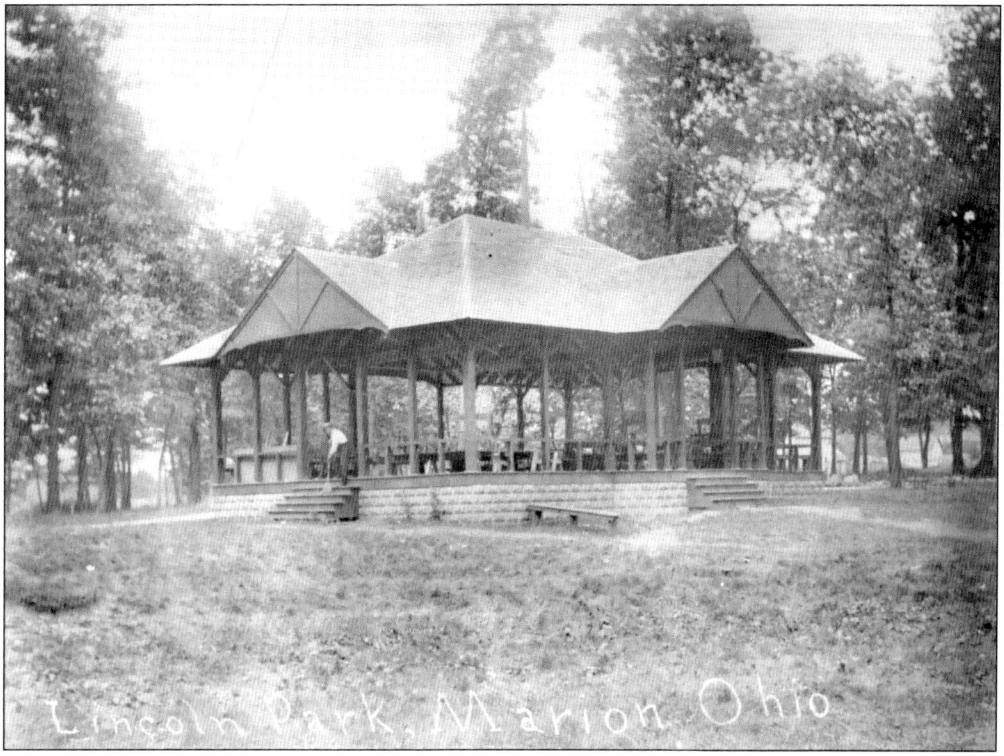

Picnic Pavilion at Lincoln Park. Originally known as Campbell's Grove, the park area was renamed Lincoln Park after being purchased by the City of Marion in 1905 at a cost of $13,000. In this view, the pavilion is being prepared for the Fourth Annual Firstenberger Reunion in 1909. Lincoln was also known for its baseball field complex, with semiprofessional games held there for many years. (Courtesy of Richard Carey.)

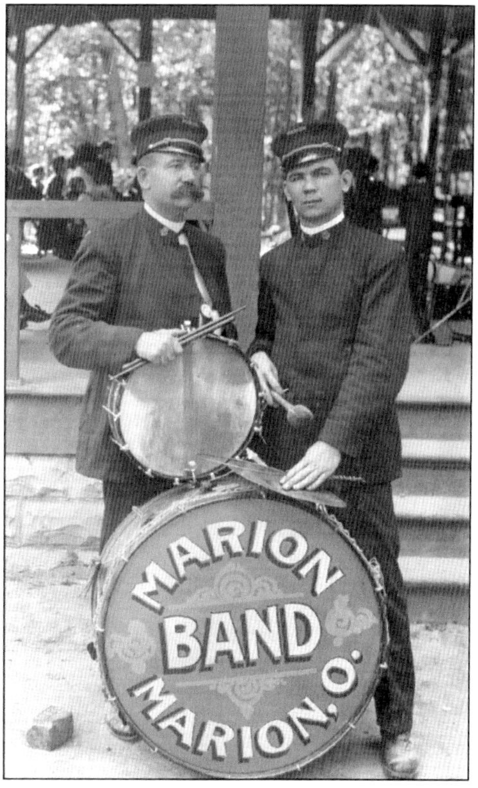

Ready for a Concert. The pavilion at Lincoln Park was also a popular venue for concerts. Band concerts and parades were a staple of Marion entertainment throughout the 1920s and into the 1930s. These two drummers are members of the Marion Band. (Courtesy of Bob Turner.)

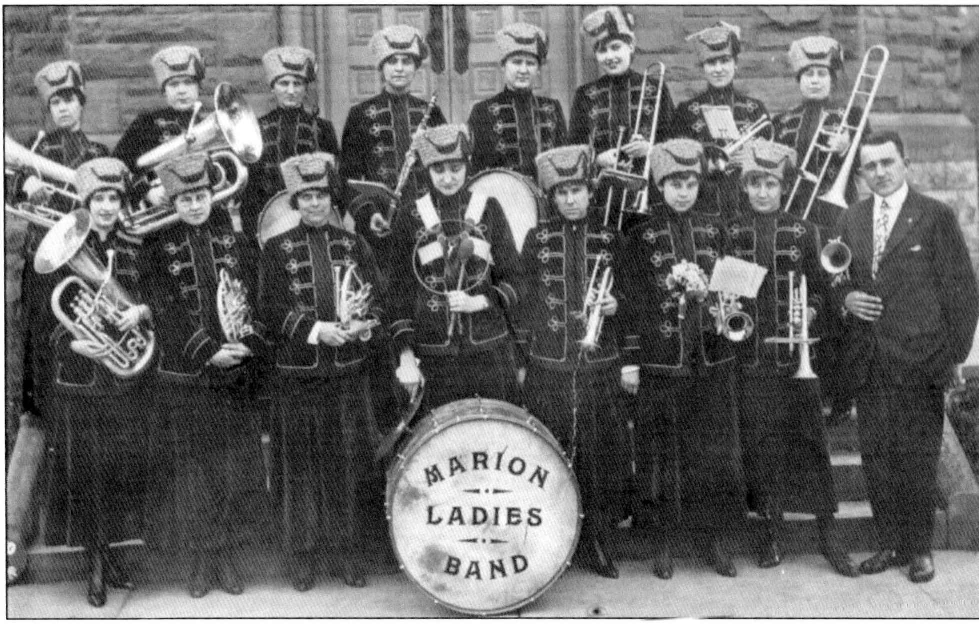

MARION LADIES BAND. While there were numerous bands in Marion, none was more unique than the Marion Ladies Band seen in this c. 1915 view with their director, a Mr. Cupp. They represented the city of Marion at events throughout Ohio and even traveled to Washington, DC, to perform. (Courtesy of Marion County Historical Society.)

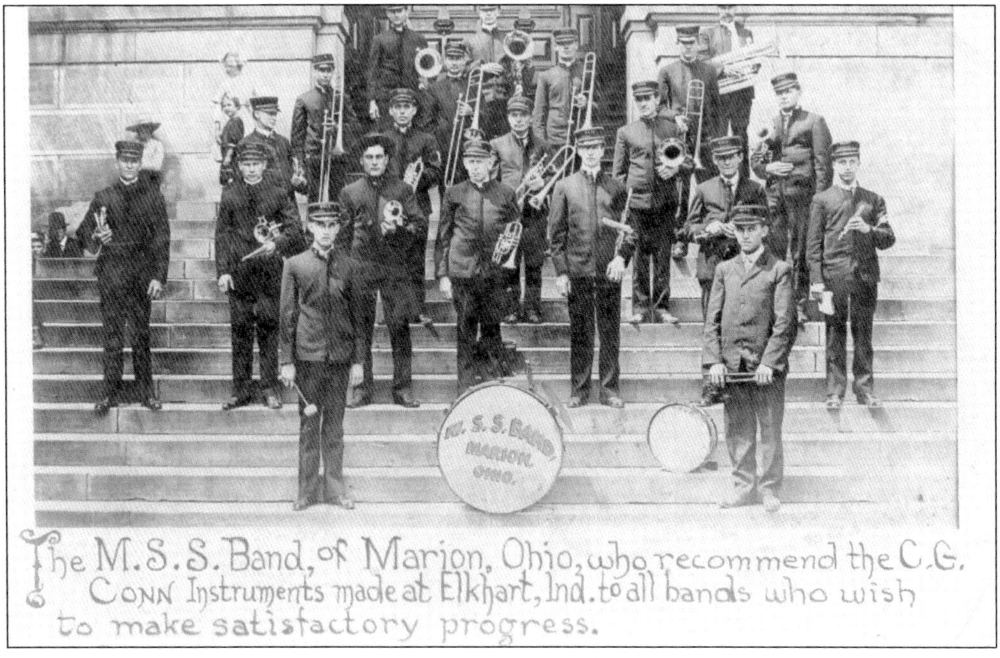

MARION STEAM SHOVEL BAND. Marion's largest manufacturer also provided entertainment by sponsoring its own band seen here on the steps of the county courthouse. The band's endorsement of the Conn Instrument Company might not have set well with Marion's own Meredith Band Instrument Company. Meredith, known for its "Open-Tone" cornets, had a manufacturing facility at 180 North State Street. (Courtesy of Richard Carey.)

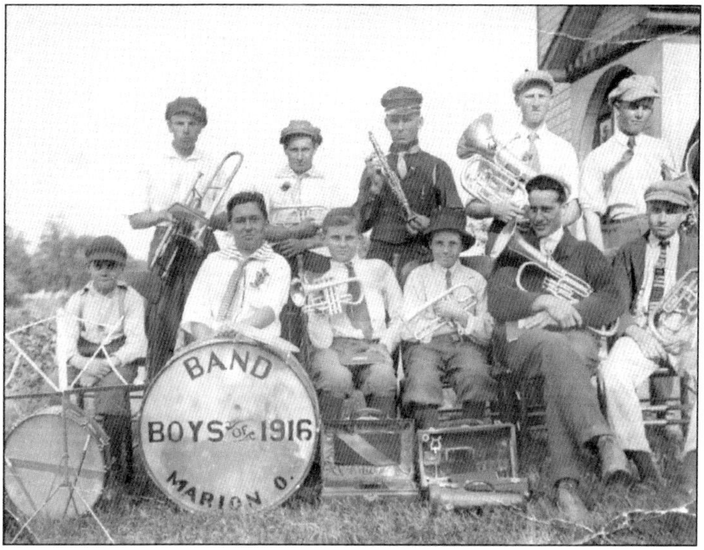

Boys Band. Fancy uniforms were not a requirement to be a member of the Boys of 1916 Band, whose members' age apparently covered a wide range under the definition of a "boy." Brass bands experienced a wave of popularity in the early 1900s. They frequently were the featured entertainment at social events such as parades and holiday celebrations. (Courtesy of Richard Carey.)

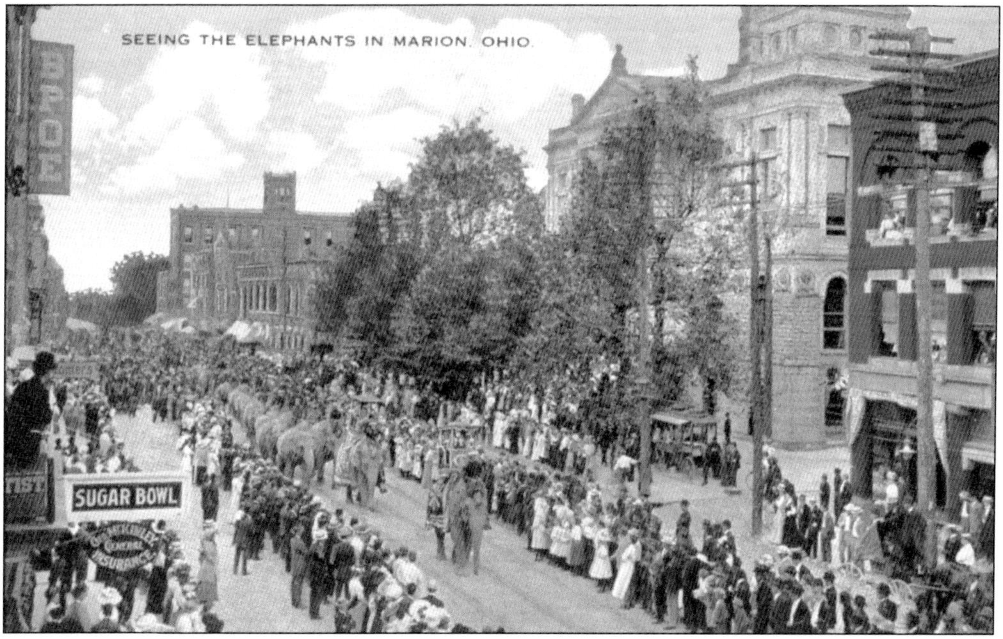

Elephants on Parade. "The circus is coming!" was certainly true when this group of 16 elephants led a circus parade up Center Street. Guests on the upper floors of the European Hotel next to the courthouse enjoy an excellent view of the parade. Legend has it a circus elephant died while in Marion and is buried near the railroad tracks by Greenwood Street. (Courtesy of Mike and Linda Perry.)

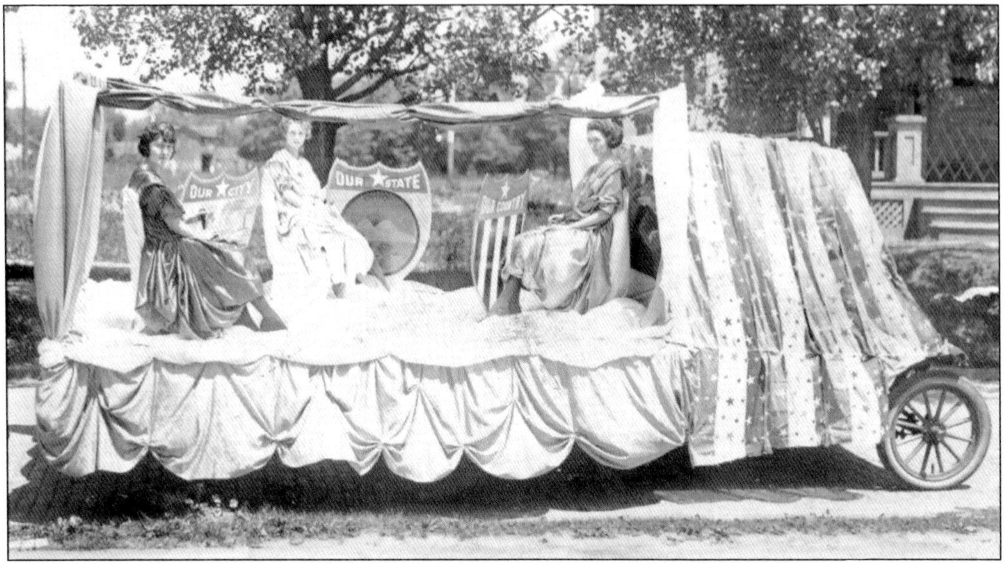

1922 CENTENNIAL PARADE. The city of Marion recognized the 100th anniversary of its founding with a massive celebration. These young ladies ride on a parade float on the back of an extended Ford Model TT truck whose driver is peeking out from behind the bunting. Pres. Warren G. Harding, accompanied by Gen. John J. Pershing, returned to Marion for the celebration. (Courtesy of Richard Carey.)

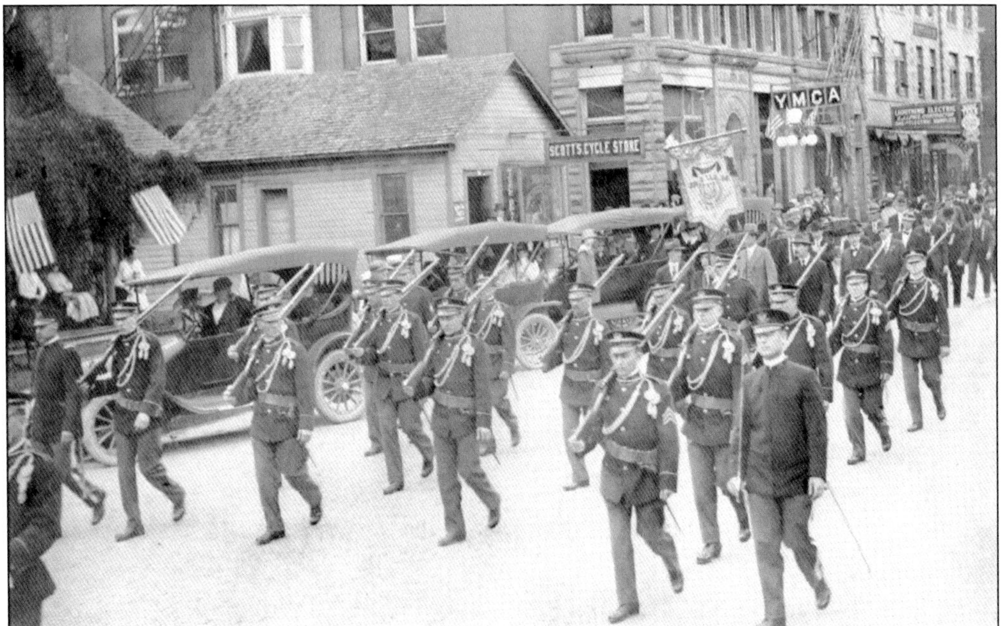

LEADING THE WAY. With the YMCA and Scott Cycle Store in the background, the Junior Order of United American Mechanics, Lime City Council No. 206, marches down State Street in 1917. Following behind are merchants who apparently supported the goals of the Order of United American Mechanics (OUAM), an American Nativist organization founded in 1844. Campaigning against the hiring of "cheap foreign labor" and patronizing only "American" businesses were both popular views during World War I. (Courtesy of Richard Carey.)

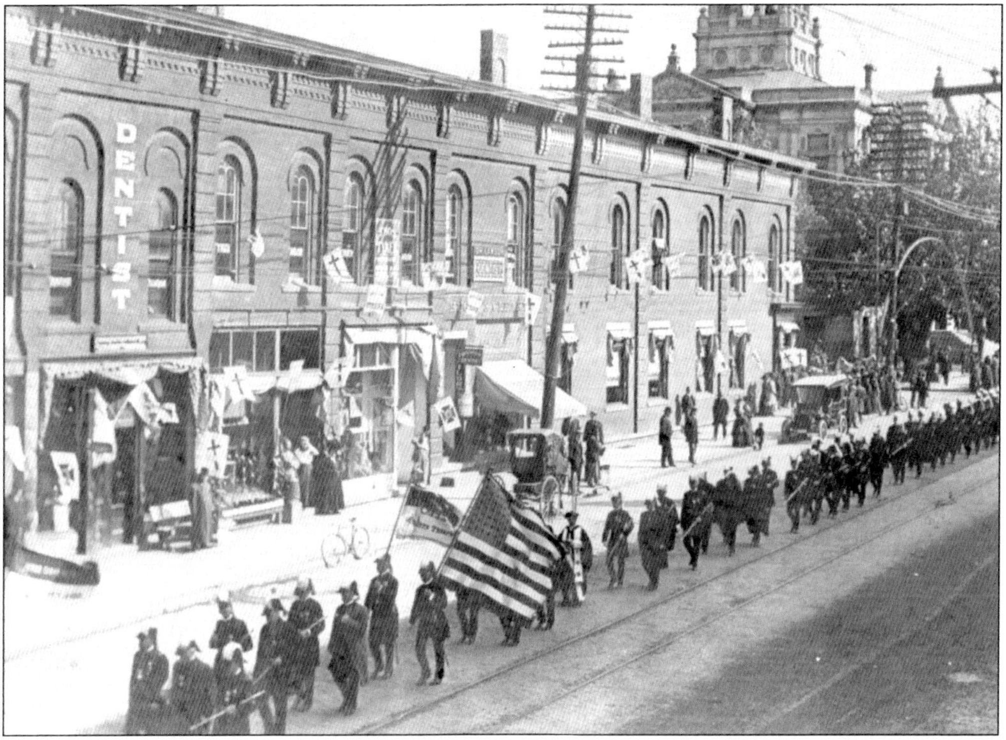

KNIGHTS TEMPLAR ON THE MARCH. Members of the Knights Templar march past the City National Bank as part of the 1909 Eagles' Parade. The Knights were members of a philanthropic chivalric order associated with Freemasonry. Banners displaying the Illustrious Order of the Red Cross (an organization within the Masons) were displayed from buildings along the parade route. (Courtesy of Mike and Linda Perry.)

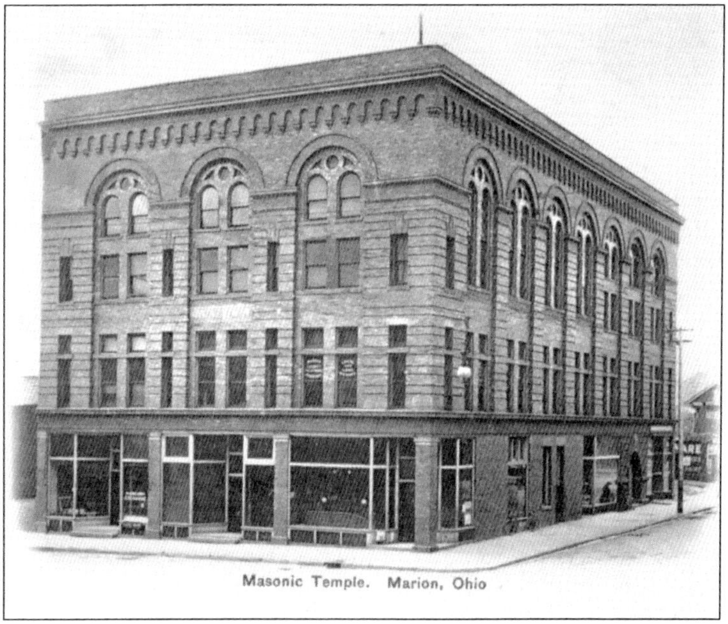

MASONIC TEMPLE. The charter for the Marion Chapter No. 70 of the Free & Accepted Masons was granted on October 21, 1841. Meetings were held in various locations until the lodge moved into its own building on Center Street in 1871. In 1903, a new lodge at the southwest corner of Main and Church Streets was dedicated. More than 23 fraternal societies existed in Marion at the turn of the 20th century. (Author's collection.)

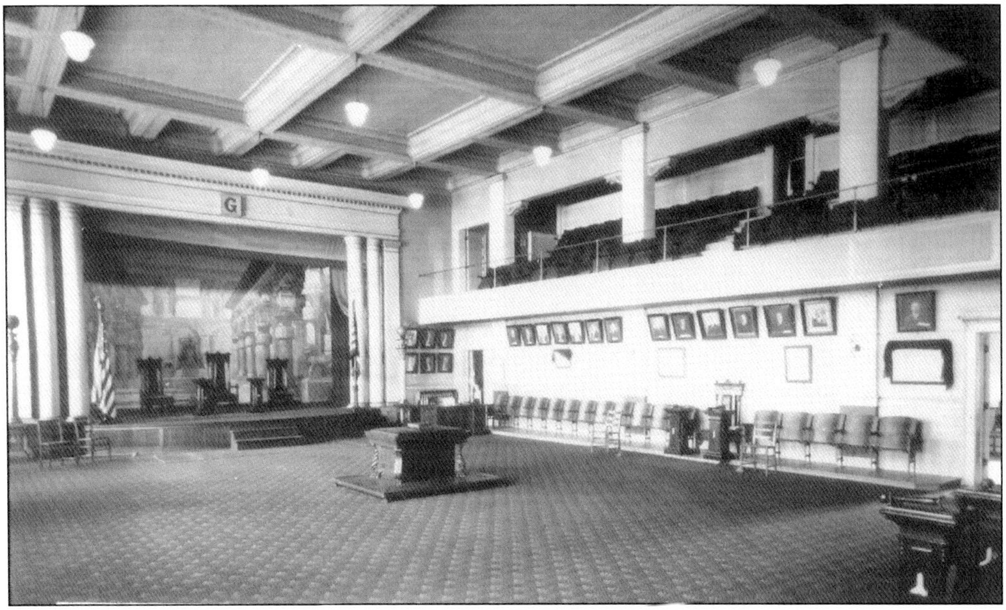

Interior of Masonic Temple. Symbolism played a key role in the interior design of Marion's Masonic Hall. A backdrop designed to emulate the Temple of Solomon and the role of its chief architect, Hiram Abiff, occupied one end of the room. The letter G, signifying the "Great Architect of the Universe," was present as were replicas of the pillars Boaz and Jachin. Every initiate passed through the pillars as part of the initiation. (Courtesy of Richard Carey.)

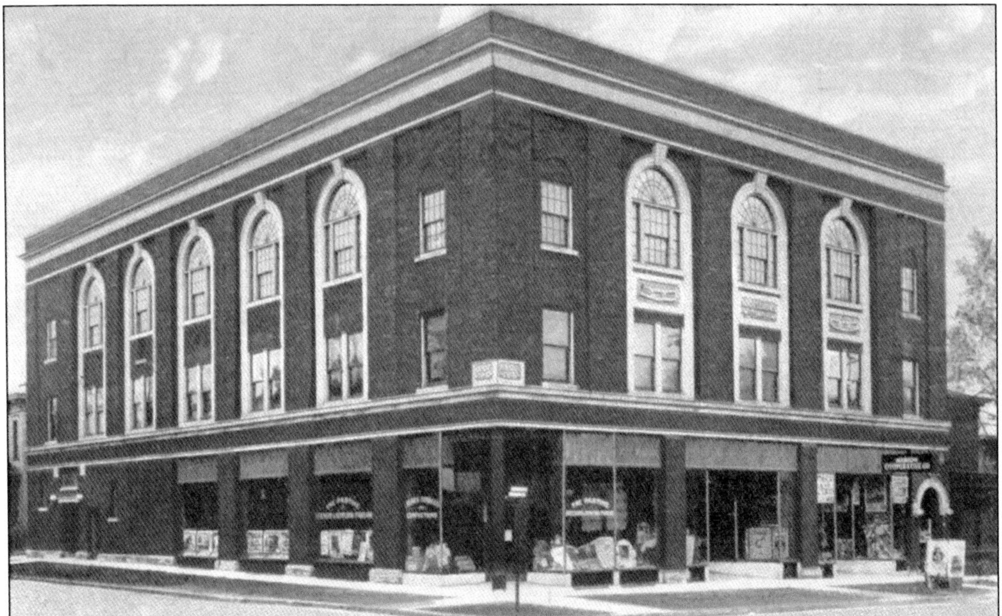

Odd Fellows Hall. Marion's Kosciusko Lodge No. 58 of the Independent Order of Odd Fellows (IOOF) was organized in 1846. The three-link emblem, representing "Friendship, Love, and Truth," served as a reminder that it was "odd" to find people who would give aid without seeking benefits for themselves. In 1903, the Kosciusko Lodge joined with the Wayside Lodge to build this temple at the southwest corner of Center and Orchard Streets. (Author's collection.)

GRAND OPERA HOUSE. The inaugural event for the Grand Opera House took place on August 19, 1896, with "the distinguished artist Mlle. Rhea presenting the romantic drama Nell Gwynne and the grand Napoleonic play, Josephine, Empress of the French." Located on South State Street, the venue played host to more than operas, with a wide variety of touring artists gracing the stage. (Author's collection.)

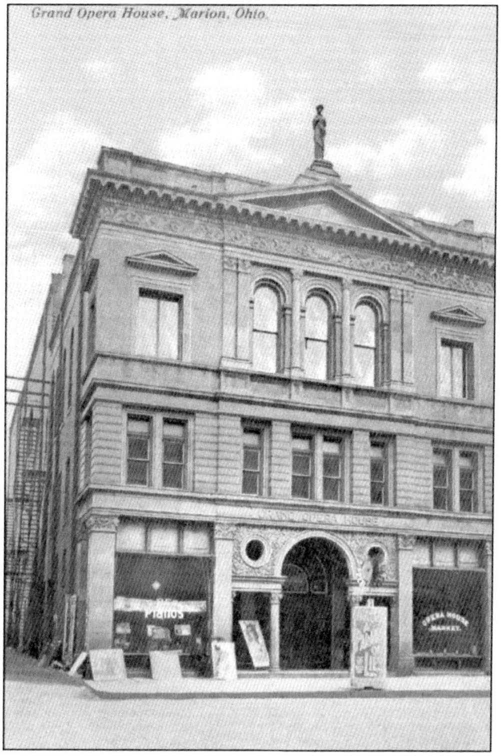

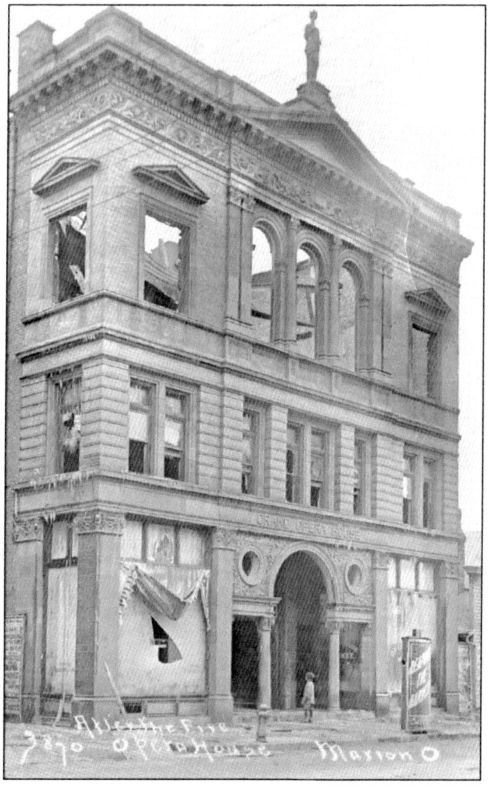

OPERA HOUSE FIRE. Although the interior was gutted by fire on December 6, 1910, the finial statue still stood tall. The property was later purchased by the Elks Club, which rebuilt the opera house and also constructed its own temple on the adjacent property. Throughout the next century, the venerable structure was known as the Opera, Grand, Alhambra, Sun, and finally the Ohio Theater. (Courtesy of Mike and Linda Perry.)

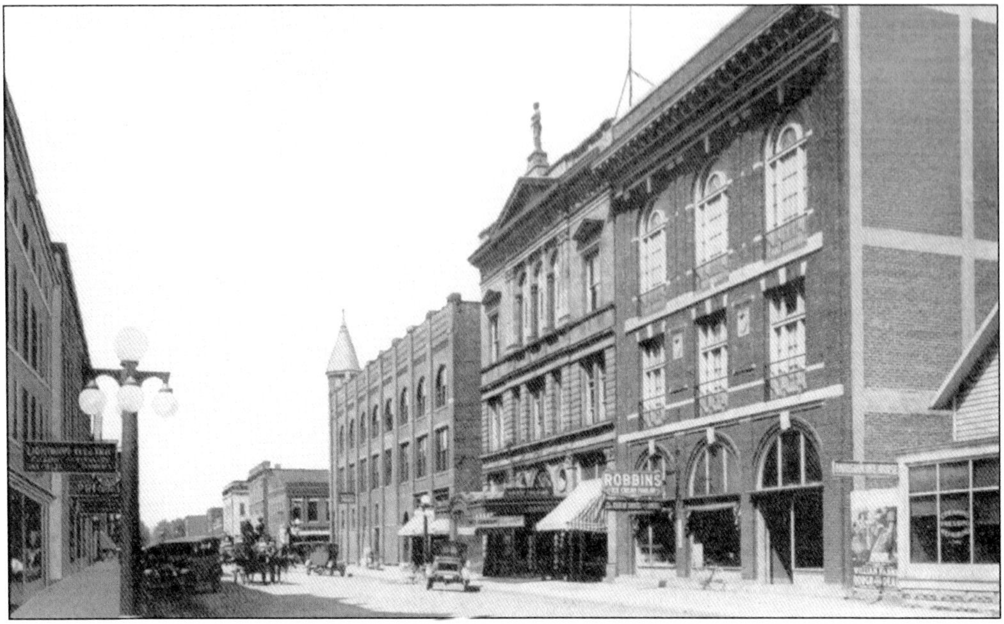

Elks Temple and Grand Theater. Marion Chapter 32 of the Benevolent and Protective Order of Elks was founded in 1885, the second lodge in the state of Ohio. Meetings were held in a variety of locations until the Elks Temple was completed in 1914 at a cost of $100,000. Perhaps the most notable member of the Marion Chapter was Warren G. Harding, who was member number 67. (Author's collection.)

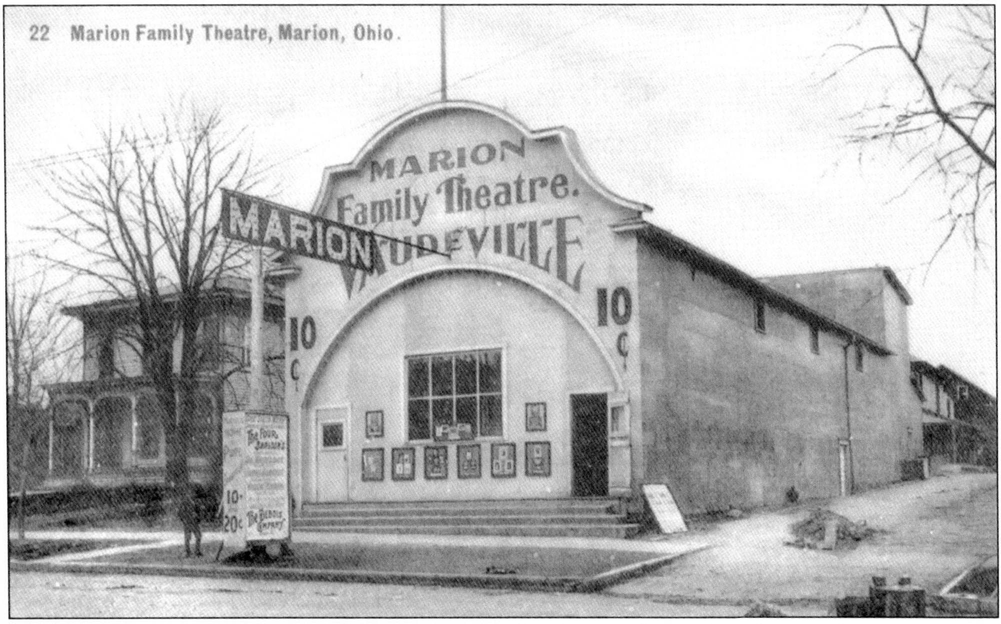

Marion Family Theatre. The Marion Family Theatre, located at the southwest corner of West Center and Union Streets, provided entertainment value with 10¢ and 20¢ admission prices. The theater was one of several entertainment options available in Marion in 1911, with the Bijou Dream, Royal, Grand Opera, Luna, and Wonderland theaters all competing for customers. The State Theater was later built on the same site. (Author's collection.)

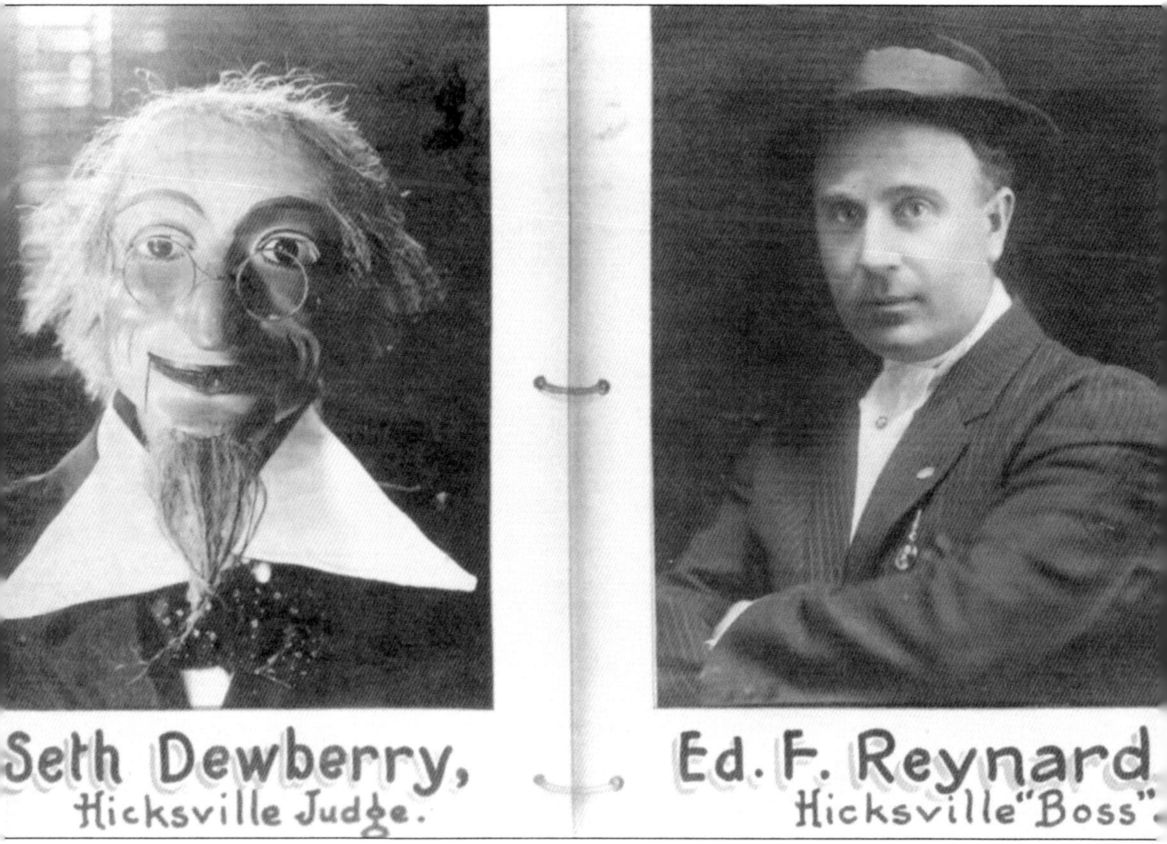

DEWBERRY AND REYNARD. Ed Sharpless, born in Marion in 1872, traveled the vaudeville circuit as a ventriloquist during the first decade of the 20th century. His entourage of 18 ventriloquial figures (dummies) and other paraphernalia was valued at over $5,000. Sharpless's most popular act focused on the actions of small town political bosses. It featured Seth Dewberry as the Hicksville Judge who would render verdicts on issues presented to him by Sharpless in his role as Ed F. Reynard, the Hicksville Boss. Sharpless later married Bianca Froehlich, prima ballerina for the New York Metropolitan Opera. Described as "plump, saucy, and Viennese," Froehlich also became known for her sultry performance of the Dance of the Seven Veils. After traveling the vaudeville circuit, the couple settled in Marion, where Sharpless formed the Marion Photo Play Company with partners Charles McMurray and George Foster. The company owned or managed several Marion theaters, including the Grand, Marion, Orpheum, and Oakland. The Hicksville Judge continued to make observations on Marion political happenings until his death in 1937. (Courtesy of Mike and Linda Perry.)

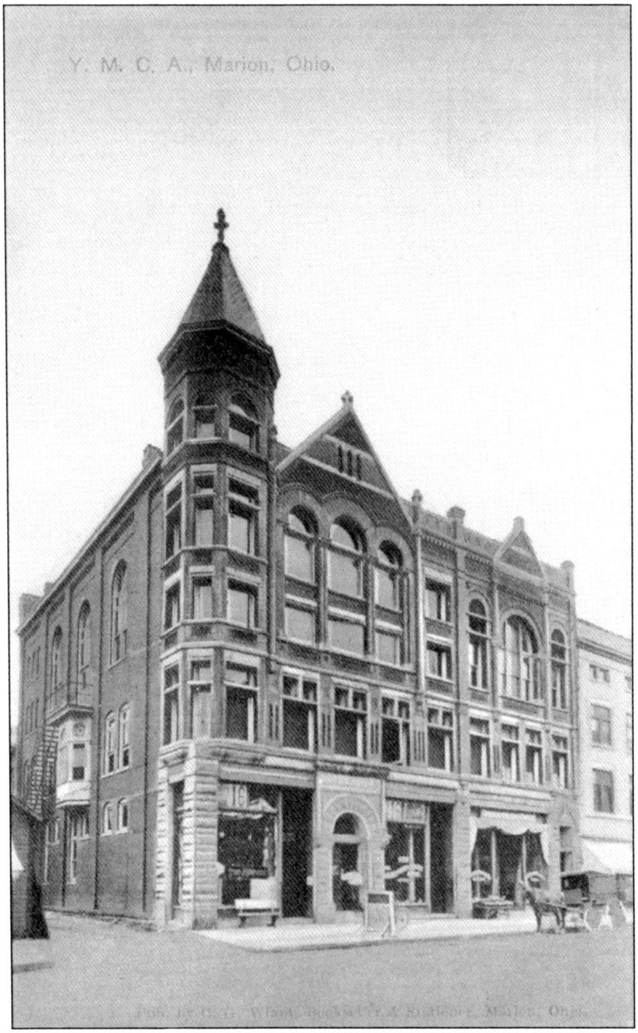

YMCA. Five hundred young men were invited in 1892 to start a chapter of the Young Men's Christian Association in Marion. Businessman Amos H. Kling offered to donate land on South State Street for the building if $15,000 could be raised toward construction costs. This was soon accomplished, and construction began in 1893. The building opened two years later, with a final cost of almost $45,000. (Author's collection.)

BOWLING ALLEYS. Spectators had a "lane side view" of the somewhat claustrophobic bowling alleys in the basement of Marion's YMCA. The Y also had a swimming pool (swimsuit not required, boys and girls separate pool times) with a ceiling so low that most adults could not stand upright. Women were also allowed to join the Y, which was an unusual policy for the late 1800s. (Courtesy of Richard Carey.)

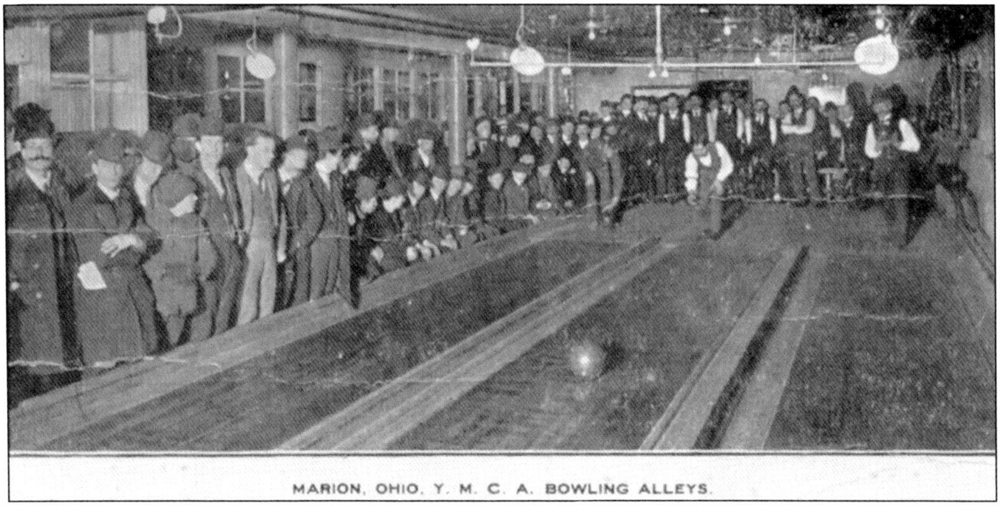

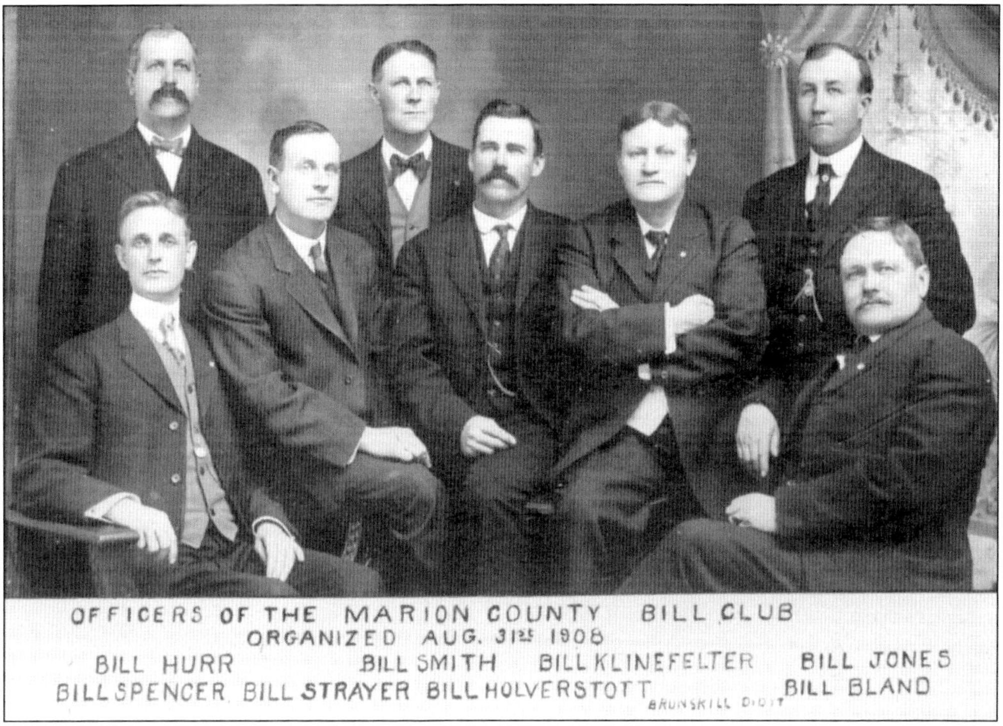

MAY I CALL YOU BILL? Social and fraternal clubs were an important aspect of the early 20th century. Many were formed with civic functions in mind. Others simply wanted to have fun, which may have been the case with the Marion County Bill Club. Organized in 1908 with chapters in Marion and Waldo, the club's primary qualification for membership was simply being christened with the correct given name. (Courtesy of Mike and Linda Perry.)

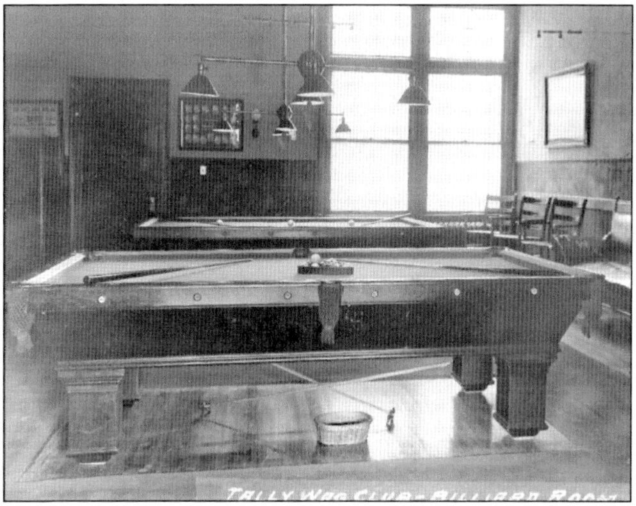

TALLY WAG CLUB BILLIARD ROOM. Marion's Tally Wag Club was founded in 1891 and offered membership to young men "of a certain means." Activities included billiards, cards, and enjoying a cigar in the smoking room. While membership was limited to men only, dances and other social events involving the fairer sex were occasionally held in the club rooms in the McNeal-Wolford building. The Tally Hos and Tick Tacks were similar clubs. (Courtesy of Marion County Historical Society.)

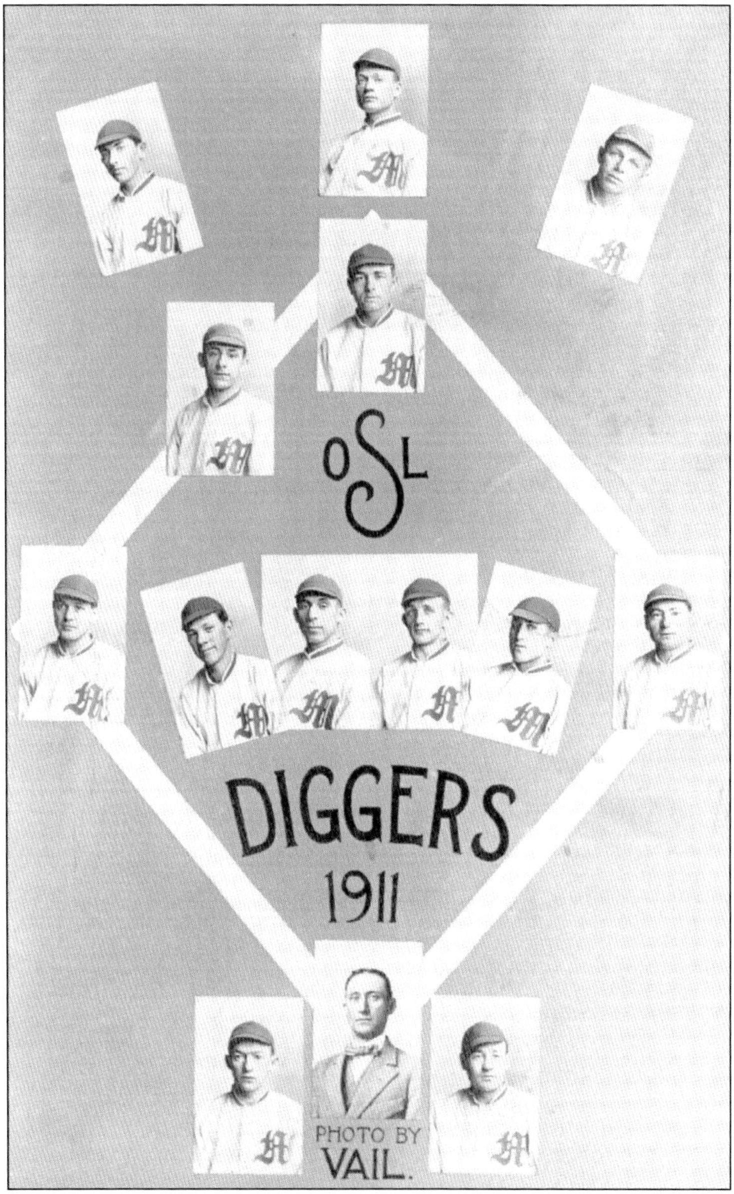

MARION DIGGERS. The first baseball team in Marion was started in 1870 by Joseph Abbott, who had learned the rudiments of the game while attending college. His Abbott's Active Baseball Club took the field in what may have been the first game in Marion when it played the Waldo Boys. The final score was 103-3 in favor of Waldo. In 1881, the Marion Mohawks became the first team in Marion with paid players. Its home field was the Diebold lot on South State Street directly behind the former Carnegie library building. Other early teams included the Drummers, Buckeyes, and Reds. In 1907, the semipro Marion Lime Burners changed their name to the Marion Diggers, with the Marion Steam Shovel Company as their sponsor. They played in the Ohio State League along with the Lancaster Red Roses, Lima Cigarmakers, Mansfield Pioneers, Newark Newks, and Springfield Reapers. The Diggers, under manager Charles O'Day, finished the season in third place, with a record of 78-71. Marion's team moved to Ironton in 1912, with the league eventually disbanding in 1916. (Courtesy of Mike and Linda Perry.)

READY FOR THE GAME. Wearing his wool uniform with pride, this unidentified young man is ready to take the field. Interest in baseball in Marion grew rapidly around 1900, with teams and ball fields springing up across the town. The Hawks, Questions, Buckeyes, Senators, Stars, Pastimes, and Hogan's Runts, among many others, could be found playing at Roosevelt Park, Webb Field, and Lincoln Park. (Courtesy of Richard Carey.)

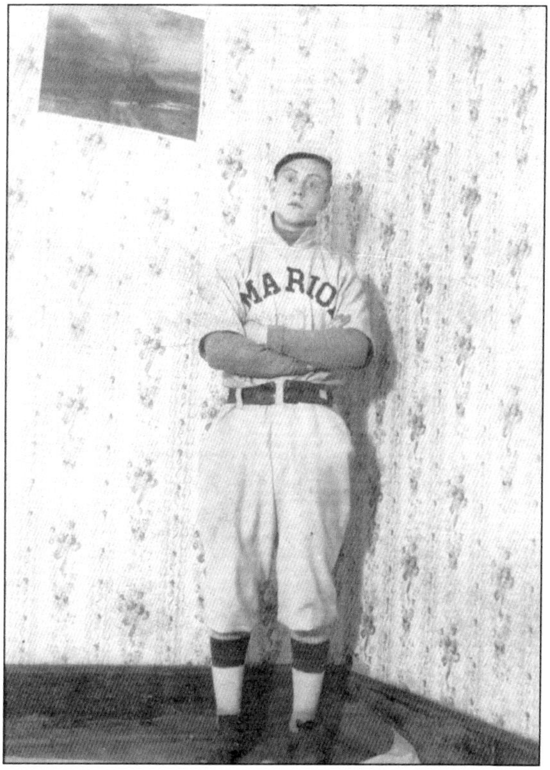

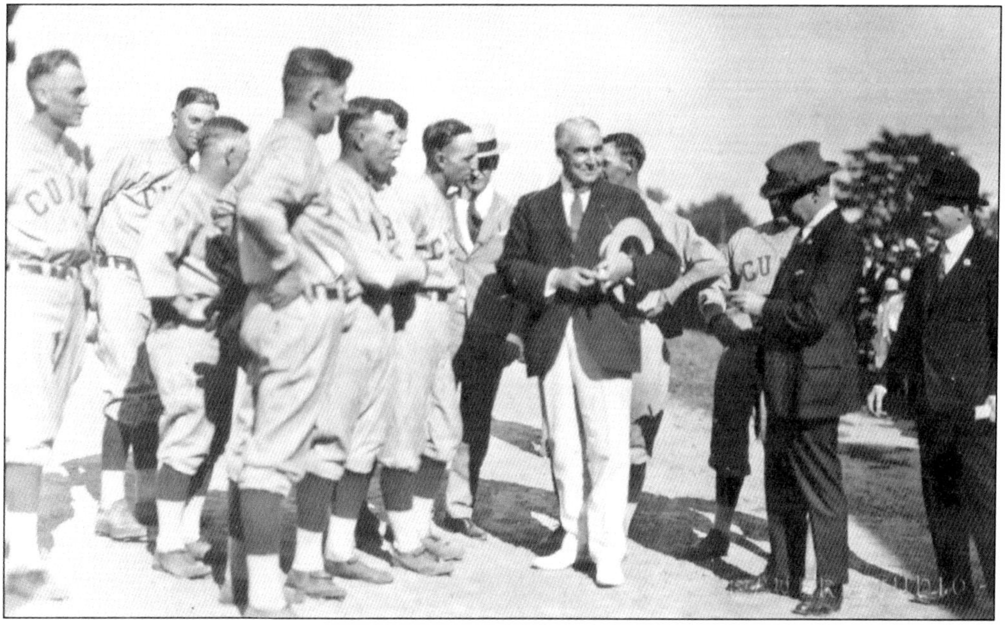

PLAY BALL. The Chicago Cubs paid a visit to Marion's Lincoln Field in September 1920 during Sen. Warren G. Harding's presidential campaign. The Cubs' ace pitcher, Grover Cleveland Alexander, took the mound against Marion's Kerrigan Tailors in front of an estimated crowd of over 5,000 fans. Senator Harding threw the first three pitches of the game. (Courtesy of Richard Carey.)

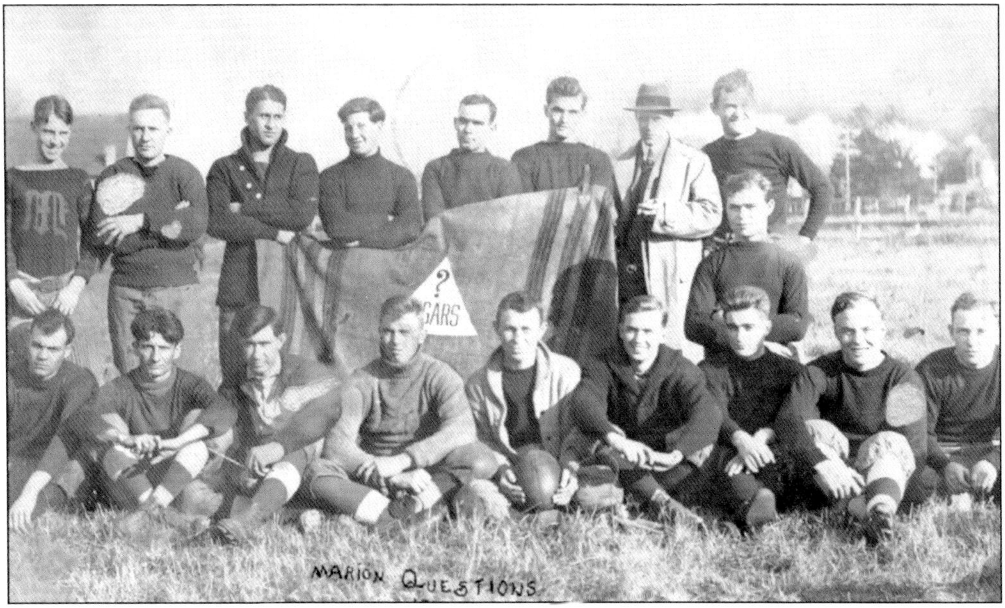

MARION QUESTIONS. Sponsored by the Marion Cigar Company from 1912 to 1915, the Marion Questions football team enjoyed success on the gridiron. Playing their games at Lincoln Park, the Questions finished the 1915 season with a 7-3 record against teams such as the Columbus Panhandles, Galion Warriors, Columbus Soderblom Smokers, Mansfield Tigers, and Akron Indians. (Courtesy of T.J. Kohler.)

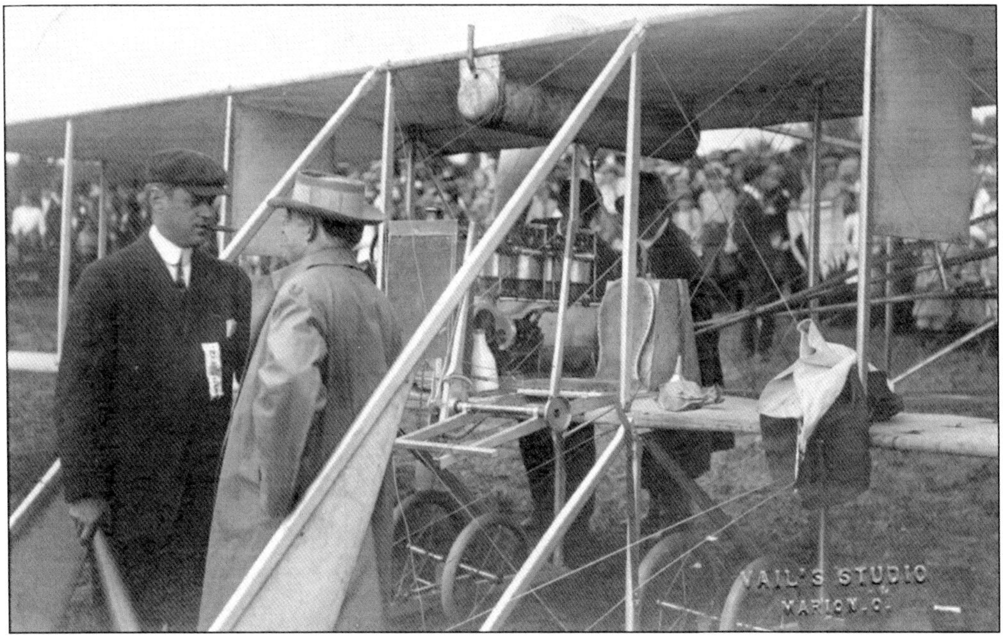

VIN FIZ. Marion buzzed with excitement on October 1, 1911, when Calbraith Perry Rogers landed his biplane in a farm field on the south side of Marion. Rogers was attempting to fly coast-to-coast to promote the Vin Fiz soft drink. After fixing a broken propeller chain and having lunch at the Pilgrim Inn, Rogers continued his journey. It was eventually completed after 49 days, 4,000 miles, and more than 20 crashes. (Courtesy of Bob Turner.)

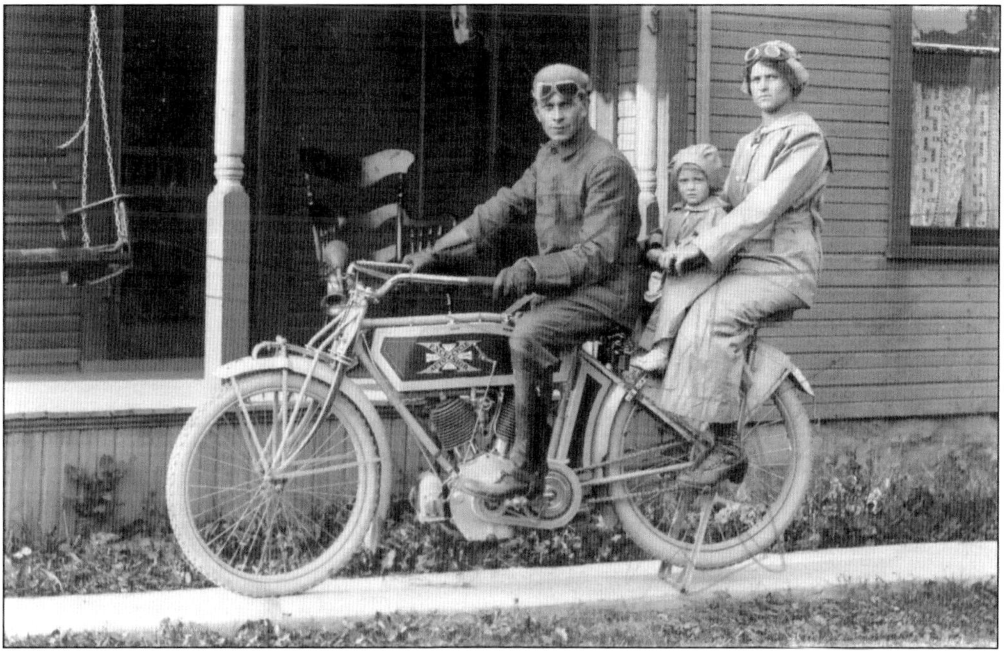

READY TO GO. This family is all set for a ride on their Excelsior Big X Auto Cycle. The four horsepower cycle with its V-twin engine and chain drive has been modified with a tandem seat and skirt guard. Excelsiors, with their exclusive Kumfort Kushion seat posts, were sold in Marion in 1912 by the F.D. Bentz Company on East Center Street. (Courtesy of Richard Carey.)

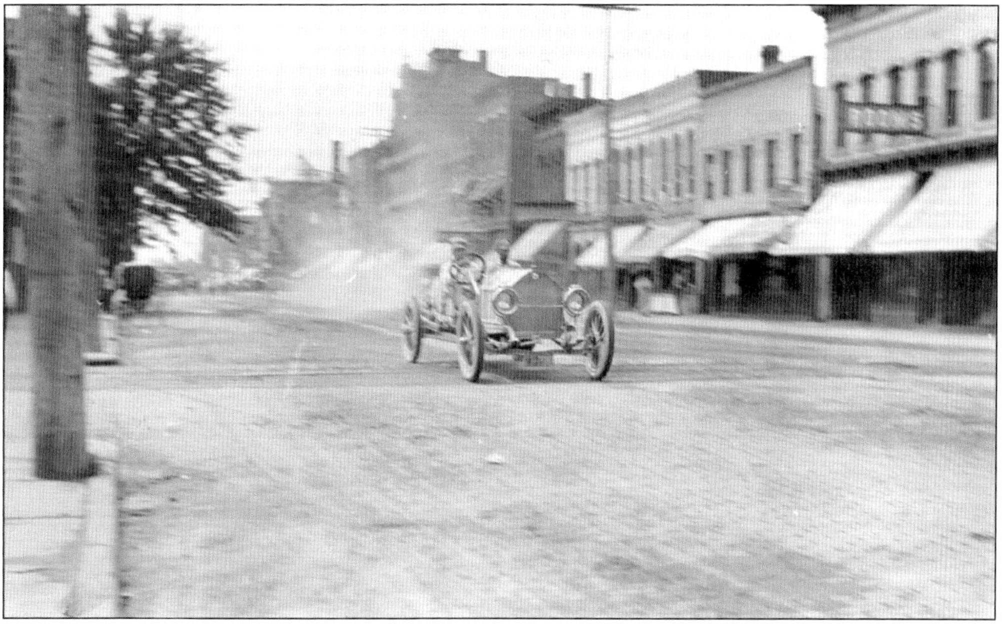

IN A CLOUD OF DUST. This pre-1907 Oldsmobile with right-hand drive and no windshield raises a cloud of dust as it tears up North Main Street across the railroad tracks. Built for speed, the car could hit a top speed of 50 miles per hour. The tall building in the background is the Railroad Block building, with the Fahey Bank as a tenant. (Courtesy of Stuart Koblentz Haley.)

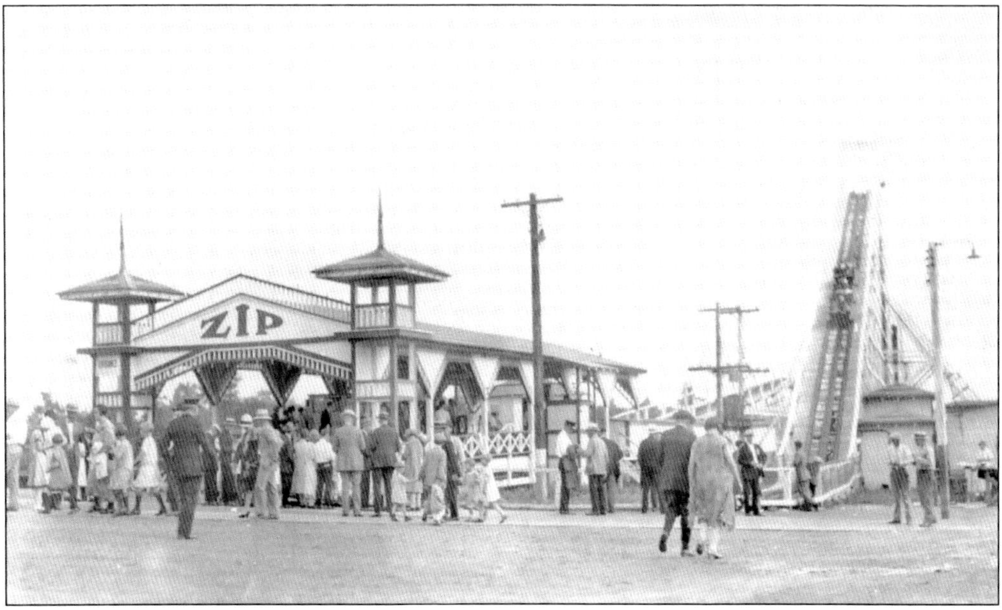

ZIP AT CRYSTAL LAKE. Located on State Route 4 north of Marion, Crystal Lake opened for business in 1922. Named for the limestone quarry that provided crystal clear water for the swimming area, the park grew rapidly. One of the favorite rides was the Zip roller coaster with its 65-foot-tall hill. Less than a week after it opened, two cousins were ejected from their car, with one later dying from her injuries. (Author's collection.)

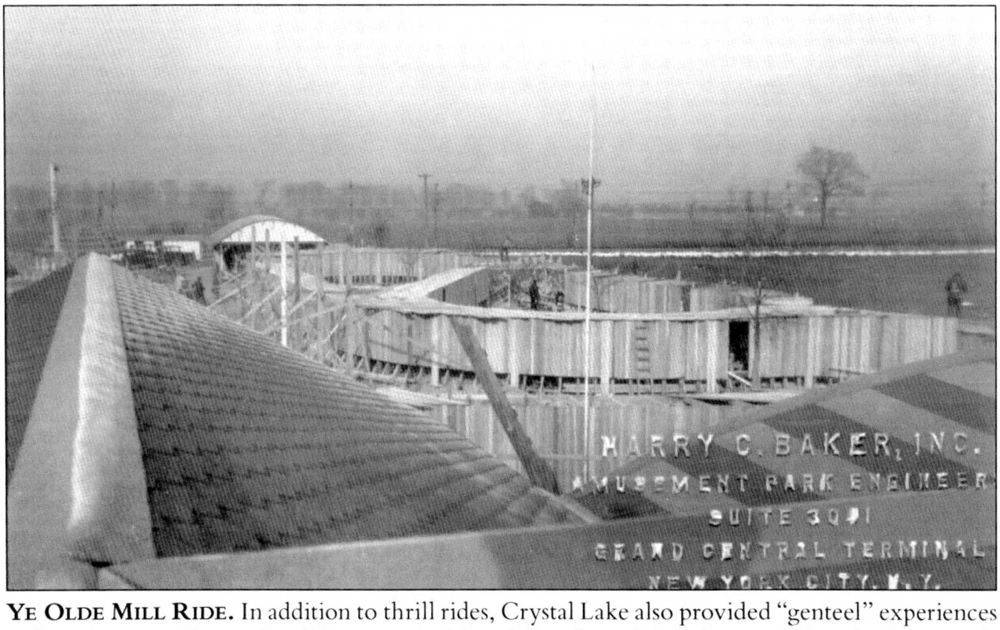

YE OLDE MILL RIDE. In addition to thrill rides, Crystal Lake also provided "genteel" experiences such as the water flume. Small boats took riders through partial darkness while enjoying murals painted on the walls. Other rides included the Skooter, Aeroplane Swing, and a merry-go-round. (Courtesy of Richard Carey.)

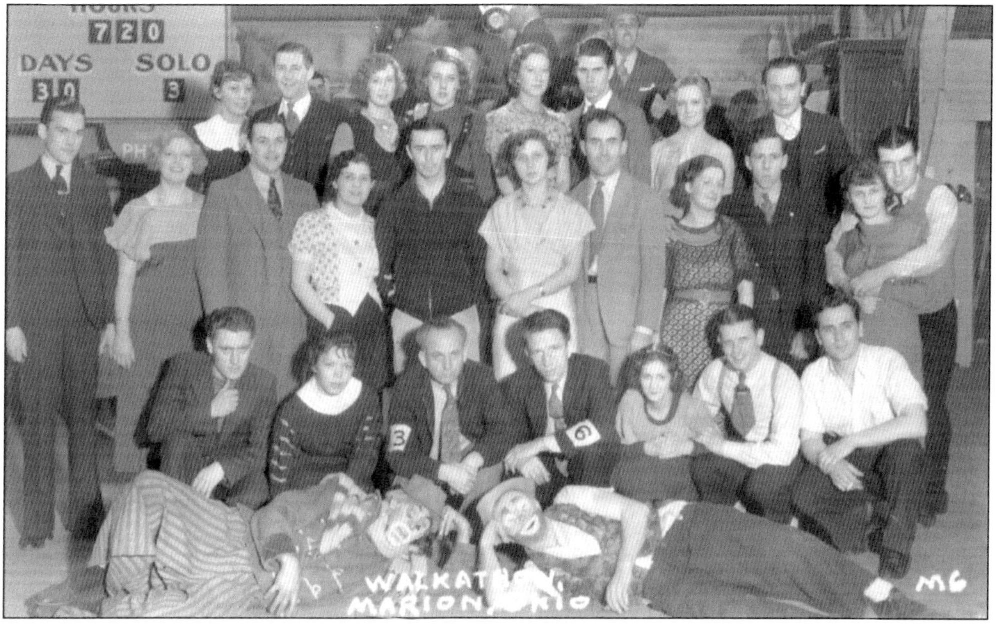

WALKATHON. A popular activity for young people in the 1920s was participating in a wide variety of "thons," such as this walk-a-thon held in Marion. Radio station WAIU, owned by the American Insurance Union in Columbus, appears to have assisted in promoting the event, which lasted for 720 hours. Dance-a-thons were also popular, with several being held at Crystal Lake. (Courtesy of Mike and Linda Perry.)

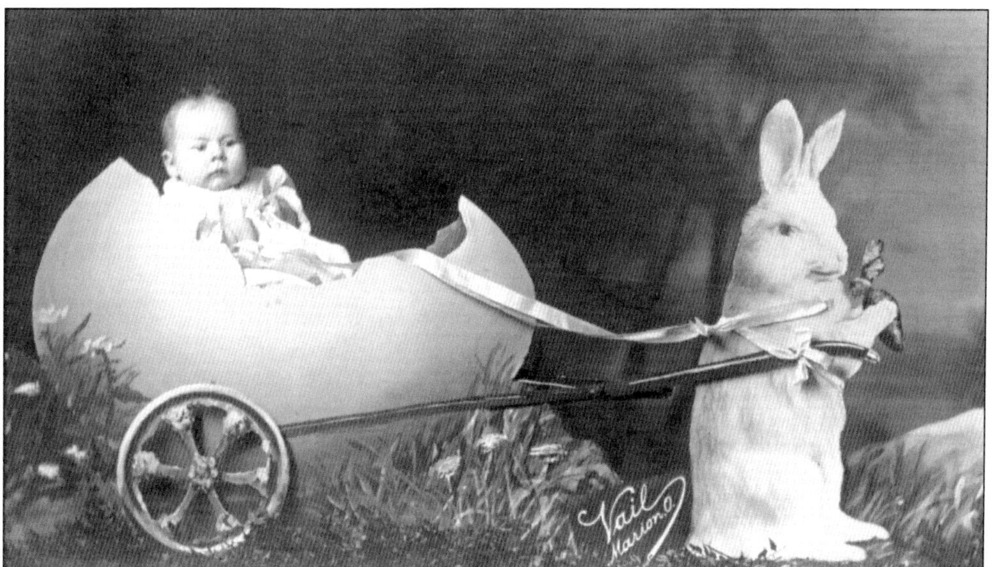

A BUGGY AND A BUNNY. Celebrating holidays with special photographs is a long-standing tradition. Vail Studios, a leading portrait studio in Marion, provided the props for this Easter-themed view. While the rabbit quietly enjoys a carrot, the baby appears to be somewhat uncertain about the entire situation. (Courtesy of Mike and Linda Perry.)

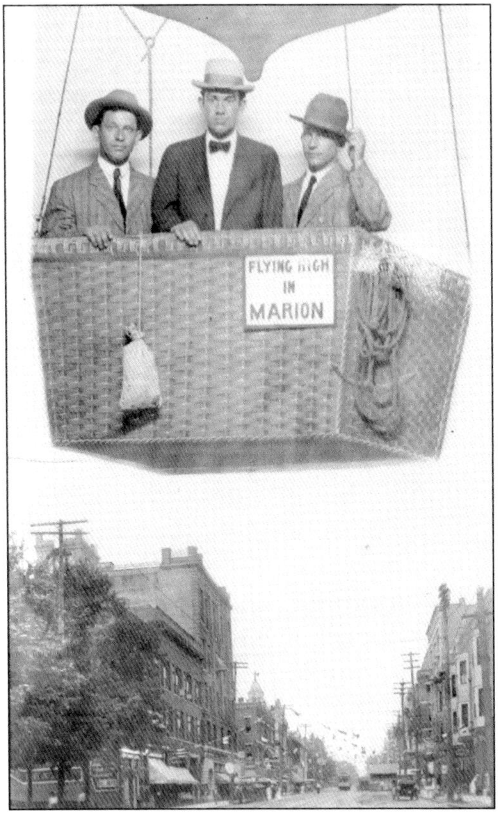

UP, UP, AND AWAY. This adventuresome trio is flying high over downtown Marion with a view of West Center Street in the background. The passenger on the right in this real-photo postcard adds to the "realism" by making sure his hat is not blown off by the gusty winds high above the ground. (Courtesy of Marion County Historical Society.)

OUT FOR A RIDE. In the early 1900s, portrait photographers traveled from town to town with their cameras and collections of props. Business was often quite good, with pictures of children posed with animals a popular seller. This young lady appears to be ready to take her pet chicken for a ride in the Studebaker wagon pulled by a goat that sports a Marion banner. (Courtesy of Richard Carey.)

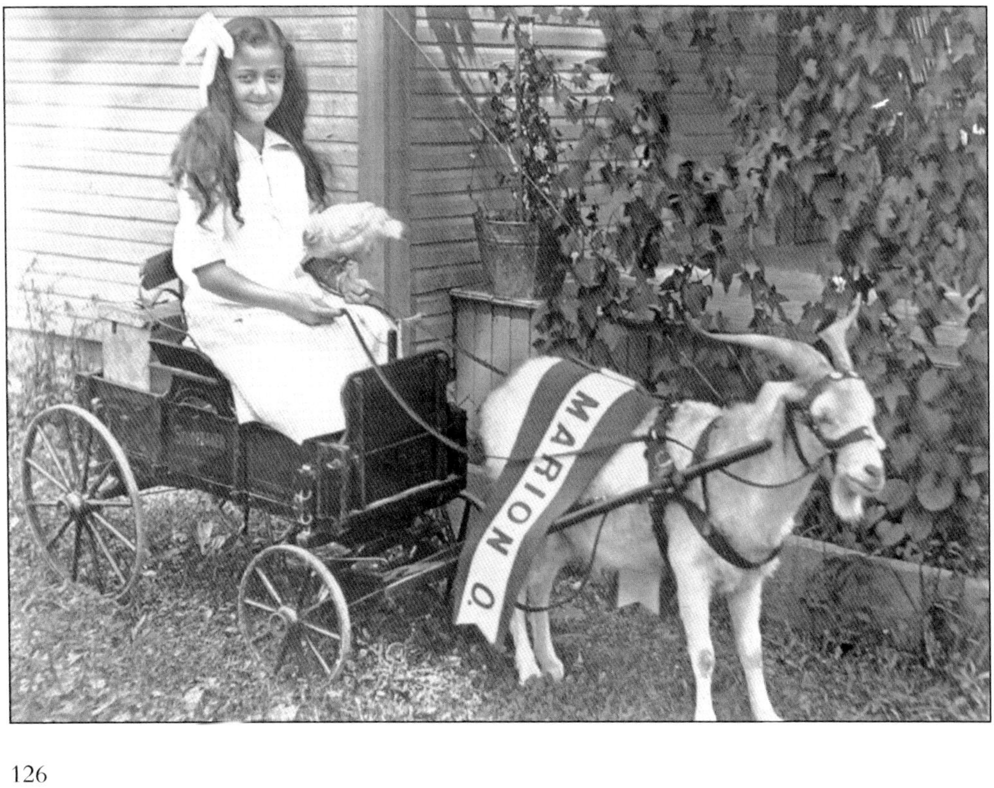

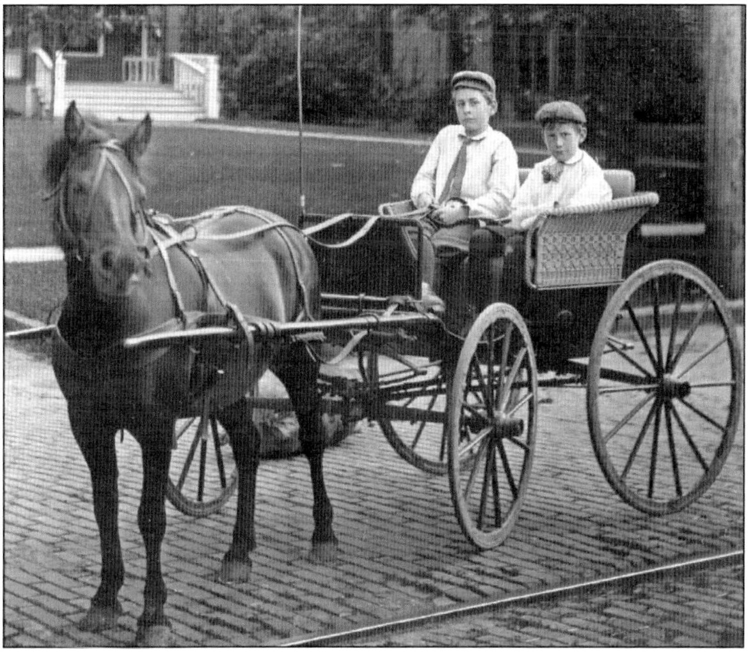

CLIPPETY-CLOCK. These two "men about town" are very stylish in their rattan-sided buggy—perhaps made by McMurray or Houghton Sulky— as they travel down the brick street. However, boys will be boys, as evidenced by the torn knee on the pants of the gentleman on the right. (Courtesy of Mike and Linda Perry.)

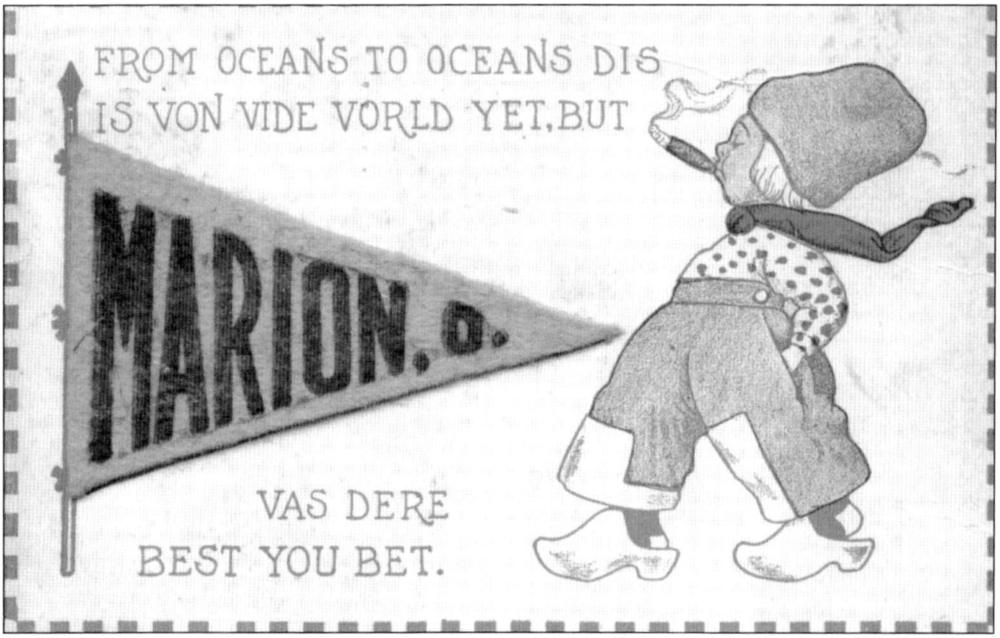

IN SUMMARY. Enjoying a cigar while strolling in his wooden shoes, the little "Dutch boy" expresses a view with which many would agree: "From oceans to oceans, this is one wide world yet, but Marion, Ohio was the best you bet." (Author's collection.)

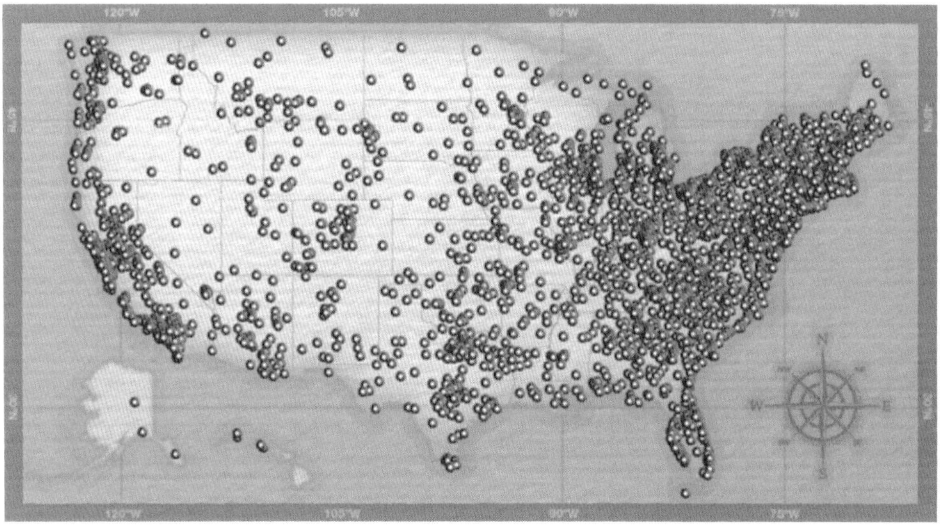

Consistent with our mission to preserve history on a local level, this book was printed in South Carolina on American-made paper and manufactured entirely in the United States. Products carrying the accredited Forest Stewardship Council (FSC) label are printed on 100 percent FSC-certified paper.

MADE IN THE USA